Nothing Superfluous

NOTHING SUPERFLUOUS

*An Explanation of the Symbolism
of the Rite of St. Gregory the Great*

BY THE REV. JAMES W. JACKSON, FSSP

SOPHIA INSTITUTE PRESS
Manchester, NH

Sophia Institute Press
Box 5284, Manchester, NH 03108
1-800-888-9344

www.SophiaInstitute.com

Sophia Institute Press® is a registered trademark of Sophia Institute.

IMPRIMI POSIT:
THE VERY REV. JOHN BERG, FSSP, *Superior General*
June 14, 2015.

NIHIL OBSTAT:
THE REV. MSGR. TIMOTHY J. THORBURN, JCL, *Censor Librorum*
February 9, 2016

IMPRIMATUR:
+THE MOST REV. JAMES D. CONLEY, DD, STL, *Bishop of Lincoln*
February 9, 2016

paperback ISBN 978-1-64413-588-4

Library of Congress Control Number: 2021943828

First printing

MARY

VIRGIN AND MOTHER

INCOMPARABLE HOST OF ABANDONMENT

IN YOUR UNIQUE

FIAT

THAT GAVE US

JESUS

I DEDICATE THESE PAGES TO YOU

(Dom Eugene Vandeur, O.S.B.)

"The Sacrifice [of the Mass] is celebrated with many solemn rites and ceremonies, none of which should be deemed useless or superfluous. On the contrary, all of them tend to display the majesty of this august Sacrifice, and to excite the faithful when beholding these saving mysteries, to contemplate the divine things which lie concealed in the Eucharistic Sacrifice. On these rites and ceremonies we shall not dwell, since they require a more lengthy exposition than is compatible with the nature of the present work; moreover priests can easily consult on the subject some of the many booklets and works that have been written by pious and learned men. What has been said so far will, with the divine assistance, be found sufficient to explain the principal things which regard the Holy Eucharist both as a Sacrament and Sacrifice." (COUNCIL OF TRENT)

CONTENTS

FOREWORD

"In the history of the liturgy" wrote Pope Benedict XVI, "there is growth and progress, but no rupture. What earlier generations held as sacred, remains sacred and great for us too, and it cannot be all of a sudden entirely forbidden or even considered harmful. It behooves all of us to preserve the riches which have developed in the Church's faith and prayer, and to give them their proper place."[1]

THE CHURCH'S LITURGY is a repository of her patrimony—a lived, and prayed, expression of the deposit of faith, in which the redeeming sacrifice of Jesus Christ is made present through the sacrament of the Most Holy Eucharist. Since the foundation of the Church at Pentecost, the Church has expressed, with beauty and grace, the meaning of salvation's mystery. In liturgy, the Church expresses through symbolism what is often inexpressible in words. Pope Benedict was right—knowing, understanding, and preserving the riches of the Church's liturgical history helps us to know Christ more intimately through the sacred liturgy.

Nothing Superfluous is a guide to the Rite of St. Gregory, the "Extraordinary Form of the Roman Rite." In clear language, Fr. Jackson reveals the rich theological meaning behind the art, architecture, words, and gestures of the Rite of St. Gregory. His work is a simple guide for those who have been moved by the beauty of the Holy Sacrifice of the Mass, and who wish to move from apprehension to appreciation—from wonder to knowledge. Of course, in the face of divine realities, knowledge itself leads back to wonder, and from wonder to love. And the instruction of *Nothing Superfluous* will

---

[1] Benedict XVI, *motu proprio Summororum Pontificum*, 2007.

help Catholics to appreciate ever more deeply the profound beauty expressed in the Mass.

In *Evangelii Gaudium,* Pope Francis expresses hope that beautiful liturgy will form "missionary disciples" of Jesus Christ. "The Church evangelizes," he says, "and is herself evangelized through the beauty of the liturgy." I believe firmly that understanding the depth of beauty expressed in the Rite of St. Gregory will serve as a source of renewal for liturgy celebrated in the ordinary and extraordinary forms, and in every rite of Holy Mother Church.

I have known Fr. James Jackson for nearly forty years. We were ordained priests together on the same day thirty years ago. I am honored to call him a friend. And I know that the meaning of the Mass is not an academic subject to him. I know that beauty, in liturgy, has captivated his heart and formed him as a disciple of Jesus Christ. *Nothing Superfluous* is rich with the insights of a pastor, a scholar, and a disciple.

I pray that *Nothing Superfluous* will be a resource for priests, scholars, students, and all those whose hearts have been moved to wonder by the beauty of the liturgy. "Ultimately," said Cardinal Ratzinger in *The Spirit of the Liturgy,* "it is the very life of man, man himself as living righteously, that is the true worship of God, but life only becomes real life when it receives its form from looking toward God." Looking toward God, in holy worship, is the transformative experience of the liturgy. May *Nothing Superfluous* aid Catholics in seeing the face of God in the Holy Sacrifice of the Mass.

— Most Rev. James D. Conley
Bishop of Lincoln

FOREWORD II

Eminent among the Popes who showed such proper concern was Saint Gregory the Great, who sought to hand on to the new peoples of Europe both the Catholic faith and the treasures of worship and culture amassed by the Romans in preceding centuries. He ordered that the form of the sacred liturgy, both of the sacrifice of the Mass and the Divine Office, as celebrated in Rome, should be defined and preserved. He greatly encouraged those monks and nuns who, following the Rule of Saint Benedict, everywhere proclaimed the Gospel and illustrated by their lives the salutary provision of the Rule that "nothing is to be preferred to the work of God." In this way the sacred liturgy, celebrated according to the Roman usage, enriched the faith and piety, as well as the culture, of numerous peoples.[1]

THERE IS NOTHING ON EARTH QUITE LIKE THE HOLY SACRIFICE OF MASS. St. Padre Pio is quoted as saying, "It would be easier for the world to survive without the sun than to do without the Holy Mass." To speak of such an exalted reality requires much humility and supernatural realism. The one who would do so must refrain from expounding mere personal opinions, not to mention whatever might be doctrinally questionable. After Our Lord Himself, only the Church, founded on the "Rock," possesses the faculty of speaking without error of this Most Blessed Sacrament. "And we have the more firm prophetical word: whereunto you do well to attend, as to a light that shineth in a dark place, until the day dawn, and the day star arise in your hearts" (2 Pet. 1:19). There must be nothing vain here. There must be nothing superfluous.

In this little gem of a book, Father Jackson has left out much. He

---

[1] Benedict XVI, *motu proprio Summororum Pontificum*, 2007.

has left aside the heated controversies over liturgical matters that so marked the latter part of the twentieth century and to our day. He has left to experts the finer points of the liturgical science and the speculations of a Theology of the Sacraments. He does not even discuss the more recent liturgical books and what has become the "Ordinary Form" of the Roman rite. There is a reason.

The purpose of this work is to place in the hands of the faithful in the pews, precisely those attending what has come to be called the Extraordinary Form of the Roman Rite or the *forma antiquior*, a simple but enriching explanation, responding to the questions that typically come to mind, as one gazes upon this traditional rite with its incomparable symbolism and harmony. It may be that something more than what is superfluous is left out here, but this book responds to a particular pastoral need. The focus is on what has been the common thread of this liturgical celebration of the greatest of the Sacraments from time immemorial, especially since it was given a more definitive form by Pope St. Gregory the Great in the sixth century.

For the rest, with the help of the light contained in these pages, it will suffice to enter into the mystery of Holy Mass, imitating the noble simplicity of the rite itself, woven of spiritual words, gestures, and sacred silence. There is no need here for ideologies or idols, whether ancient or of the more modern sort. There is not even any need for human creativity, however valuable in other walks of life. Let there be nothing profane, nothing shallow, nothing superfluous.

—The Right Rev. Dom Philip Anderson, O.S.B.

ACKNOWLEDGMENTS

I WISH TO THANK MY PARENTS, the late Dr. and Mrs. Dale E. Jackson, for having first impressed upon me the importance of reverent silence in church. Most Protestant churches—like the one we attended when I was growing up and, alas, like many Catholic churches—had an established practice of talking out loud about all kinds of things before the service began. But my father would bow his head, fold his hands, and pray in silence. And if I tried to ask him a question or pester him with an observation, my mother would say, "Shhh. Your father is praying." Thus I conceived a notion of reverence, connected to silence, very early in my life. This has only grown.

I thank the good monks of the Benedictine abbey of Notre Dame de Fontgombault. They give the Sacrifice of the Mass and the Real Presence of Our Lord the utmost human respect, and the attention and devotion they lavish on every aspect of the liturgy, from practicing their chant to taking care of the vestments, impressed upon me a great desire to imitate them in the parish. They were my first contact with solemnity in the Mass and the Divine Office, a blessed contact.

I thank my godfather, the late Dr. John Senior, whose superb skills as a teacher, kindness as a friend, and support as a mentor were an enormous influence on my love for the Gregorian Rite. If there is someone else who loved the Mass as much as he did, I don't know of him.

I thank Mr. Alan Hicks, who invited me to Dr. Senior's home for a Low Mass, celebrated with great love by the late Fr. Harry Marchowski. It was the first time I saw the ancient rite of the Mass. Though a living room is no basilica, there was a perfect devotion there.

I thank my brethren in the Priestly Fraternity of St. Peter, whose desire to serve Holy Mother Church in perfect obedience to the Holy See and perfect fidelity to the ancient liturgy have been an inspiration to me.

I thank my parishioners. It was their questions about the Mass (which I was unable to answer) that set me on a quest to find out why we do this or that. No priest could want a better flock than mine.

I'm especially grateful to Nora Malone for her work as my editor. She was wonderful to work with, as was Ted Fritz, who accomplished the layout and did the illustrations. They did this pro bono, thinking that this small book might give some glory to God.

And Fr. Hubert Bizard, FSSP, in spotting the slightest theological or historical error was very helpful, as was the support of my superior general, Fr. John Berg, FSSP. This could not have been accomplished without them.

Lastly, this is a book that is meant to be read as though it were a parish adult education class. It is purposely without footnotes; it is not an academic text.

A PEARL OF GREAT PRICE

Face to face, Thou hast made Thyself known to me,

O Christ; I have found Thee in Thy mysteries.

—St. Ambrose of Milan

THERE IS A PEARL OF GREAT PRICE, a treasure hidden in a field, that gives life its meaning and that the contemplatives of the Church search for and would not exchange for all the gold in the world. It is the discovery of the indwelling of God. When we receive Holy Communion, we receive the Holy Trinity into our soul.

The greatest benefit of the liturgy (because it is not an end unto itself) is to lead us with a steady hand into the sanctuary of the soul, so that we may grow in the supernatural life.

There are special vocations in the Church that search for God without images. I think of the Desert Fathers or the sons of St. Columba or St. Colmcille of ancient Ireland. But most of us draw from an immense treasury of signs, words, and ritual actions in order to nourish our meditation and help us come in contact with this great pearl. Many of these signs, words, and actions are found in the liturgy. The purpose of this book, therefore, is to say some things about the liturgy so that those who read it can better participate in it.

The Language of the Liturgy Speaks to Our Hearts

The prayers of the liturgy are almost entirely structured on Sacred Scripture, and one of the difficulties in grasping the meaning of the texts is that much, if not all, of the mentality and culture from which they stem has disappeared. The images of God that the texts convey show this problem—e.g., the God who sleeps, the God of wrath, et cetera.

The modern proclivity to dump these difficult texts and gestures (such as the washing of feet on Holy Thursday) on the grounds that they are passé, or old-fashioned, or medieval, or monastic is passé itself. I remember a lecture in which the priest pleaded for the removal of the word *Easter* on the grounds that the word came from the name of the Babylonian goddess Ishtar. "We should say *Resurrection Day* instead." His whole lecture reminded me of the Austrian emperor who didn't like one of Mozart's operas because it had too many notes. "Which notes do you want taken out?" replied Mozart.

Does the fact that we no longer see shepherds and flocks every day mean that such images are no longer comprehensible? Is it because no one at our parish has ever met a seraph that the metaphorical power of this messenger no longer speaks to us? Half of all the poetry ever written makes use of images and terms that are not part of daily life. These words and symbols are a part of a biblical and liturgical mother tongue that simply cannot be replaced. It is a language that must be learned, not replaced.

Divine realities only gradually yield their full significance. So understanding the liturgy is a lengthy and progressive process of becoming familiar with a particular reality. This is one of many reasons why the liturgy must have a great stability, not just in texts but also in gestures, vestments, and music.

Consider for a moment a powerful scene in the film *The Shawshank Redemption*. Actor Morgan Freeman's character provides the voice-over (and what a voice he has!), and the central character, Andy Dufresne, has taken control of the warden's office. He plays an LP of some opera and then broadcasts it over the prison loudspeaker system. What follows is a mesmerizing scene in which the prisoners stop what they are doing to absorb the beauty of the music. Freeman recites these lines:

> I have no idea to this day what them two Italian ladies were singin' about. Truth is, I don't want to know. Some things are best left unsaid. I like to think they were singin' about something so beautiful it can't be expressed in words, and makes your heart ache because of it. I tell you, those voices soared. Higher and farther than anybody in a gray place dares to dream. It was like some beautiful bird flapped into our drab little cage and made these walls dissolve away . . . and for the briefest of moments—every last man at Shawshank felt free.

Analysis or dissection, then, is out of place when considering the liturgy. I use the word *consider* purposefully, since it's from the Latin and means "with starlight." That's not a very bright light. This approach will not be analytical but dialogical instead, like a dialogue or conversation, allowing the liturgy time to say what it has to say, listening attentively to its overtones, and allowing its deeper meaning to unfold. The liturgy needs time and silence to deliver its riches.

The Liturgy Is Transcendent

One of these riches is transcendence. To understand transcendence, look for a moment at pagan religion in the West, which had in its favor that it was waiting. Recall the statue dedicated by the Athenians to the unknown god (Acts 17:23), which St. Paul said was really Christ; He was the one for whom they longed. God's mercy on the pagans in lavishing on them such great saints as Peter and Paul seems to indicate (as the late Abbott Gerard Calvet, O.S.B., pointed out) that He prefers to be adored without being known (like the unknown god in Athens), as opposed to being known but not adored (which describes how He is regarded by many in our society).

What is adoration? In the widest sense it is a free and loving submission of the whole being to God. Revelation adds to this by correcting the pagan idea of the supernatural. Rather than the Divinity appearing as a superior force in nature, like Zeus, true Divinity appears as being infinitely superior to all nature. And *supernatural* does not carry in this thought some banal modern connotation meaning the unexplainable or unusual. It means a reality that is infinitely above any natural conception of sanctity that man can have. The word *sanctus* (usually translated as "holy") in Latin means "separated." Our Lord spoke forcefully about this in the Gospels. "You are from beneath, I am from above. You are of this world, I am not of this world" (Jn. 8:23).

From this we see a second effect of revelation (a Latin word that means "to draw aside the veil"), which enables us to see that God is three times holy; thrice separated from the nature that He created. The burning bush on Mount Sinai was enough to make Moses fall to his knees immediately. But far from crushing Moses with His splendor, God revealed Himself as a Father and ultimately raises us to the dignity of sons through our Baptism. So adoration does not exclude tenderness, which is why the liturgy has both the awe-inspiringness of the Consecration and the tenderness of Communion. The world has turned away from God's transcendence. And we are living perhaps in the beginning of the great apostasy spoken of in the Scriptures. In this country alone, Catholic apostates (from a Greek word meaning "to stand outside of") are the second largest denomination after practicing Catholics. We are not immune from the fallen world in which we live, and the state of this world is worse than the old paganism, because the ancient pagans rejected Christ from ignorance, and modern pagans reject Him from contempt.

Modern man glorifies himself, and this naturalism has entered even into prayer. It appears in liturgy as a hunger for novelty and adaptation; the invasion of modern forms of music and flat, vulgar language mixed with creativity, which, when imposed on the liturgy, is one of the subtlest forms of pride. Modern man has given in to the temptation to adapt religion to man, rather than what the Church has always striven to do: to adapt man to religion.

This is an important concept to grasp in our liturgy. It does not cater to the individual. The passing centuries have continually polished, elaborated, and adapted things (colors, gestures, melodies, et cetera), divested them of their singleness of purpose, and given them universal currency. The liturgy is not the work of an individual, but the work of an organic unity composed by the Catholic Church. This vital or living formula concentrates its whole attention on the next life, while using the things of this life. So over the centuries a style of celebration was perfected; Jewish in its roots, with the addition of the manners of the courts of Byzantium, and the medieval and renaissance courts of Europe. It employs a classic language, remote from everyday life. But there is a problem with this in our times, expressed very well by Romano Guardini:

It cannot, however, be denied that great difficulties lie in the question of the adaptability of the liturgy to every individual, and more especially to the modern man. The latter wants to find in prayer—particularly if he is of an independent turn of mind—the direct expression of his spiritual condition. Yet in the liturgy he is expected to accept, as the mouthpiece of his inner life, a system of ideas, prayer and action, which is too highly generalized, and, as it were, unsuited to him. It strikes him as being formal and almost meaningless. He is especially sensible of this when he compares the liturgy with the natural outpourings of spontaneous prayer. Liturgical formulas, unlike the language of a person who is spiritually congenial, are not to be grasped straightaway without any further mental exertion on the listener's part; liturgical actions have not the same direct appeal as, say, the involuntary movement of understanding on the part of someone who is sympathetic by reason of circumstances and disposition; the emotional impulses of the liturgy do not so readily find an echo as does the spontaneous utterance of the soul. These clear-cut formulas are liable to grate more particularly upon the modern man, so intensely sensitive in everything which affects his scheme of life, who looks for the personal note. He easily tends to consider the idiom of the liturgy as artificial, and its ritual as purely formal. Consequently he will often take refuge in forms of prayer inferior to that of the liturgy, but which seem to have one advantage over the latter—that of contemporary, or, at any rate, of congenial origin.

In an age of selfism—an age of pride—the way Holy Communion is received in the Gregorian Rite grates the modern soul, though it is a perfect expression of man's adapting to religion and not the other way around. With hands folded and eyes downcast or looking at the crucifix, the faithful approach the Communion rail, which is like a division between heaven and earth. They go up to *receive* Communion, not to *take* it. And when anyone goes up to someone far greater than he to petition for a gift of some kind, his whole body and demeanor ought to express humility, so he kneels because he is begging.

Even very young children can grasp this. Long before they have any knowledge about transubstantiation, they see the adults giving 100 percent of their attention and devotion to the Blessed Sacrament. These children are learning. They see with their own eyes the reality of Holy Communion. Our good Lord does not wait for them to study theology so that they might understand Him. He communicates to their souls, through the liturgy and through the reverence of those participating in it.

I was recently at the Ordination of seven priests for the Fraternity of St. Peter, in the magnificent St. Cecilia's Cathedral in Omaha, Nebraska. I was seated in choir with the other clergy, and as the Ordination proceeded, I noticed a couple of boys and a girl who had come up to the end of the nave to get a closer look. A few minutes went by, and there were nine or ten children. Five minutes later there were about thirty. They were watching intently, reverently, with wonder in their young eyes. It was beautiful. They were participating in the Ordination.

If we turn our backs on naturalism, we see in our liturgy an expression, an unfolding of the delight of Baptism that transcends the fashions of the moment. It is perfectly adapted to that instinct for the sacred and that thirst for adoration that man carries within himself. That which never rises to God will never descend to man. "He that is of the earth, of the earth he is, and of the earth he speaketh" (Jn. 3:31). The language of the liturgy (not just words, but what those children were looking at) must come down from God before we can expect it to make us ascend toward Him.

To remedy this danger of naturalism, not only does the Sacred Liturgy avoid prayers made up on the spur of the moment; it gives us an altar on which God is central. The altar ascends to God. The priest and the people face the altar. The Gregorian Rite is about adoration. "There is a danger when the communitarian character tends to transform the assembly into a closed circle. The community must not enter into dialogue with itself; it is a collective force turned towards the coming of the Lord" (Cardinal Ratzinger).

This turning to the Lord, to the thrice-holy God, is symbolized by the priest and the faithful facing the crucifix, facing the Lord (ideally all facing the East, whence will come the Lord). "How greatly it is to be desired that Christianity should once more come to discover this primary meaning of the Mass: the reorientation of the whole of mankind, of the whole universe, towards its true center which is God: this universal return, wrought in Christ crucified and ascended up to heaven; this resumption of all things in the immense flood of divine love, flowing back finally in filial love towards its source, the Father" (Fr. Louis Bouyer).

THE LITURGY AS A WORK OF ART

The Council of Trent taught that the Church's liturgical rites "contain nothing unnecessary or superfluous." This challenges us to look at the liturgy as a work of art. A masterpiece of art, such as the paintings of the Sistine Chapel, contains gaps, flaws, less felicitous parts, repetitions, and things that are hard to understand or even contradictory, but they are never unnecessary or superfluous.

Our beautiful liturgy has been developed over two thousand years—not constructed, or fabricated, but developed. Is there human invention to be found in it? Of course. In His guidance of this development, the Holy Ghost makes *use* of human ingenuity, but the Mass is not the *result* of human ingenuity.

The purpose of development is to make the Mass more perfectly into what it already is. Take the addition of St. Joseph's name to the Canon, which took place during and not before Vatican II. Blessed

John XXIII did so by a *motu proprio* (Latin for "on his initiative"). It changed nothing in the Mass. It is based on a timeless and universal devotion to a great saint. It does not change the character of the Canon in the slightest. Rather, it makes the Canon more perfect—makes it more into what it already is. This is an example of legitimate development.

The question of what is not legitimate development is a larger question than this little work can address. But a guiding principle may be taken from Vatican II, which said that no change was to be made to the liturgy unless it could be demonstrated that the change would be of positive benefit to the faithful. This is easy to see in the case of adding St. Joseph's name to the Canon. It is not easy to see in the removal of the Last Gospel. In what way do the faithful benefit from not hearing the most perfect thanksgiving for the Mass ever written? Granted the Last Gospel was a new thing in the Middle Ages; the Dominicans would say it on their way back to the sacristy after Mass. But the faithful wanted to hear it, and it caught on like wildfire throughout the Church, with the priests beginning to say it at the altar. Adding it to the Mass was in perfect harmony with what had gone before. It's about the Incarnation. Christ has entered our world. He has entered into us. We leave the Mass girded with this great truth.

The point is that our liturgy is received, not constructed. Every time someone tries to construct liturgy, he will be off track. Go back to the Old Testament for a moment. God took Moses up the mountain and told him how the people were supposed to worship. He was very specific. He did this because He is merciful, since every creature has as its primary duty in life to worship God. But we did not know how to worship Him. So He taught us.

But the people complained in the desert. "We don't like manna! We want meat!" Okay, God let them have meat. "We want a king just like the other nations!" Okay, God let them have a king. "We want to marry other women, not just Jewish women!" Okay, God let them marry other women. His indulgence was extraordinary. But the one thing He would not allow was liturgical straying. The entire Jewish nation was punished for the liturgical straying of a king.

How the Faithful Partake of the Mass

Let us be particular about participation at this point. The word *participation* is from the Latin: *partis* ("part") and *capio* ("I take"). So what does it mean to partake of the Mass? Here are some good answers from the 1958 Instruction *De Musica Sacra*, from the Congregation of the Rites. Keep in mind that this Instruction is based on a number of previous Instructions from Blessed Pius IX, St. Pius X, Benedict XV, Pius XI, and Pius XII.

> The Mass of its nature requires that all those present participate in it, in the fashion proper to each. This participation must be primarily interior (i.e., union with Christ the Priest; offering with and through Him). But the participation of those present becomes fuller if to internal attention is joined external participation, expressed, that is to say, by external actions such as the position of the body (genuflecting, standing, sitting) ceremonial gestures (Sign of the Cross), or in particular, the responses prayers and singing.... Perfect actual participation (*participatio actuosa*), finally, is obtained when there is added sacramental participation (by communion). Deliberate actual participation of the faithful is not possible without their adequate instruction.

A few comments on these words are in order. First, notice that the participation is required. This is not referring to the Third Commandment directly, but in the sense that if you come, you cannot sit and be an idle or mute spectator and expect the blessing of the Lord, except in very difficult circumstances, such as poor health.

Secondly, participation is not the same for everyone. That is a pipe dream, impossible to achieve. This means that the role of the altar boy is different from the role of the priest, which is different from the role of the usher. It also means that, for some, full attention to the Mass can be impossible, such as if they are grief stricken. The Church is a good mother and does not insist that all her children must be doing the same thing at the same time in the same way, though good order in the congregation assists peace.

Thirdly, at the heart of participation is union with Christ the Priest at the altar, and this union is especially interior, just like that of His Mother and St. John standing at the foot of the Cross. They gave Our Lord their attention, devotion, sympathy, time, and everything else they could give Him while He was on the Cross, but did so silently. *That* is participation. It is the essence of participation, and it is primarily interior. So although praying the Rosary during the Mass is a very low form of participation—and a form that appeals to very few—Pius XII made it clear that it is not to be condemned, since it is quite possible to be in union with Christ through the Rosary.

Fourthly, the gestures need to be well made. A sloppy Sign of the Cross or a distracted and irreverent genuflection sets the soul up for poor participation.

Fifthly, singing. Trying to move Catholics to sing is often like trying to persuade them to have surgery that they deem unnecessary. But the Church will not budge on this, and neither should pastors. "He who sings well prays twice," as St. Augustine put it. Nevertheless, the faithful must be provided with a Low Mass, during which there is no music at all.

Some distinctions are in order regarding the Latin phrase *participatio actuosa*, a phrase used during the Second Vatican Council. It is often translated as "*active* participation," although the translation "*actual* participation" is more accurate. To understand this, go back to what Our Lord said when He promised, "I will be with you all days even unto the end of the world" (cf. Mt. 28:20). He lives with us, even though He is at the right hand of the Father. The Church is His Mystical Body. So when the Church acts, it is the activity of Christ, the Head of the Church. Thus, the teaching, governing, and sanctifying of the Church are done through the hierarchy and the faithful, but when the priest sanctifies by blessing someone, it is really Christ who blesses through the priest. The sacrament that enables us to be part of that activity, that divine life of Christ, is Baptism. A baptized Christian has not only the right to participate in that life but also a duty to do so.

The baptized then can *actually* participate in the Mass, but the unbaptized can participate only in an *active* way. In other words, the unbaptized can make the Sign of the Cross, and be blessed in doing so, but not in the same way as the baptized.

An example of both is listening. As the Scriptures say, *"Fides ex auditu"*—"faith comes from hearing" (Rom. 10:17). A deacon or a priest reads the Holy Gospel at Mass, but we participate actively and actually by listening attentively. The better we listen, the better we participate. The unbaptized can learn the Faith by hearing it; the baptized can learn but also worship God with it.

In his Apostolic Exhortation *Sacramentum Caritatis*, Pope Benedict said that the two modes of actual and active participation are: (1) through the union of the mind and heart of the individual faithful with what is happening on the altar; and (2) through the reception of Holy Communion, which defines participation.

PARTICIPATION IN THE MASS CARRIES OVER INTO DAILY LIFE

"Imitamini quo tractates," says Pope St. Leo the Great in the ancient text from the Liturgy of Ordination to the priesthood: "Do in practice what you do in the liturgy." So the application of the liturgy

to everyday life should be a sign of actual participation in the Mass. For example, do you have problems respecting God's Holy Name? Then bow your head at the Name of God every time you hear it in the Mass. Do the same when you leave the Mass, and it will do wonders for helping you to refrain from misusing God's Name. This bowing is required of the priest during the liturgy, and it not only fosters respect for God's Name but can also make reparation for the misuse of His Name. It's hard to correct the people at work who misuse His Name, for instance, but you can secretly bow your head each time you hear Our Lord's Name, or the name of the Blessed Virgin or of the pope or a saint, and make reparation for others' disrespect.

Do you have problems with custody of the eyes? Then use the example of the priest, who is under orders not to let his eyes wander during the Mass, but rather to keep them focused on something holy, whether it be the crucifix or our good Lord Himself. At every moment of the Mass he is required to look at something, and not just anything to which he is inclined. The Mass can be a perfect training for custody of the eyes. Altar boys learn fast that if they want to serve well, they must keep their eyes on their task and not look around at the congregation.

Of course, practicing this outside of Mass is most helpful to participation. That is, if we allow our eyes to wander all the time outside of Mass, we will have developed a habit, or rather a vice, of distraction, which we will likely take with us to Mass, concentrating on the person in the pew in front of us. This practice also applies to the mind: if we allow our mind to wander all over outside of Mass, chances are we'll bring that vice into the Mass with us.

Dangers to Participation

What are some of the dangers to participation? One is the lack of silence. If the celebrant is convinced that his role is to keep the congregation interested—or worse, entertained and anything but bored—then he can be tempted to think that the daily Mass without a sermon is sorely lacking; that Mass without his speaking from the pulpit is missing the key element. With too much of an intellectual approach, the imagination, emotions, and aesthetics are not given enough room, and only the intellect is fed. The Gregorian Rite does not have catechesis for its essence. Liturgy is its own end, which is worship.

Another danger to participation is using the liturgy as a primary means to disseminate information. DVDs played on a big screen in the sanctuary to stir up the faithful to give more money might be successful in some places, but this has no place in the Mass.

The liturgy should never be used as a warm-up for some other activity. For instance, if there is to be a parish picnic, the Mass must not be seen as a way to get everyone together first. It must always remain elevated over every other activity of the parish.

The Church Fathers adhered to a principle that held that the deepest catechesis (called *mystagogia* in Greek) should be given only after the faithful had received the sacraments of initiation: Baptism, Confirmation, and Holy Eucharist. Prior to Baptism, Confirmation, and Communion, which were received on the same day, the instructions they received were naturally limited in scope, but their instructions were clearly continued after their entrance to the Church. The entire method of teaching was structured around a framework of questions and answers, such as "Did you notice that . . . ? Did you hear when . . . ?" Celebrate and worship first, then seek to understand. That is the tradition. This is very different from the modern conception that all must be understood immediately.

We do not adhere to the letter on this pedagogical approach. Pius XII warned about archeologism, which seeks to yank some practice from an earlier century and bring it willy-nilly into ours (my language, not his!). But the principle is sound. No catechism will succeed unless it is grounded on a stable, solid, reliable, and faithful celebration of the Mass. Many a convert has seen a great lack of continuity between the catechism and a sloppy, irreverent celebration of Mass.

Another problem arises when celebrants see the liturgy as a terrain for their "creativity." This leads to a kind of liturgical coup by which the sacred is obscured or pushed aside altogether, the language is trivialized, and worship is turned into a social event or a fun-fest for all. The real subject of the liturgy is no longer God but the person celebrating and the community that celebrates with him.

This is not to say that all creativity is and must be banned from the liturgy. The organ was broken in an Austrian church one Christmas Eve, and the pastor asked a guitarist to come up with a hymn accompanied by the guitar, and we received "Silent Night." But to rearrange the whole liturgy?

A priest does not create the liturgy; he is a servant and guardian of its mysteries. The danger of trying to make the readings more interesting by rhetorical devices and theatrics must also be avoided. I remember being instructed in seminary (not an FSSP seminary) not to read the Word of God, but to "proclaim" it. This leads the reader or priest to impose his emotions and emphases on the texts—emotions and emphases that the texts simply lack. Reading the Scriptures in the liturgy in Latin, or before the sermon in the vernacular, is not acting; rather, the reader must allow himself to be a humble instrument of a word that comes from heaven. His eyes ought to be downcast, his voice plain, and his gestures nonexistent. He must not be the focus.

The Mass Leads Us to a Deeper Love of Prayer

A taste for mental prayer and for silent prayer, which helps us to participate more fully in the Mass, is not acquired by a process of reasoning. It is instead the result of a mysterious merging of the soul with the Bride of Christ (the Church). The taste—even the relishing—of prayer depends on our union with the Church and her way of prayer. Here is what Dom Romain Banquet, a Benedictine abbot once said to his monks:

> Prayer, such as it was understood by St. Benedict, has as its theme the very text of the *Opus Dei* ["the work of God," i.e., the Divine Office]. It springs from the womb of this office. Let yourself be caught up in it. God is bowing down to you at this moment. In silence, question the ideas that have been planted in this way. This kind of interior prayer is the most intimate part of the *Opus Dei* during its celebration; it becomes afterwards its reverberating echo, a precious perfume, a personal fruit suited to the dispositions and needs of each one of us according to the promptings of the Holy Ghost." (*La Doctrine Monastique*)

> To be caught up in the sacred Liturgy takes silence. Supernatural good makes itself known without noise and hides itself in silence.

But this is not true just for contemplatives. Laypeople can experience it too if they could give themselves to the liturgy for a time each day. George Bernanos, the superb French novelist, is an example of this:

> Each day he read the newspaper and listened to the radio. However each morning, whatever happened, he set aside half an hour as sacred. Before his family awoke, before the house filled with noise, he would read, in his old, worn missal, the Mass of the day in Latin, with all the concentration of mind and soul he was capable of: this predestined soul had received the divine privilege of attention. He nourished himself avidly with the unchanging formulas of the liturgy, finding in them each morning a note of startling freshness. It was as if, each morning, these words were

being said for the first time in the entire history of the world and to him alone. They were his daily and supersubstantial bread. It was in this way that he started his day. On Sunday he went to Mass with his family and usually received communion. (*Bernanos Vivant*, by F. Bruckberger)

It would be wonderful if our churches were filled each day with the faithful, but few have the time, the energy, or the ability to do so. Heaven knows that the village with the steeple as the tallest structure and the bells as the most prominent sound seems like a dream nowadays. But what Bernanos did in his home you can do too. Taste and see. In the Propers of the Mass, and in particular, in the Gregorian Rite, you will find the answers to the problems each day presents.

This taste for the interior life, this education of the soul takes place not just in the Mass itself but also in the liturgical season. Like the light from a star that went extinct thousands of years ago but is just now shining on us, so are the central events of Our Lord's life; His Passion, Resurrection, and Ascension, accomplished at a particular point in time, and finished forever at least with regard to their historicity, are conveyed and prolonged by liturgical action. This is what St. Leo the Great meant when he said that that which was visible in the life of our Redeemer has passed into the mysteries.

The words *mysteria* and *sacramenta* are synonymous for the Fathers. They describe a sacred action in which the work of our redemption is made present, not just as a symbol, but as something that conveys a great reality. In the sixteenth century, men like Martin Luther were going about stressing the individual and psychological aspects of prayer, which was very detrimental to an objective piety centered on the mysteries. One thinks of Luther *alone* in his cell, poring over the Scriptures and determining what true faith is from the poring; and ranting and raving against those who did not share his opinions about what those mysteries meant.

But when the liturgy unfolds the Scriptures to us, it does not just tell a story likely to favor this or that personal meditation, in which to be engaged later. Instead, it realizes the actual presence of the Lord, with which we are free to communicate through the length of worship. It is the Church in her entirety—and we with her—taking part in the death and Resurrection of our Savior. This is not merely the fruit of the effort of the mind or imagination. It is objective.

If we consent to let the liturgy accomplish in us the divine work of redemption (as Bernanos consented), then, as Dom Gerard put it, "It is then that the judicious choice of scriptural texts and their calm repetition, their power of expression, the art of Gregorian chant, the sacraments and the mysteries of the life of Christ which pass back and forth unceasingly before our eyes, imprint on our souls the image of the Son, who transforms them and reconciles them with the Father."

The Mass Enables Us to Think
and Feel with the Church

"Nothing is more educative for man in his totality than the liturgy. The Bible is certainly a marvelous teacher of prayer, of the sense of God and of the adult convictions of conscience. Used alone, the Bible might produce a Christian of the Puritan tradition, and an individualist and even a visionary. The liturgy, however, is *the authentic method instituted by the Church to unite souls to Jesus*" (Dom Maurice Festugiere).

> The sort of Christian produced by an enlightened and docile participation in the liturgy is a man of peace and unified in every fiber of his human nature by the secret and powerful penetration of faith and love in his life, through a period of prayer and worship, during which he learned, at his mother's knee and without effort,

the Church's language; her language of faith, love, hope and fidelity. There is no better way of acquiring *the mind of the Church* in the widest and most interior interpretation of this expression. (P. Yves Congar, quoted by Geoffrey Hull in *The Banished Heart*, 2010)

Sentire cum Ecclesia: this phrase sums up what the study of theology hopes to accomplish: "to think and feel with the Church," or, as Fr. Congar put it, to acquire the mind of the Church. It's a kind of supernatural sensitivity by which the faithful feel, as if by intuition, whether something is in conformity with the Faith and with the Tradition of the Church. You see this in children with their strong sense about whether something is in keeping with their house. "Our family does not do it that way." Perhaps they cannot articulate why the subject in question is out of line with the family, but they have a *sense* that it is. And that sense should not be ignored. When Catherine Vianney, the older sister of St. Jean Vianney, first heard their new parish priest in the pulpit, she was the first in her family to sense that something was wrong. She was twelve years old. Indeed, the priest had sworn allegiance to the republic that was born of the French Revolution. She could not say why the priest was a traitor to the Faith; she just knew he was.

This sense comes especially from the liturgy, more than from any other source. "It was the celebration of the divine liturgy that kept the faith of the faithful intact during the centuries of Muslim persecution," stated Maximos V, the Melkite Rite patriarch, at a synod of the Melkite bishops (this rite is in union with Rome) in 1977.

The famous Archbishop Bossuet of Meaux—who might have been the greatest preacher of the seventeenth century—said that the liturgy was "the main instrument of Tradition." He thought that the liturgy was "Tradition professed," as opposed to the declarations of councils that represent "Tradition defined."

The popes know very well that most people do not read their

encyclicals. When Pius XI wrote *Quas Primas*, his intention was to fight against the spiritual disease of secularism. Here is how the pope announced a new feast that had not been celebrated before and how he would change the missal. "In the task of helping the truths of the faith reach the people and of raising them to the joys of the interior life, the annual solemnities of the liturgical feasts are much more effective than all the documents, even the most serious, of the Church's magisterium: the latter are usually only read by a small number of the most cultured; the salutary influence of the former reaches the heart and the intelligence, and thus the whole man." The feast he instituted was that of the Sacred Heart.

After Vatican II a destructive clergy discarded genuflections, sacred rites, Gregorian Chant, reverence for angels and saints, beautiful vestments and architecture, et cetera, et cetera, but the faith of many was saved by reverence for holy things. I was once involved with a parish that, having come back to its senses, searched for the sacred things that had once adorned its church, in order to restore them. A long section of the original Communion rail had been carefully and lovingly stored in a barn by an old woman who could not give you quotes from documents on the liturgy, as could the priest who had had the rail torn out, but I dare say she knew more about the mind of the Church than he did.

Time after time, converts to the Faith attest to this great truth: that the liturgy and the things that properly accompany it (really beautiful altars, vestments, statues, music, et cetera), move the soul more than argument.

> The young man I was at 18 years old, who was searching amidst a great cloud for a truth which presented itself to him confusedly—a living truth, made for the soul and not just for the mind—had sanctity revealed to him by Gregorian chant. In its bareness and its simplicity it took me much further than secular music, it allowed

me to catch a glimpse of mysteries which I never suspected; it filled me with this "plenitude of God" of which St. Paul speaks; it told me that his plenitude was for me if I wanted it; I was certain that it was God Himself who spoke to me through this chant. (André Charlier, *Le Chant Gregorien*)

Let us look, then, at the liturgy and the things that properly accompany it, for an understanding of the symbolism of the Rite of St. Gregory will deepen our appreciation for what is going on at Mass and lead us to that pearl of great price.

For this looking, however, keep in mind that this will not be a study or explanation of the historical signification of the liturgy, or of the contemporary traditional Mass movement, if I may call it that. Better men than I have already written on these subjects, and I would have little to add to them.

THE HOUSE OF THE LORD

CHURCH CAN REFER TO MANY THINGS. It is a material building in which the divine offices are celebrated. It's also a spiritual fabric—people assembled by ministers and collected in one place by "Him who maketh men to be of one mind in an house" (Ps. 68). It is also called in Sacred Scripture:

✛ A congregation, or synagogue, or ecclesia

✛ Sion—with the expectation of heavenly rest

✛ The House of God

✛ The Lord's House, My Father's House

✛ Temple

✛ Tabernacle of God

23

+ A chapel, which comes from the Latin word *capella*, meaning "little cloak," referring in the early church to a place that kept the cloak of St. Martin

+ Monastery

+ Oratory

+ Virgin—"That I might present you as a chaste virgin to Christ" (2 Cor. 11:2)

+ Bride—"He that hath the bride is the bridegroom" (Jn. 3:29)

+ Mother—she bears children in baptism

+ Widow—"She sitteth solitary through her afflictions, and, like Rachel, will not be comforted" (Durandus; Lam. 1)

+ Harlot—"She is called out of many nations, and closeth not her bosom to any who return to her" (Durandus).

+ City—the communion of her citizens

God commands the building of a church. He commanded that Moses build a tabernacle on Mount Sinai. It was divided into two parts: the Holy of Holies, where the priests ministered to the Lord, and the Holy Place, where the people attended the sacrifices. The Temple of Solomon also had these two great divisions. The tabernacle was first a tent—suitable for wandering. The Temple was not built until the Hebrews took possession of the Holy Land. As Christ came not to destroy but to fulfill, so God's command to build a church carries over into the New Testament. All in the old Temple was symbolic of what was to come.

Let's now look at the symbolism of a traditional Catholic church, using the thought of Bishop Durandus.

BEAUTY IN THE CHURCH BUILDING

The qualifications to speak authoritatively on how a church ought to look are daunting. So much knowledge must be understood, compiled, harmonized, and adapted practically, that to find a man with such qualifications seems impossible. Yet God provided His Bride with just such a man. Fourteen years after the Council of Trent, a young archbishop put together specific directives regarding the design of Catholic churches, affirming the authority of tradition. He was an expert in architecture and in liturgy (he was instrumental in the revision of the Roman Pontifical, Missal, and Breviary under St. Pius V), in priestly formation (he was instrumental in the decree of 1563 regarding this formation), in Canon Law (he was the Papal Delegate to Italy), and in art and music. As if that were not enough, he was extremely well read in the Fathers of the Church and in the medieval doctors (especially St. Thomas Aquinas), so his ability in dogmatic theology was used frequently at the Council of Trent.

His name is St. Charles Borromeo, and the document he wrote is called *Instructiones Fabricae et Supellectilis Ecclesiasticae* (*Instructions on the Building and Furnishing of Churches*). He wrote it so that it could be applied to cathedrals, monasteries, and humble parish churches. He understood well why mostly odd numbers should be used (1, 3, 5, 7—in recognition and honor of the Unity of God, the Holy Trinity, Pentecost, and the Seven Sacraments respectively), so that a composition would always have a clear center. This would result in symmetry (a reflection of divine order). When symmetry could not be achieved, then the right side was favored in keeping with the Mass. So, for example, if a church could not afford two bell towers, it could build one tower, but it must be on the Epistle side of the church. He understood well why and what kinds of circles, domes, or vaults should be used for the ceilings, to reflect the perfection of heaven.

During his time, when Protestants were rejecting the idea that man could encounter the sacred through the senses, St. Charles strove to integrate all the visual arts (such as sculpture and stained glass) with the preeminent auditory arts (hearing the text of the Mass, music, the sermon) so that everything was in harmony with and in support of the sung Mass. He did not favor any particular aesthetic style. Romanesque, Byzantine, Gothic, Baroque—many styles could be used to achieve this harmony. But note the hierarchy here: First is the Mass, and then come singing, then sermons and instructions, then at last come statues and paintings.

The building should be so prominent and identifiable with the Catholic Church as to be unmistakable. St. Charles thought of a church as being a building that any Catholic, even from another land, would recognize it as Catholic on sight. He was a proponent of the recognition by Catholics of the Blessed Sacrament such that they could walk or ride by and tip their hats or make the Sign of the Cross in honor of the Sacrament. Non-Catholics should also be able to identify our churches, in regard to their uniqueness and beauty.

The *Catechism of the Catholic Church* states that "visible churches are not simply gathering places but signify and make visible the Church living in this place, the dwelling of God with men reconciled and united in Christ" (no. 1180). You wonder how a building could accomplish that, even given the *Instructions* of St. Charles. But it can, especially it if reflects in stone and wood the Gregorian Rite through three natural laws: permanence, verticality, and iconography.

Permanence

In the Mass of the Dedication of a Church, we read in the Tract: "They that trust in the Lord shall be as mount Sion: he shall not be moved for ever that dwelleth in Jerusalem." Just as the sacred liturgy should be permanent (and not subject to change unless for a very grave reason) so the church building ought to be permanent to reflect this. This is done in several ways.

The church ought to be a building that will serve for generations. It should transcend time and culture. In other words, to construct a church according to the latest fad will ensure that the structure will be passé or obsolete in a few years. It is the same principle with church music, vestments, and so on. If Fr. Skip tries to rap his sermon, he'll sound like a buffoon, not a messenger of the Holy Gospel. As the Sacred Liturgy is durable, so should the church building be durable.

The church ought to be of significant mass, built with solid foundations and thick walls. This is related to durability, and integral to verticality. A good, solid mass of stone enables the church to be an icon of Christ and reflects the solid base of the Sacred Liturgy, the massive prayer of the Roman Canon.

Just as any change in the Sacred Liturgy should be done only in continuity with what came before (this is called "organic development"), so the church design should come from what has been done before; what is tried and true. For example, the semicircular arch of Romanesque architecture was handed down from the earliest time of the Church. It reflects perfectly the structure of Gregorian chant. By this I mean that chant—when sung properly—does not "hit" the highest notes or lowest notes with volume, but softens and tapers the sound to achieve *melisma* (a Latin word whose root is "honey"). Gothic architecture retains all the qualities of the Romanesque, but adds a soaring verticality. This reflects two things that were occurring in the Church when the Gothic was developed: devotion to our Lady, and the growth of polyphony. The Gothic arch then accommodates both the sweetness of chant and the great soaring melodies and glorious harmonies of polyphony.

Verticality

"Glory to God in the *highest*": the vertical should dominate the horizontal. This reflects the primary purpose of the Church—to get us into heaven. The church building should be like the Elevation of the Host in the Mass.

It is not a coincidence that the Epistle for the feast of a Dedication of a Church is taken from the vision of St. John the Evangelist of the heavenly Jerusalem: "In those days I saw the holy city, the new Jerusalem, coming down out of heaven from God, prepared as a bride adorned for her husband. And I heard a great voice from the throne, saying: Behold the tabernacle of God with men, and He will dwell with them" (Apoc. 21:2-3). The solid foundation is the main altar and the tabernacle, which in themselves ought to point up to the New Jerusalem.

It is the dramatic sense of height that enables a man to look up. If there is no height, there is no physical lifting of the head and the eyes toward heaven. If there is no lifting of the eyes and head, the formation of transcendence in the worshipper is very hard to accomplish. This can be seen also in forms of music that are especially earthbound and stuck in some time period, such as the 1970s. Therefore everything in the church ought to be firmly rooted *here*, but point to *there*—to what is beyond this world. The altar rails, the Stations of the Cross, the candlesticks—everything should point to heaven. Verticality also forms the worshipper in the recognition that Christ is a King. Our ancestors in the Faith called their great churches *basilicas*, a word that comes from the Greek meaning "a house of the king."

Iconography

Iconography refers to the value of a church building as a sign or icon. The church should remind us of the next world. However, "Do not conform yourselves to this age" (Rom. 12:2). Just as the Mass we celebrate should not be conformed to this world, so the church building shouldn't either.

The building should point beyond itself. It will do so not by graphic art (such as clever marquees outside the church that attempt to lure new customers), but by veiling the church with symbols, as the Mass is veiled in Latin. To this day, people flock to see the cathedrals of Europe, not necessarily because they are Catholic, but because they are drawn to the mystery of beauty. Those churches allow one to think of a different world beyond this one.

The Introit of the Mass of the Dedication of a Church begins, "Terrible is this place: it is the house of God, and the gate of heaven; and it shall be called the court of God." The very appearance of our churches should call this great truth to mind.

So if we follow those three simple laws of church architecture— permanence, verticality, and iconography—we will have a building that will help us go to heaven. As one parishioner put it, after he had seen the Gregorian Rite in the Denver basilica, "The cathedral was a participant in the liturgy."

The Church's Structure

Let us now consider the parts of the church and their meanings. The first step in building a Catholic church is the laying of the cornerstone. "It fell not, for it was founded upon a rock" (Mt. 7:25). The bishop lays the stone with a cross engraved upon it, and then he sprinkles it with holy water. This stone represents Christ and His Vicar, St. Peter. Then larger stones are laid on top of the cornerstone. These represent the faithful who undertake the painful labors of fraternal charity—the people who do the work in a parish. The lighter stones that are then placed above the larger ones represent people who do no labor in the church but depend on others to do that work for them. But all these are dependent on the cornerstone, which holds them all together.

The cement between the stones represents charity, which is the bond of peace.

The arrangement of the building is like the body of Christ—His head at the top, His arms in the transepts, His heart at the altar. It is in the shape of a cross, since, "if any man will come after me, let him deny himself, and take up his cross, and follow me" (Mt. 16:18).

It has four walls, as there are four evangelists.

The foundation symbolizes faith. Height represents courage and hope, which leave behind adversity and prosperity. Length is fortitude and perseverance. Breadth is charity, having two sides—the love of friends for the sake of God and the love of enemies for the sake of God. These two walls are concord and peace.

The roof is charity, which "covereth a multitude of sins" (1 Pet. 4:8). The roof's tiles are soldiers and police who protect the church from external and internal enemies in the land in which the church is built.

The door of the church is Christ—"I am the door" (Jn. 10:9)—but to enter through the door one must strive to keep the commandments. "If thou wilt enter into life, keep the commandments" (Mt. 19:17).

The floor of the church is the foundation of our Faith. Spiritually it is the poor in spirit, who humble themselves in all things: "My soul cleaveth to the pavement" (Ps. 119:25). It also represents the multitude by whose labors the church is sustained.

The four walls of the transepts—what Durandus called the hands of the church—are the four cardinal virtues: prudence, justice, fortitude, and temperance. The windows are the sayings of the saints and also hospitality with cheerfulness. The choir loft is the angels, who sing in praise of the Savior. The original word *choir* (*chorus*) is from the Greek, meaning a band of singers who, in ancient tragedies, gave expression to the moral and religious sentiments evoked by the actions of the play.

The Bell Tower

The bell tower represents the bishop, whose mind should ascend to heaven and who also stands as a defense of his flock. "Thy neck is like the tower of David builded for an armory" (Cant. 4:4).

The rooster on the weathervane of the bell tower is like the earthly rooster in the chicken coop, who is vigilant during the night and predicts the morning with his crow but slaps his sides before the prediction. The nighttime is this world, and the sleepers are the children of this world who are asleep in their sins. The rooster is the preacher, who seeks to awaken sinners and exclaims, "Woe to them that sleep! Awake thou that sleepest!" (Eph. 5:14). The preacher is to speak of the Day of Judgment and the glory that is to come, but first he must slap his sides like the rooster; that is, he must mortify himself for his sins.

The weathervane always turns to face the wind. This is symbolic of the preacher, who must turn to face the rebellious in the flock and the wolf that seeks to do harm to them. He must do so, lest he be guilty "when the wolf cometh, of leaving the sheep and fleeing" (Jn. 10:12). The iron rod pointing to heaven on which the rooster sits represents the discourse of the preacher, in that he must speak of God and not of man, according to the saying "If any man speak, let him speak as the oracles of God" (1 Pet. 4:11).

Windows

The glass windows are the Holy Scriptures, which keep out the wind and rain (that which is harmful to the flock) but let sunlight (which is God) into the hearts of the faithful. These are wider on the inside than on the outside (a common architectural feature of the Romanesque and Gothic styles), signifying that the truth of God is greater than the defense from what is wrong. The windows have two shafts, which signify the two great precepts of charity (love of

God and love of neighbor), which were accomplished by Christ's sending out the apostles two by two.

Pillars and Beams

The pillars on the inside represent the apostles, "who seemed to be pillars" (Gal. 2:9). The bases of the columns are the apostolic bishops, while the capitals are the Fathers and the Doctors. The ornamentation of the columns is the writings and examples of the saints.

The beams that join the columns together are the preachers, who bring to the faithful the wisdom of the apostles, the Doctors, and the bishops.

Steps

Circular staircases, a feature borrowed from Solomon's Temple, represent the hidden knowledge that only those who ascend to celestial things may know. The steps leading up to the altar represent three things: the knowledge that will be granted in the Beatific Vision; the sacrifices of the martyrs; and the virtues, as we approach Christ through the virtues: "They go from virtue to virtue" (Ps. 84:7).

The Pulpit

The pulpit is sometimes elevated not just so that people can hear and see better, but so that the speech that comes from it should be elevated from common discourse, and because of its root in the preaching of Solomon, "who made a brazen scaffold, and set it in the midst of the temple, and stood upon it, and stretching forth his hands spake to the people of God" (3 Kings 6:13).

The Sacristy

The sacristy, where the priest and the sacred ministers put on their robes, is the womb of the Blessed Virgin, where Christ put on the robes of humanity. The priest proceeds from the sacristy into the public view as Christ left Mary to be seen in the Temple.

The Sanctuary

Each church has an altar: "Thou shalt offer burnt offerings on mine altar" (Ex. 9:2). St. Peter used to travel around with a small wooden altar. But as soon as the Church came out of the catacombs, the pope took that altar and reverently enclosed it in the high altar at St. Peter's, which is what St. Peter always wanted to do. Ideally, all altars are made of stone.

The altar represents Christ above all. It is also a table: "Thou preparest a table before me in the presence of mine enemies" (Ps. 22:5). It's not that the church is filled with enemies, but at every Mass one may assume that enemies (betrayers of the Cross) are present. And certainly our enemies from hell hover in and around churches and lurk in the parking lots. The altar is also a clean heart, and the fire that burns near it—the holy lamp or sanctuary lamp—represents Christ: "I am the light of the world" (Jn. 8:12). This lamp also reminds us that charity should always burn in our hearts: "The fire shall always be burning upon mine altar" (Lev. 6:9).

The shape of the altar is wide, and by this expanse is understood charity, which ought to extend even to our enemies.

The white cloths that cover the altar signify the flesh of the Savior—that is, His humanity. They also represent our own garments: "And put on white garments, that the shame of thy nakedness do not appear" (Apoc. 3:18). A pure heart is adorned with good works, and nakedness is the lack of good works. "Let thy garments be always white" (Eccles. 9:8); that is, let our works be clean.

The reason for the number of candles on the altar may be understood from the Jewish menorah used in the Temple before the

Holy of Holies that had seven branches (there is another menorah used just for Hanukah that has nine branches). It had two meanings attached to it: one was that there were six branches on either side to represent the twelve tribes of Israel, and the seventh branch in the middle to represent the presence of God with His people. It also represented the presence of God in the burning bush. The original menorah is lost to history, and the only picture of it is found on the Arch of Titus in Rome.

The candles on the altar are six, which varies from what Moses ordered, viz., seven lights—six for the twelve tribes, one for the presence of God. The candlesticks are representative of the Church Militant and also stand for the light of good works, which enlighten and enflame the charity of others. The seventh candle is not normally used; in the Temple, it was in the center and represented the presence of God in Israel. The tabernacle has replaced the seventh candle, as God is no longer represented on the altar but is truly present. The seventh candle is still used, however, for the Mass of a bishop, who is the chief representative of God in a diocese.

Two candlesticks are used for Low Mass, to portray the joy of the Jews and the Gentiles at the Nativity of Christ. The one on the left represents the Gentiles, as does the Gospel side of the altar. "Ye were sometimes darkness but now light in the Lord" (Eph. 5:8). The one on the right (the epistle side) is for the Jews and is lit as a prayer. "Arise, shine, thy light is come, and the glory of the Lord is risen upon thee" (Is. 60:1). The cross between them is Christ, who is the Mediator between the two peoples, the cornerstone, "who hath made both one." (Eph. 2:14).

The altar has a triumphal cross, raised high, to signify the victory of Christ on the Cross. A triumphal cross is made of good-quality metal, with or without jewels. It represents many things to us: Christ, without Whom no gift is acceptable to the Father; the Mystical Body of Christ; mortification of the heart, in which our carnal motions are consumed by the fire of the Holy Ghost. This consuming fire is especially represented in the consecration of the altar.

IMAGES

The images (stained glass, the Stations, statues) around the church are the Scriptures of the unlearned. We do not adore these pictures, but as St. Gregory the Great says, by them we *learn* what to adore.

Our Lord is represented in many ways, but good art has a care not to confuse images. For example, St. John the Baptist called our Lord the Lamb of God, and He was crucified for our sakes, but we do not place a lamb on the Cross. There is no problem depicting a lamb at the foot of the Cross, or a lamb with blood coming from his side—even into a chalice—and putting that image into a nativity scene. But we do not put a lamb into the crib. Neither do we confuse mysteries, by putting the resurrected body of Christ on the Cross. The triumph of the Cross in the Resurrection is depicted by an ornate cross; one that is of precious or semiprecious metal and may be with or without a corpus.

Artists depict angels as being very young, almost like babies, since they cannot age due to their incorporeal nature.

The four evangelists are presented as a man (St. Matthew), a lion (St. Mark), an ox (St. Luke), and an eagle (St. John). These were the four creatures in the vision of Ezekiel.

St. John the Baptist is presented as a hermit; martyrs are pictured with instruments of torture, such as St. Bartholomew with the flaying knife and St. Lawrence with the gridiron. Sometimes the saints are portrayed with palms: "The righteous shall flourish like the palm tree" (Ps. 92:13), because the palm tree grows best under adversity (very hot weather) from outside, when well watered below by grace. Confessors are shown with the signs of their office, abbots with their cowls, bishops with miters, some saints with lilies, which denote chastity. Doctors have a book in their hands, and virgins have lamps (cf. Mt. 25:1). St. Paul is shown with a book and a sword. The sword is his zeal, and the book depicts his conversion and that he is the first Doctor of the Church. Flowers and trees are often used to portray the fruit of good works.

Gold, the most precious of metals, is used especially to symbolize charity, which is the most precious of virtues.

All the sacred images are veiled during Passiontide, since our Lord's divinity was concealed as He gave Himself up to be betrayed and scourged. "But Jesus hid himself, and went out of the temple" (Jn. 8:59). The virtue of His divinity is hidden. The veiling of the images also symbolizes that the understanding of Scripture before the Passion was veiled, hidden, and obscure. Many of the Fathers also see this lack of understanding as the sword that prevented man from returning to Paradise.

On Holy Saturday, the veils are removed, because at our Lord's death, the curtain or veil of the Temple was rent, and His Resurrection made it possible for us to enter heaven and also to understand the mysteries.

The church is adorned gloriously within, but not without. There are practical reasons for this of course, but the theological reason is the indwelling of God. "Know you not, that you are the temple of God, and that the Spirit of God dwelleth in you?" (1 Cor. 3:16).

Bells

Bells were first used in Campania in Italy; large bells are called *campanae*. It is clear in the rite of consecration of bells that they are meant to serve many purposes: that the faithful may be cheered on to their reward; that the devotion of faith may be increased in them; that the fruits of the field and the minds and bodies of the parishioners may be defended; that the hostile legions and all the snares of the Enemy may be repulsed; that the violence of storms may be restrained; that the spirits of the storm and the powers of the air may be restrained; that sinners might find refuge in Holy Mother Church.

The bells signify the silver trumpets by which people of the Old Law were called to the sacrifice. They also signify the priest preaching. The Lord commanded Moses to make a vestment for the high priest and ordered seventy-two bells to sound when the high priest entered into the Holy of Holies (Ex. 28:35). This sounding of the bell exhorts the faithful to pay attention to the preacher. But the cavity of the bell reminds the preacher of humility and of the warning of St. Paul: "I am become as sounding brass or a tinkling symbol" (1 Cor. 13:1).

The hardness of the metal signifies the fortitude that should be in the mind of the preacher: "Behold I have made thy face strong against their faces" (Ez. 3:8).

The clapper that strikes the two sides of the bell is the tongue of the preacher, who should preach from both the Old and New Testaments. A bishop who cannot preach is like a bell without a clapper. St. Gregory the Great calls him a dog that cannot bark!

The striking of the bell signifies the striking of vices in the preacher, and because the word of God is a two-edged sword, the sermon is first for the correction of the preacher ("lest having preached to others, he himself should be a castaway" [cf. 1 Cor. 9:27] and, second, for the correction of the faithful.

The link by which the clapper is joined is moderation, by which the tongue of the preacher should be ruled.

The wood of the frame on which the bell is fastened stands for the wood of the Cross, lifted high. The rope to pull the bell comes from this wood, which reminds the preacher that he must preach Christ and Him crucified (cf. 1 Cor. 1:23). A rope is usually composed of three strands, so preaching should comprise morality, allegory, and history. The rope goes high and low when it is rung, for sometimes the preacher should speak of lofty things, and at other times of simple things, as St. Paul said, "Whether we exalt ourselves it is for God, or whether we humble ourselves it is for you" (2 Cor. 5:13). When the priest pulls the rope downward, he descends from contemplation to the active life. But when holding on to the rope he is drawn upward; he is raised in contemplation.

In a Catholic culture, the bells were usually rung twelve times a day, since the day is canonically divided into two parts of twelve hours each. These correspond to the Divine Office. This scheme of ringing the bells was meant to sound the death knell of the Passion and death of Christ. At Matins and Lauds (6 a.m.), He is arrested and bound. At Prime (8 a.m.), He is reviled. At Tierce (9 a.m., the third canonical hour), He is condemned to death. At Sext (12 p.m., the sixth canonical hour), He is nailed to the Cross. At None (3 p.m., the ninth canonical hour; notice the connection here with the Hour of Divine Mercy), His side is pierced. At Vespers (6 p.m.), He is taken down from the Cross, and at Compline (9 p.m.), He is laid to rest. The bells can also be rung three times a day at the hours of the Angelus—at 6 a.m., 12 p.m., and 6 p.m.—in honor of the Incarnation and of the Holy Trinity.

There was quite a science to the ringing of bells. In English the words *ringing, tolling, knelling, chiming,* and *chanting* all refer to different ways of sounding the bells. This art has largely been lost, and I pray that someday it will return.

Bells were also rung when someone was dying, so that the parish would know to pray for the person. This was called the Passing Bell. Bells were rung for processions so that evil spirits might hear and flee, as a tyrant hearing the trumpets of the king coming to depose him would flee in fear.

Bells were silent in case of an interdict (an ecclesiastical punishment for a congregation or a town): "I will make thy tongue cleave to the roof of thy mouth, for they are a rebellious house" (Ez. 3:26). This was considered a severe punishment.

THE DEDICATION OF A CHURCH

A church is dedicated to God, and there are five reasons for this dedication:

1. That the devil and his power may be entirely expelled from it.

2. That those who fly for refuge into it may be saved, as when Joab fled into the tabernacle and laid hold of the horns of the altar.

3. That prayers may be heard there, as Solomon prayed might happen at the dedication of the temple (3 Kings 8:30).

4. That praises may be offered to God, under the head of the Church, who is Christ.

5. That the sacraments may be administered there worthily.

In the Rite of Dedication or Consecration of a Church, the bishop writes the alphabet in Greek and Latin upon a St. Andrew's cross of sand on the floor of the church. It represents how both testaments are fulfilled in the Cross and how one testament is contained in the other. It is done on the floor, since it is really the ground that is being consecrated. For if something happens to the building, the ground is not reconsecrated. But the new building is blessed with Gregorian water. The same goes for an altar. Once it is consecrated, it remains consecrated. (There are exceptions to this, such as after an act of profanation.)

Twelve special candlesticks are placed around the walls of a consecrated church. These twelve lights signify the Twelve Apostles, who have enlightened the world through their teaching: "All prophecy is versified in the faith of the Crucified One" (St. Bernard, *Vexilla Regis Prodeunt*). These candles may be anointed with balsam to signify purity of conscience and the savor of a good reputation, which is essential to those who would imitate the apostles.

CONSECRATION OF AN ALTAR

An altar is consecrated for three reasons:

1. Because of the Sacrament which will be offered upon it. This was prefigured among many ways by Noah, who built an altar to the Lord and offered a sacrifice upon it, taking some of all clean birds and beasts (cf. Gen. 8). But we have the Body and Blood of the Lord.

2. Because of the invocation of the Name of God that takes place there. This was foreshadowed by Abraham, who built an altar to God, Who had appeared to him, and called there upon the name of the Lord (cf. Gen. 12). The invocation that is done on our altar is called the Mass.

3. Because of the chanting that takes place there. "He gave him patience against his enemies, and caused singers also to stand before the altar, that by their voices they might make sweet melody." (cf. Ecclus. 47:9)

Four materials are used for the consecration. These are the ingredients of the Gregorian Water: water, wine, salt, and ashes—the four things that expel the devil:

1. Water signifies the outpouring of tears.

2. Wine signifies the exultation of the soul and spiritual intelligence.

3. Salt, symbolic of wisdom, signifies natural discretion.

4. Ashes signify profound humility.

These acts that are represented in the Gregorian Water are needed for salvation. For example, without humility there is no remission of sins. An adult who has sinned must have the humility to confess his sins; if he does not, they are not forgiven.

The order is significant, since the church is consecrated outwardly by water and inwardly by the Holy Ghost. "Unless a man be born again by water and the Holy Ghost, he cannot enter the kingdom of heaven" (Jn. 3:3). So the water is first, but into it are put the lifting up of the soul, wisdom, and humility, which are effected by the action of the Holy Ghost. This action of the Holy Ghost upon the soul calls to mind the Creation of the world: "He moved upon the face of the waters" (Gen 1:2).

Four crosses are carved into the stone of an altar, to represent the four loves the priest ought to have: of God, himself, his friends, and his enemies. God told Abraham in the book of Genesis, "Thou shalt spread into the east, and the west, and the north and the south." (Gen. 28:14). Another cross is made in the middle of the altar to represent the Passion, which was made in the middle of the earth—that is, in Jerusalem.

The five crosses on the altar represent the five wounds of Christ, by Whose stripes we were healed. They also denote the five feelings of pity that are necessary for us:

1. Pity toward Christ, in sympathizing with His Passion, as Job, in the person of Christ says, "Pity me, pity me" (Job 19:21).

2. "The pity of a man towards his neighbor" (Ecclus. 18:12), when we see his calamity.

3. The pity of man toward himself in three ways: first, for his sins of commission by bewailing them. "There is no one who hath

penitence for his sin, saying, 'What have I done?'" (Jer. 8:6). Second, for his sins of omission, "Woe is me, for I have held my peace" (Is. 6:5); i.e., I should have spoken but did not. Third, for himself because he has done good deeds for less pure motives. "When we have done all good deeds, we must say that we are unprofitable servants" (Lk. 17:10). Of this threefold compassion Ecclesiasticus says, "Have pity on thy soul and please God" (Ecclus. 30:24).

In the Middle Ages, during the Rite of the Consecration of an Altar, the bishop goes seven times around the altar, to implore God that those who celebrate and attend Mass at it might have the sevenfold virtue of the humility of Christ and might have similar movements of humility in their lives. These movements of Christ are as follows:

1. From being rich He became poor.

2. From His throne in heaven He was laid in a manger.

3. From being at the right hand of the Father He was made subject to His parents.

4. From having command of the angels He bowed His head under the hand of a slave.

5. From the company of the nine choirs of angels He bore a thief and a betrayer as disciples.

6. From the perfection of the judgment of His Father He stood gentle before an unrighteous judge.

7. From being able to loose the angels in judgment upon the world, He mercifully prayed for those who crucified Him.

They also indicate the seven journeys of Christ: from heaven to the Virgin's womb, from her womb to the manger, from the manger into the world, from the world to the Cross, from the Cross to the sepulcher, from the sepulcher to the place of spirits, from the place of spirits to heaven.

Then the bishop sprinkles the altar. The altar is sprinkled seven times to symbolize the seven gifts of the Holy Ghost that are conferred especially in Confirmation and also to symbolize the seven outpourings of the blood of Christ, which made those gifts possible for us: His circumcision, His sweating of blood, His scourging, His crowning with thorns, His pierced hands, His pierced feet, and His pierced side.

These aspersions are made with a hyssop, an herb that grows naturally on a rock in the Sinai desert. It is a humble herb that signifies the humility of Christ, and that is what breaks through the obstinate heart. Our altar is our heart; the heart is in a man what an altar is in a temple. On this altar is made the sacrifice of joy, "The sacrifices of God are a broken spirit" (Ps. 50:17). On this altar is made the commemoration of the Body and Blood of the Lord. From it prayers rise to heaven, because God looks at the heart.

Relics of the martyrs are enclosed in the altar with three grains of frankincense. A stone slab is placed over the relics as they are encased in the altar, because by the example of the saints, charity arises in us that is sweet smelling to God, an acceptable sacrifice "which covereth a multitude of sins" (1 Pet. 4:8).

The altar is anointed with chrism in five places. As the bishop pours oil on the altar, so does Christ pour grace upon our heart, which is our altar in the temple of the Holy Ghost. But as the altar also stands for Christ, so is He the Anointed One. "The Lord hath anointed thee with the oil of gladness above thy fellows" (Ps. 44:8).

Unction with oil also signifies mercy: "Anoint thy head with oil, and wash thy face" (cf. Mt. 6:17). For as oil is among other liquids, rising to the top, so is mercy to other works: "The Lord is loving to every man, and His mercy is over all his works" (Ps. 144:9).

After the anointing, incense is burned in the five places that were anointed, so that our good works might be known to others. The chrism is burned with this prayer: "We are the sweet savor of Christ in every place." (2 Cor. 2:15) The flame itself represents our work before men: "Let your light so shine before men that they may glorify God" (Mt. 5:16).

Consecration of the Entire Church

The whole church is illuminated with flame, in twelve places on the walls of the church, which are also anointed. The twelve small candelabras that are in our church are from its consecration. "Then shall the just shine, as sparks run swiftly among the stubble" (Wis. 3:7). The whole body of the church is consecrated then, for as St. Bernard of Clairvaux wrote, "Present your bodies a living sacrifice holy acceptable unto God which is your reasonable service; mortifying upon the altar of your heart your members which are upon the earth."

Like the great cathedrals of Europe, the traditional Roman rite is a work of art; and like any work of art, every element must be understood in context, even authorial "mistakes." What may be an accident, a later interpolation, or even a defect, can, with or without the author's intention, contribute to a larger unified whole. Sometimes, these "happy faults" can even be the best or most interesting part of the work. And if this is true on a purely human level, imagine how much more it is true when the art in question involves the providential guidance of the Holy Ghost.

A SERIOUS PLAY

OUR GOOD LORD SAID THAT we would have to become like children to enter the kingdom of God, and in fact it is only with childlike wonder that we can best appreciate the Gregorian Rite with its symbolism and even the architecture that goes with it.

Henry Adams once wrote about the great cathedral of Chartres, France, one of the world's finest examples of Gothic architecture. He was Protestant, so he had no background in Catholic theology, but he was a good student of architecture. He had heard of the Catholic ability to express theology in stone as much as in a painting or a hymn. So he traveled to Chartres, and by just looking at, reflecting on, and wondering about the cathedral, he was able to understand much about what the theology of the time taught about the Blessed Virgin. Here is an example of what he learned through his keen observation:

To the Church, no doubt, its cathedral here has a fixed and administrative meaning, which is the same as that of every other bishop's seat and with which we have nothing whatever to do. To us, it is a child's fancy; a toyhouse to please the Queen of Heaven—to please her so much that she would be happy in it—to charm her till she smiled.

The Queen Mother was as majestic as you like; she was absolute; she could be stern; she was not above being angry; but she was still a woman, who loved grace, beauty, ornament—her toilette, robes, jewels; who considered the arrangements of her palace with attention, and liked both light and color; who kept a keen eye on her Court, and exacted prompt and willing obedience from king and archbishops as well as from beggars and drunken priests. She protected her friends and punished her enemies. She required space, beyond what was known in the Courts of kings, because she was liable at all times to have ten thousand people begging her for favors—mostly inconsistent with the law—and deaf to refusal.

She was extremely sensitive to neglect, to disagreeable impressions, to want of intelligence in her surroundings. She was the greatest artist, as she was the greatest philosopher and musician and theologian, that ever lived on earth, except her Son, Who, at Chartres, is still an infant under her guardianship. Her taste was infallible; her sentence eternally final. This church was built for her in this spirit of simple-minded, practical, utilitarian faith—in this singleness of thought, exactly as a little girl sets up a doll-house for her favorite blond doll. Unless you can go back to your dolls, you are out of place here. If you can go back to them, and get rid for one small hour of the weight of custom, you shall see Chartres in glory.

This is a way to understand the Gregorian Rite, a mystical way similar to how the Fathers understood Sacred Scripture.

THE DOOR OF BEAUTY

People usually enter Holy Mother Church by one of two doors: the door of the intelligence or the door of beauty. The first is open to scholars and intellectuals. The second is open to anyone—especially those who see with childlike wonder. "It is necessary to lose the illusion that the truth can communicate itself fruitfully without that splendor that is of one nature with it and which is called beauty" (Henri Charlier).

The Church in her mystery needs an earthly epiphany (a Greek word meaning "manifestation") accessible to all—from the child to the senior. This is why the church building itself should be majestic, the liturgy splendid, and the music sweet. When a group of Japanese tourists visits Notre Dame Cathedral in Paris, they are entranced to watch Solemn Vespers. Beauty has opened its doors for them. Notre Dame Cathedral and the *Summa Theologica* of St. Thomas are products of the same era, but how many have read the *Summa*? How many even can?

The beauty of the liturgy can be called the splendor of the truth (philosophers distinguish five kinds of beauty, and splendor is the first of these; it is a shining forth, a compelling beauty of power). Among the small and the great, the beauty of the chant or the polyphony, the texts, the candles, the vestments, and the dignity of bearing all exercise an influence on the soul, which it touches directly even before the soul perceives that influence. But this is a very delicate art. "The liturgy is not a show, a spectacle requiring brilliant producers and talented actors. The life of the liturgy does not consist in pleasant surprises and attractive ideas but in solemn repetitions," says Cardinal Ratzinger (*The Spirit of the Liturgy*).

What is the solemnity to which the cardinal refers? First, it is a behavior opposed to sentimentality and the domination of emotion. When the priest faces the people for Mass, it is particularly difficult for him to keep his emotions from dominating the liturgy. If he is sad, this becomes burdensome and a distraction to the one who desires joy. If he is in a particularly happy mood, then this is burdensome and distracting to the one who needs to mourn. Solemnity expresses the supernatural; it raises us out of the everyday and is not bound to this or that emotion. It is not an emotional flatline, but a *gravitas*, a seriousness becoming the proclamation of the death of the Lord, which is what St. Paul called the Mass.

Certainly the priest must be on guard so that solemnity does not degenerate into pomposity and affectation. Adornment succeeds especially when it is almost forgotten, but accusations of triumphalism are an insult to the poor, who love to see greatness exalted. "There is no trace of triumphalism in the solemnity with which the Church expresses the glory of God, the joy of the faith, the victory of truth and light over error and darkness. The richness of the liturgy is not the richness of some priestly caste: it is the richness of all, including the poor, who in fact desire it and are by no means scandalized by it" (Cardinal Ratzinger).

Prince Vladimir of Kiev, while still a pagan, wanted to worship the one God, and so he listened to Moslems, Jews, and Greeks, each of whom came to show him their religion. He sent a delegation of ten men to go and see how each of the groups practiced their liturgy. When he heard their reports, he was most impressed by their account of the Greek Christians: "We went to Greece and they led us to the place where they worship their God. From that moment on we did not know if we were in heaven or on earth; there is no other sight like it here below, and there is nothing of such beauty. We simply cannot describe it; all we know is that it is there that God lives amongst men; and their worship is more marvelous than in the other countries" (*The Chronicles of Nestor*). Vladimir converted, and that is how Christianity was brought to what is now the Ukraine. The Greeks had put on their best vestments, enlisted the help of their best choir, and chosen the best priests to sing the liturgy. We can't do that each day in the parish, but we can strive to imitate their virtues and approximate their solemnity, even at a Low Mass.

REFLECTIONS OF GOD

Symbolism helps to show that God lives among us. Where did Catholic symbolism come from? It is very unlikely that it was understood and then expressed in writing or in stone; it is far more likely that the architecture grew naturally from the Mass, and then it and the Mass were understood after much reflection, such as that of Henry Adams.

One sees in the earliest times of the Church various symbols: the fish with its connection to our Blessed Savior's Holy Name; the Resurrection set forth in the phoenix; the Passion symbolized by the pelican; the Holy Eucharist by grapes and shocks of wheat; the Word of God by the eagle; the Church by the ark; partridges, peacocks, lions, horses, strange fishes, oxen, stars, the moon—the list is long.

The prevalent use of numbers is also deeply significant. One—the unity of God; two—the divine and human natures; three—the Holy Trinity; four—the Gospel; five—the wounds of Christ; six—the attributes of God; seven—the gifts of the Holy Ghost; eight—spiritual regeneration; twelve—the apostles; these are just a few of the ways in which numbers are used as symbols. The Fathers of the Church often made use of numbers to expound the significance of Sacred Scripture.

The Old Testament is full of symbolism for what was to be fulfilled in the New Testament. Spiritual regeneration and the Church can be seen in the ark and the Flood; the bread and wine of the Eucharist can be seen in the manna and the stricken rock; the Old and New Covenants are plain in the story of Sarah and Hagar.

Nature and the Church are the implicit and explicit revelations of God. Artists talk about a trinity of effect in every picture; musicians talk about a trinity of tone in every note; philosophers speak of a trinity of power in every mind and a trinity of essence in every substance. So there should be no surprise to see the Trinity reflected in nature—from St. Patrick's shamrock to a man's body, mind, and soul. The Resurrection is also mirrored in nature—from the setting and rising sun to springtime—and our Blessed Savior taught that excellent doctrine by referring to a grain of wheat that, "if it die bringeth forth much fruit" (Jn. 12:25).

In music we can see the same principle: Franz Joseph Haydn said the trombone is deep red, the trumpet scarlet, the clarinet orange, the oboe yellow, the bassoon deep yellow, the flute sky blue, the diapason deep blue, the double diapason purple, the horn violet, the violin pink, the viola rose, the violoncello red, the double bass crimson. The symbols hold amazingly true in his magnificent composition *The Creation*. It starts with a soft-streaming sound from violins; then each instrument is added until the sun appears in its glory. Thus, the expressions of one art may be translated into another. In a similar way, the Holy Trinity is reflected all over in a traditional Catholic church.

The parables of the Gospel are a sure source of the origin of Christian symbolism, as much as the liturgy of the ancient Jewish Temple. Tradition has it that when Jesus was once in sight of the Temple, He pointed toward it and uttered those gracious words: "I am the door" (Jn. 10:9). St. Paul does not hesitate to allegorize the Temple: the Holy of Holies was heaven; the High Priest, Christ; the veil, His flesh; et cetera. No wonder St. Charles Borromeo insisted on the importance of the doors of the church in his great work on church architecture, *Instructions on the Building and Furnishing of Churches*. In fact, beautiful doors are the key to the entire façade of the church.

Think of Chartres for a moment, or any of the great Gothic cathedrals. One of the first things you notice is their vertical dimension.

They soar upward; they emphasize height. Compare this with pagan temples, which emphasize the horizontal. It has been observed by more than one author that in this architecture we see a movement from the pagan, who worships only in fear, to the Christian, who keeps the fear yet aspires to go to heaven. "*Ad supernas semper intenti*," said St. Paul. "Always intent on the higher things" (1 Cor. 12:31).

As a sacrament is "an outward sign instituted by Christ to give sanctifying grace," so the church building should be sacramental—an outward sign of what is really happening inside it, and above all what should be happening in the soul.

Here are some examples:

1. The Holy Trinity is symbolized in many ways, such as by the three steps leading up to the altar from the nave; by the sanctuary, the nave, and the narthex; and by having three altars.

2. Spiritual regeneration—an octagon is preferred for the baptistery. St. Ambrose points out that the old creation took seven days; hence, the eighth was the new day. The Resurrection was considered the eighth day. The main symbol used in this sacred octagon is three fishes intertwined in an equilateral triangle, typifying our regeneration in the Trinity. The fish is the emblem of the Christian, who was born again of water.

3. The Atonement is reflected in the church's cruciform shape. Even the triumphal cross embellished with foliage and flowers or jewels signifies the continual flourishing and increase of that which was planted on Golgotha. The arms on a crucifix extended straight out to symbolize our Lord's embrace of His Passion and death and His undying love for sinners.

4. The stained glass, the statues, and the votive lights express well the doctrine of the Communion of Saints.

5. Doors—"I am the door" said Christ. If a serpent is used for the door handle, it is symbolic of the passage from St. Mark's Gospel, "They shall lay their hands upon serpents and shall not be harmed" (Mk. 16:18). Ideally we enter from the west end of the church, signifying that it is by way of the Church Militant that we can hope to enter the Church Triumphant (the east end). There is a reason why the animals could enter into Noah's ark only through the door in the port side of the ark. As the ark stood for the vessel of salvation and had only one entrance, so the symbolism of the doors in the west side is significant. The Gothic doors start somewhat wide, but narrow with successive smaller doors, because Christ said, "Strait is the path and narrow the door" (Mt. 7:14). From the door to the main altar, we should see a straight path.

6. Gargoyles represent evil spirits fleeing from the holiness of Christ.

SERIOUS PLAY

It's not that everything has to be a symbol. But everything in the liturgy—and the building in which it takes place—is in one sense a kind of play, like the gargoyle. This is not childish play but very serious play.

To understand the concept of serious play in the liturgy, I'm going to use some of the thought of Fr. Romano Guardini (a favorite author of Pope Benedict XVI), which is in a fascinating little book called *The Spirit of the Liturgy*, but adding some of my own comments to it.

Certain grave and very serious people who see moral problems in everything, and demand a definite purpose to all things at all times, are inclined to regard the liturgy as superfluous pageantry that is somewhat aimless. What is the purpose of it all? Why not just have the sacrifice and the following meal and be done with it? According to this thinking, if something is nonessential to a thing's purpose, it is more or less wasteful, or at least trivial and beside the point.

But look at nature for a moment. Are the various kinds of leaves or the myriads of flower varieties useful? According to this kind of mindset, they are useful to some extent, but *not* the seemingly indiscriminate extravaganza of nature, which gives us an endless variety of shapes, colors, sizes, and scents of flowers, unless to attract a bee or two. Still, that does not account for the variety. It simply is not necessary that apples be red or green, and the fact that an apple is red does not seem to serve any real purpose (unless Eve had a particular fancy for that color, but that's another subject). It is a fact that some things might not have a purpose. But they could have meaning or significance. And their significance consists in being what they are. And their meaning is that they should be the image of eternal God.

Art (when at its best) has no purpose. The wall will stand up fine without any pictures hanging on it. But art is full of meaning. Idealists in the Enlightenment wanted to force it to have purpose—so that art would teach virtue, say—but the more they succeeded in this, the uglier the art became. It reminds me of those dreary games sold by those who insist that all play must be a "learning moment." Anxious parents buy these, frightened that their children might not be getting a leg up on the other kids as they prepare for Harvard.

So both purpose and meaning are needed in life, but things must not be forced into a rigid framework of purpose. Canon law gives a whole system of purposes, constitution, and government. Thus, sacraments act as channels of graces. They have a purpose and are regulated by law, and grace is given every time they are properly celebrated. But the liturgy has no thought-out, detailed, systematic plan of instruction.

Compare a gymnasium with an open field at the edge of a wood. In the gym, everything is organized to a particular development and discipline. And it is lifeless in itself. The field and woods are filled with life but are rather unorganized. The abundance of prayers, ideas, symbols, and gestures in the liturgy create a world where the soul is rather free to wander about at will and to develop itself there. As when taking a walk in the woods and the field, the soul can stop at any time and marvel at a flower or the color of the grass or the smell of the trees, or, in the liturgy, to linger over this prayer or wonder about that vestment.

So our liturgy does not have a purpose in the sense described above—existing essentially for the sake of humanity—but it exists for the sake of God. It's like the small flower turned toward the sun, delighting in its Maker. In the liturgy man is no longer concerned about himself (thank God), but for a brief time his gaze is turned toward God. He is in a forest of sacred life, in the midst of a thousand, thousand adorations. This is described in the first chapter of the book of Ezekiel, when the saintly prophet saw the flaming cherubim.

> And I saw, and behold a whirlwind came out of the north, and a great cloud, and a fire infolding it. And in the midst thereof the likeness of four living creatures. . . . And every one of them went straight forward. Whither the impulse of the spirit was to go, thither they went. . . . This was the vision running to and fro in the midst of the living creatures, a bright fire and lightning going forth from the fire. And the living creatures ran and returned like flashes of lightning. . . . And I heard the noise of their wings, like the noise of many waters. . . . And when they stood, their wings were let down. . . . As the appearance of the rainbow when it is in a cloud on a rainy day.

These angels will not be neatly fitted into a purpose. How aimless their action appears! They are pure motion, powerful and splendid, acting immediately according to the Spirit, desiring nothing except to express the inner drift and glow and force of the majesty of God. They are the living image of the liturgy.

There is another image from Sacred Scripture—a favorite passage of mine—used on the feast days of Our Lady about her Child, with Whom she is eternally united. "I was with him forming all things: and was delighted every day, playing before him at all times; playing in the world. And my delights were with the children of men" (Prov. 8:30, 31). This is the delight of the Eternal Father that Wisdom (the Logos, the Son, the perfect Fullness of Truth) should pour out His essence before Him in all His ineffable splendor. We are not talking about purpose here; the Son "plays" before the Father.

The play of children has no purpose really; it does not aim at anything. I was a guest at some parishioners' house for dinner, and the children insisted I watch their play. "Not quite like Shakespeare," they warned. Chairs were arranged, props were assembled, and the dialogue began, with much audience participation. There was a dinosaur, a castle, "Lady Lava," birds, plenty of chatter and laughter, and an indecipherable plot. This was life! It was life pouring itself out without aim, drawing from riches in its storehouse of humor and story and dance and rhyme. It was wonderful.

But as life progresses, conflicts arise, and life appears at times to grow ugly and discordant. Man sets himself a goal, but many obstacles are in his way, and it is very seldom that he can attain his ideal. He tries to reconcile the contradiction between what he wishes to be and what he is, and this is the vision of good art. People who contemplate art should not expect immediate results, or great lessons, or advice about their troubles. But they should be able to linger before it, moving freely, becoming conscious of their own better nature.

The liturgy is this, but much more. With the aid of grace, a man is given the opportunity of becoming what he is destined to be and longs to be: a child of God. In the liturgy, he goes to the altar. "I will go unto the altar of God. Unto God who giveth joy to my *youth*" (Ps. 42:2).

This is not work. It is play in the highest and most profound sense. To be at play on this supernatural plane is not to create but to exist.

Profound earnestness and divine joyfulness are mingled. The fact that the liturgy gives a hundred careful directions about language, color, vestments, gestures, and instruments can be understood only by those who take play seriously. Children gravely draw up the rules for their games, and the meaning for this stick and that tree. They don't have to be taught this; they do it instinctively. Similarly, the liturgy lays down the serious rules of the sacred game that the soul plays before God.

Only those who are not scandalized by this will understand the liturgy. The practice of the liturgy means that by the help of grace, under the guidance of the Church, we grow into living works of art before God, with no other aim than to live and exist in His sight. It means to become as a little child. It means to confine oneself to play for a while, as David did when he danced before the Ark.

> It is in this very aspect of the liturgy that its didactic aim is bound, that of teaching the soul not to see purposes everywhere, not to be too conscious of the end it wishes to attain, not to be desirous of being over-clever and grown-up, but to understand simplicity in life. The soul must learn to abandon, at least in prayer, the restlessness of purposeful activity; it must learn to waste time for the sake of God, and to be prepared for the sacred game with sayings and thoughts and gestures, without always immediately asking "why?" and "wherefore?" It must learn not to be continually yearning to do something, to attack something, to accomplish something useful, but to play the divinely ordained game of the liturgy in liberty and beauty and holiness. (Guardini)

With these things being said about the liturgy, we should take a look at the building in which it is celebrated in a similar fashion. To do so, it is wise to go back to the Middle Ages, which are the ages that best understood serious play. The Gothic cathedrals of the thirteenth century were masterpieces of serious play.

Of all the guides for this, one of the best is the thirteenth-century French bishop William Durandus. He was influenced by many holy sources, such as St. Isidore of Seville. He wrote a great work called the *Rationale Divinorum Officiorum*, the first book on church buildings. He sees a great connection, a great harmony, between the building, the vestments, the music, and various things used in the liturgy. He explains this harmony by the symbolism hidden in them.

Of course, some liturgical scientists will dismiss this kind of explanation. They prefer to explain that the reason for the chalice veil was to protect the chalice from bat dung, since bats were a real problem in the big medieval churches. "But we no longer have that problem so that's why the veil is obsolete." I actually heard this once. There is some logic to it, in that if that's all there really is to the veil, then the heck with it (or death to bats). But what if the veil is supposed to symbolize the stripping of the garments before the Crucifixion? Then it has great meaning, but little purpose, as Guardini might say.

Listen for a moment to good Bishop Durandus talk about the serious play of the divine things of the liturgy.

> All things, as many as pertain to offices and matters ecclesiastical, be full of divine significations and mysteries, and overflow with a celestial sweetness; if so be that a man be diligent in his study of them, and know how to "draw honey from the rock and oil from the hardest stone". But "who knoweth the ordinances of heaven or can fix the reasons thereof on the earth"? For he that prieth into their majesty, is overwhelmed by the glory of them. Of a truth "the well is deep and I have nothing to draw with": unless He giveth it unto me Who "giveth unto all men liberally and upbraideth not": so that "while I journey through the mountains" I may "draw water with joy out of the wells of salvation." Wherefore, albeit of the things handed down from our forefathers, capable we are not

to explain all, yet if among them there be anything which is done without reason, it should forthwith be put away.

Durandus saw the Mass as wonderful, and he wondered as to what it all might mean. And I feel this—the Gregorian Rite excites in me a great wonder in the sense of a classical definition of wonder, which might be as follows: "Wonder is the passion that arises from consciousness of ignorance." As Dennis Quinn put it in his superb book about wonder (*Iris Exiled: A Synoptic History of Wonder*), "To that species-and-difference definition one might wish to add a final cause: this consciousness leads to the seeking of knowledge of things in their causes." The Rite of St. Gregory almost forces me to learn more of God, to seek Him in the ordinary things of this Extraordinary Form of the Roman Rite.

But wonder can be lost. Quinn writes about this:

> Painters and poets speak of keeping a fresh eye for things, and undoubtedly the child has freshness of vision, the "innocent eye," as Ruskin called it, that can see the events and facts of experience as marvels: but undoubtedly freshness stales and childhood innocence ends. The freshman becomes a sophomore, who, possessing Sophia (in his own estimation), is "wise". Sophistication has of late become a term of almost ultimate praise for whatever is technically advanced, but the Sophisticated Lady of Duke Ellington's song expresses well the jaded shallowness of those who are "in the know". Actually, the sophists of Plato's dialogues are men of this type, while Socrates himself has a childlike quality about him which his enemies often ridiculed or regarded as a pose. If there is one thing a sophisticate hates, it is to be "caught out", to have his ignorance revealed. How important to such is the appearance of knowledge—to know the names of things, the lingo, the "right" opinions, to be *au courant*, to have the right look, be seen with the right people in the right places. Is not the ultimate solecism

of the sophisticate the expression of wonder? But, as Donne suggests, we all have trouble retaining our sense of wonder; we cease to notice, much less marvel at, those things about us that are worthy of wonder.

Although it is true that repetition tends to dull the sense of wonder, the poet and the philosopher testify that some are able to overcome the tendency; and everyone is to some degree poetic and philosophical. Teachers, who treat the same subject over and over again, if they are to be effective, have to overcome the wonder-dulling effects of repetition. They have, or course, the ignorant and (one hopes) the fresh-eyed young to help keep their own wonder alive.

Take away the ceremonies from the Church, and you will straight-away destroy the worship of God among the greater part of Christians. Make sure no one raises his hands, or bends his knee, or strikes his breast, or bares his head to pray, or stands to hear the gospel read, or does any similar thing, and you will see that within a few days, what we call devotion fades quite away. For the devotion which remains in the hearts of a few Christians, feeble spark of worship though it may be, is kept alive by ceremonies. (St. John Fisher)

THE IMPULSE TO ADORN IS A PART OF LOVE

Preparation in the Sacristy

THE PREPARATION FOR THE MASS in the sacristy represents the hidden life of Christ in the home at Nazareth. As we shall see, the Mass reenacts the principle parts of the life of Christ here on earth, when He walked among us. We are privy to very little that went on in the home at Nazareth or in the carpenter shop, but we know that the Savior worked and prayed in preparation for His public ministry, which began in the thirtieth year of His life here on earth.

In a similar way, when the faithful come to Mass, they are not privy to all the preparation that goes into the Sacrifice of the Mass. The long hours of preparation are not accomplished just by the priests; the laity work hard too, from the altar boy who practices his service, to the choir that rehearses, to those who repair the vestments and clean the sacred linens. All this work is hidden from most of the faithful, and on Sunday they see only the fruit of that labor, if they care to look.

PRECIOUS ARTICLES USED IN WORSHIP

First let us understand that the things that are used for the Mass must be beautiful, ornamental, and artistic. And all articles used in worship should be excellent. Just as it was in the sacrifices of the ancient Temple of Solomon, nothing that is defective may be offered to the Lord. No lame animal could be used, not even an animal that had some flaw in its coat or skin. Only the best could be sacrificed to the Lord. This is not because God is fussy and turns His nose up at low-quality items! It is because it all prefigured the Lamb of God, who was spotless in virtue. The Church therefore has at heart "the beauty of the house of God and the place where His glory dwelleth" (Ps. 25:8).

He has no need of the gifts that the creature does or can offer Him (Ps. 15:2), but it is necessary that we consecrate to Him that which He first gave to us. It shows our love and gratitude to Him. It is the gift of St. Mary Magdalen, who anointed the Lord with precious ointment. "She hath wrought a good work upon me" (Mt. 26:10). So the first reason to use the best things possible is to glorify God; to do a good work upon Him.

A second reason is that when precious vessels and vestments are used in divine service, the faithful are better able to grasp the sublimity and wonder of the mysteries celebrated. This helps them to have the proper disposition for these mysteries, which is awe and reverence for holy things.

Of course, this is not enough for divine worship. To adore the Lord in spirit and in truth means fighting the good fight against sin;

striving for a moral, devout, and learned clergy; and never neglecting the poor and the suffering, who are living temples of God.

But only religious ignorance or indifference can accuse the Church of excess and extravagance in decorating the House of the Lord. It is to be deplored that frequently the most wretched, ugly buildings in town are churches. Evelyn Waugh wrote an account of a two-month journey he made through Mexico in 1938. The revolution had quieted down by then, but the reminders of the oppression of the Marxists were everywhere, especially in the churches. He was struck by the efforts of the poorest villagers to fix up their churches, and in an excellent little book called *Robbery Under Law*, he summed up rather well why sacred things should have splendor: "For the impulse to adorn is a part of love; and those who see in the glories of Mexican church decoration only the self-advertisement of a clerical caste and the oppression of a people, do not know love."

With that being said, certain religious orders should not receive censure or blame if through poverty and the love of poverty, they use sacred vessels and vestments of lesser monetary value. This is another way to express adoration of God, so that what is offered to God is the very best in the monastery.

Clear Creek Abbey in Oklahoma is like this. The vestments used there are rather simple, yet they are of far greater quality than the monastic habit. The monks really *are* poor. But if in the suburban parish where the houses of parishioners are far more splendid inside and out than the church they worship in, then we see not religious poverty and simplicity but a sign of disregard and want of reverence for God. Under a cloak of charity, the hypocrite Judas Iscariot concealed a base avarice. "Why was not this ointment sold for three hundred pence and given to the poor?" (cf. Jn. 12:1-6). He said this, remarks St. John, not because he cared for the poor, but because he was a thief and had neither faith in Jesus nor love for Him. As a rule, who possesses the most ardent and practical love of neighbor? It is the one who is the most generous and cheerful contributor to the splendor of the house of God.

Magnificence is a virtue that St. Thomas Aquinas treats in the *Summa Theologica* as a part of the virtue of fortitude. This is the virtue of doing something great: "It belongs to the magnificent man to provide himself with a suitable dwelling.... No end of human works is so great as the honor of God ... [and] for this reason magnificence is connected with holiness, since its chief effect is directed to religion or holiness" (II-II, Q. 134).

But however perfect the vessels and vestments are for the Mass, they are not fit to be used for divine worship until they are blessed. They must be withdrawn from profane use and be especially dedicated to the service of the Most High. And traditionally, only those who had received the minor order of Tonsure could touch one of the sacred vessels. This was due to their temporary promise of celibacy. This is why our altar boys do not touch the vessels, but hold them with gloves or with some cloth.

It is good to ponder the touching of the sacred. We remember Oza, the servant of David, who was instantly killed by God because he touched the Ark of the Covenant as it fell (1 Para. 13:10-11). This event sounds strange in the literal sense and even capricious or vindictive, but consider that Eve could not touch the tree in the Garden of Eden without experiencing spiritual death. Also consider that after the Resurrection, Jesus told St. Mary Magdalen, "Do not touch me: for I am not yet ascended to my Father" (Jn. 20:17). The great point of this is not to teach us that the laity cannot have contact with the sacred, but that no man can touch God, for He is pure Spirit.

VESTMENTS

Vestments must not be used for everyday life, nor can we enter the sanctuary in our everyday clothes. That would defeat the purpose of the ritual. Vestments remind us to put off the old man with all his acts and put on the new man, who is created in justice and holiness of truth (cf. Eph. 4:22-24). This is written in our nature; if we were only spirit, our religion would be completely spiritual. But we are spirit and body—spiritual in our soul and corporal in our body—so our religion must be both spiritual and corporal. As the body without the soul is dead, so the vestments and rites must be filled with or express the truth.

Vestments originated in the Old Law, for when the Hebrews were delivered from the power of Pharaoh, they had no ceremonies to keep the faith fresh in their minds, and they fell quickly into idolatry and adored a golden calf. So God ordered Moses to consecrate Aaron and his sons and clothe them in holy vestments, in garments of glory and of beauty, so that, washed and purified as the Law required, they might fulfill the high dignity of priests of the Most High (Ex. 32:4). For forty days Moses exercised them in the holy ceremonies, in the use of sacerdotal vestments and in the ornaments and linens.

Here is a magnificent description of the vestments in the Old Law:

He [the high priest Simon] shone forth in his day as the morning star amid lowering clouds, and as the moon with the fullness of her beauty. And as the sun in his glory, so did he shine in the temple of God. And as the rainbow shedding its light in the brilliant clouds, and as the blooming of roses in the spring time, and as the lilies on the banks near the waters, and as the sweet frankincense on the summer air. As a bright fire, and frankincense aflame. As a massy vessel of gold, adorned with precious stones. As an olive-tree budding forth, and a cypress-tree rearing itself on high, like unto such was he, when he put on the robe of glory and was clothed with the perfection of power. When he went up to the holy altar, he honored the vesture of holiness. (Ecclus. 50:6-12)

Also, the vestments of the Old Law were to be made of gold,

jacinth, purple, scarlet twice dyed, woven linen, and other precious things. These represent for priests of the New Law the many virtues that the priest should acquire and keep for the service of the Lord. The vestments for the New Law signify the virtues covering or informing the soul. The celebrant is powerfully reminded that he must pursue virtue, lest he become a sepulcher, whitewashed and beautified on the outside but inside filled with rottenness and death (cf. Mt. 23:27). No one can *take* the honor of serving in the priesthood but must be *called* to do so, as Aaron was called by God. This is why, in the Ordination of a priest, the man being ordained cannot put the vestments on himself but is instead clothed in them by the bishop.

The Vestments Used for Mass

I won't go into the pontifical vestments, but I want to mention the bishop's *Cappa Magna* (a huge red garment with a long train that requires many servants to carry it). Some might cry "Triumphalism!" when they see it, but they miss the point. The point is that the bishop cannot move unless he has the laity supporting him. The "great cape" is heavy, like the responsibility of his office. It is a striking symbol of the dignity of the episcopal office and of its burden and our duty to help the bishop carry it. Bishops wear many vestments, but at Mass they cannot be seen largely, since this is a prayer, and God is glorified in secret.

Let us consider each of the vestments of the priest as they are laid out in the sacristy and their significance.

First, the priest or sacristan lays the chasuble down on a vesting table, above which is a cross. It is laid down with its front on the table. Next, he lays down the stole in the shape of an H. Then comes the maniple, going straight down, and over them is put the cincture in the shape of an S, so that the stole, maniple, and cincture form an IHS, since all must be done in the Name of Jesus, of which IHS is an abbreviation. Over them is carefully placed the alb, and lastly the amice, so that they can be put on in proper order. Now let us look briefly at each of these vestments and see their significance from the prayers that are said while the clothing takes place, and also from events of Our Lord's life.

Before he puts on the vestments, the priest rinses his hands with water, and prays, "Give strength to my hands, Lord, to wipe away all stain, so that I may be able to serve Thee in purity of mind and body." There is a special container of water set aside just for this washing, but if a parish does not have one, a plain sink is used, and if there is no sink in the sacristy, a basin, pitcher, and towel are used.

Once he has washed his hands, the priest may take off his fascia (a different cincture is used for the Mass, but he can certainly keep on the one he is wearing) and his wristwatch (though there is no rubric to do so). The Mass has a certain pace, and it does not belong to the priest. The time used in the Mass belongs to God and must be given generously to God. The priest can be tempted to be stingy with the time given to God, but good preparation normally takes care of this.

Amice

The first vestment the priest puts on is the amice, which goes around the neck and is meant to cover up his street garb (the cassock and Roman collar). As he briefly places it over his head (a monk's amice covers the cowl), the priest prays that the Lord might give him the grace to guard his thoughts and his tongue: "Lord, set the helmet of salvation on my head to fend off all the assaults of the devil." Devils seek to disrupt all his prayer, and even when there is no external distraction in the sacristy, the priest is often besieged with distracting thoughts, which he must fight off, since his recollection is crucial to the faithful's being able to recollect and therefore to pray.

The amice also reminds us of the shameful veiling of the eyes and face of Jesus at Herod's court. Those who placed the veil on Him struck Him on the head and in the face, saying derisively when He could not see, "Prophesy to us, Christ, who struck Thee?" (Lk. 22:64). This garment then—like so many sacred articles and gestures used in the Mass—is one of the many reminders of the great price Christ had to pay in order for us to have the Mass.

When he puts it on, the priest can move it from left to right, in keeping with the movement from left to right that will be seen all through the Mass (though this is not obligatory here); it was an ancient gesture in the Temple of Solomon to express the blessing of God. You will see the Sign of the Cross made from left to right, the incensation of the altar done from left to right, Holy Communion distributed left to right, et cetera. This is also expressed in the New Testament, when Our Lord informed us in the Sermon on the Mount that on the Day of Judgment the sheep shall be separated from the goats. "And he shall set the sheep on his right hand, but the goats on his left" (Mt. 25:33).

The strings of the amice are crossed over the breast and tied over the waist. It is doubled over the neck, if you will, to signify the chastising of the voice and useless words. The benediction (a word from Latin meaning "good speech") of a priest does much to build up the kingdom of God. The malediction ("bad speech") of a priest does much to tear down the kingdom. We know from Scripture that on the last day all of us shall have to account for our words. "But I say unto you, that every idle word that men shall speak, they shall render an account for it in the Day of Judgment." (Mt. 12:36) The priest above all must strive to keep a guard over his words.

Alb

When the priest puts on the alb, he prays: "Make me white, O Lord, and cleanse my heart; that being made white in the Blood of the

Lamb, I may deserve an eternal reward." The priest prays that his soul should be white with innocence and free from sin.

When he puts on the alb, he is reminded of the humiliation of Christ, who was sent back to Pilate from Herod's court dressed in a white robe (cf. Lk. 23:11). In those times, the white robe was the costume of a clown. Since we are "fools for the sake of Christ" (1 Cor. 4:10), we wear this as an honor, not as a humiliation. In the early Church, it was the practice that those newly baptized wore a white robe for a week. It is no accident that visions of heaven show "white-robed martyrs" (cf. Apoc. 7:9; *Te Deum*).

You may notice that there are different styles of albs, from plain to lacy. There is no law concerning this, though the habit of distinguishing the classes of feast days may be reflected in the alb. For example, for penitential days or fourth-class feasts, a plain alb might be worn; one with a little lace might be worn for third- and second-class feasts, and the best alb for first-class feasts.

Fine linen was traditionally used for the cloth, since "the fine linens are the justification of the saints" (Apoc. 19:8). Linen becomes white by much washing and bleaching. Just so, we are not born saints, but by much labor and mortification and overcoming of self, we arrive at the purity necessary to celebrate the Mass. The whole body of the priest is covered in this white cloth, while the priests who assist in choir wear only the cassock and surplice, signifying that the freedom from sin required from the celebrant is greater than for those who assist.

Cassock and surplice

I should mention at this point the symbolism of the cassock and surplice, though they are not vestments per se for the Mass. The cassock—from an ancient word meaning "house"—covers the priest from neck to feet. It is black, because the priest is to be dead to this world. The white collar symbolizes the purity to which he is bound by a vow, and the cincture symbolizes the purity that he must practice in deed. The traditional Roman-style cassock has thirty-three buttons, which stand for each year Our Lord lived on the earth. As he buttons them in the morning, the priest can thank Jesus for each year He walked among us. Also, when he puts the cassock on, he can pray, "O Lord, the portion of my inheritance and my chalice, You are He who will restore my inheritance" (cf. Ps. 15:5).

The surplice is a short white garment used to assist at the Mass or the Divine Office and to distribute sacraments. It serves to remind the priest and the faithful of the connection between the sacraments and the life of heaven, where the saints are clothed in white garments (cf. Apoc. 4:4).

Cincture

Next, when vesting for Mass, the priest puts on the cincture, tying it around the waist in some way, as with a Franciscan knot. He binds his loins like Jeremias (Jer. 1:17), telling of chastity. The prayer he says when he puts it on is: "Gird me, O Lord, with the cincture of purity, and quench in my heart the fire of concupiscence, that the virtue of continence and chastity may abide in me."

Again and again the priest is reminded of the grave responsibility to live a chaste life. I wonder if the lack of chastity in the lives of too many priests (especially as we saw in the news at the beginning of this millennium) is not connected to the fact that many priests no longer say these prayers and no longer use these vestments, given that they are not required in the Ordinary Form of the Mass. And not only are the prayers important, but to feel the vestment on the neck or the waist is an essential reminder to the priest, since we are not angels but are made of flesh and blood. Even if the priest is living a chaste life, he must not let down his guard and think that he is strong or has somehow conquered nature. No, he must be sober, vigilant, watchful, and pray often and every day to remain in chastity, a sorely needed virtue for our times.

The priest may use the cincture to recall the cords with which Our Lord was bound when taken captive by the soldiers in the Garden of Olives, in order to drag Him to His trials before Pilate and Herod. The priest may also use the cincture to give thanks to God for the ropes that tied Our Lord's innocent all-powerful hands to the pillar and also the strands of the whip used in the scourging there.

Maniple

Next, the priest puts on the maniple. He picks it up from the vesting table and kisses (more about ceremonial kissing later) the small cross on the center of the maniple, praying, "May I deserve, O Lord, to bear the maniple of weeping and sorrow in order that I may joyfully reap the reward of my labors."

So the maniple is first a symbol of the labor of the priest. It reminds him to engage in the hard work of recollection and prayer throughout the whole Mass; to give Our Lord the utmost human respect possible through speech and gestures; and above all to do everything in the Mass with love.

Originally, the maniple was a garment used by Romans as a fancy handkerchief, to wipe away sweat caused by labor. The priest can use the maniple to remind himself that he must collaborate with Our Lord in wiping out not only his own sins but the sins of this flock through penance.

It is worn on the left wrist, since the left in our liturgy signifies this world, and the right signifies the world to come. So the left hand is tied to the business of this world (that is part of the priest's life—to make sure the bills are paid), and the right hand is free for the things of the next world, such as blessing.

It is interesting that the word *manipulus* in Latin is mentioned as a sheaf of wheat in Scripture. "They that sow in tears shall reap in joy. Going they went and wept, casting their seed; but coming they shall come with joyfulness, carrying their sheaves [*manipulos suos*]" (Ps. 125:5-7). So the maniple shows, on one hand, penitential tears and grief, the toil and hardships of sowing, the suffering and combating, the work and labors of this perishable life; but on the other hand, it shows the fruit of good works and sheaves full of merit, as well as the abundant harvest of happiness and joy, of peace and rest reaped in eternity. That is why it is worn only for the Holy Sacrifice of the Mass, in which the sufferings and cruel and bitter death of Christ are represented. It is not worn outside of Mass, because no sorrow can compare with the sorrow that should penetrate our hearts during Holy Mass. When the priest gives a sermon or homily, or even a ferverino, he takes off the maniple and places it on the altar or on the missal. This is to signal the faithful that the Mass is to be interrupted briefly, since the sermon is outside the Mass.

Lastly, when he puts the maniple back on after the sermon, the celebrant is reminded of the fetters with which the hands of Our Lord were bound after His arrest by Pilate, and His being presented to the mob to see if they would prefer Him or Barabbas. For the greatest labor of Christ was done in His Passion and death.

Stole

Next, the priest puts on the stole, the preeminent symbol of the priesthood. He kisses the small cross in its middle (we kiss what we love), then places it over his neck while praying, "Lord, restore the stole of immortality, which I lost through the collusion of our first parents, and, unworthy as I am to approach Thy sacred mysteries, may I yet gain eternal joy." As our first parents lost Paradise through disobedience, so the priest must submit to the yoke of obedience and place the burden on his neck voluntarily. A stole weighs next to nothing, however, since the yoke of Christ is light. In fact, the bishop says to a priest when he is ordained, "Receive the yoke of Christ, for his yoke is sweet and his burden light" (cf. Mt. 11:30).

You might notice that a deacon wears his stole on the left shoulder, draped across front and back, and crossed just at the end at his right side. It is on the left to bind him from the things or temptations of this world, but the right is free, in a sense, to symbolize that he is free to seek the things of God.

Priests wear the stole for Mass crossed over the chest so that the ends of the stole are on his right and left. This tells him that he must fight the devil with "the armor of justice on the right hand and on the left" (2 Cor. 6:7). The stoles lies on his chest in the form of the cross of St. Andrew, reminding him to carry his cross. He does not wear it like the cross of St. Peter, however, since an upside-down cross is an inappropriate symbol to use. It is also in the form of St. Andrew's cross to signify the difference of hierarchy, as the priesthood is lower in dignity than the episcopacy (St. Andrew was below St. Peter in hierarchy); a bishop wears his stole so it hangs straight down. The priest wears the stole crossed for the Mass, but at other times and for all other sacraments, he wears it hanging straight down, as in a state of repose, to remind him of eternal rest in heaven. A bishop does not cross his stole, however, even for the Mass. This is to remind him that he is to have arrived at the repose gained by perfect virtue.

A stole is also a sign of spiritual power, and the priest should not administer a sacrament without it. This spiritual authority is a gift from God through the Church, but it comes also from innocence, one of the greatest sources of strength for a priest. This innocence was lost by Adam's disobedience but regained through the obedience of the priest to his superiors; the stole is a symbol of the yoke of submission and obedience to the will of God.

When he puts the stole on, the priest can think of the heavy burden of the Cross, which our exhausted Lord voluntarily and patiently accepted. It is light to the priest, reminding him that whatever trials he might have pale in comparison to the trials of Christ.

Thomas à Kempis, in his magnificent work *The Imitation of Christ*, wrote a beautiful passage about the service of God, which is symbolized by a stole:

> It is a great honor, a great glory to serve Thee, O Lord, and to despise all things for Thee. For they who willingly subject themselves to Thy most holy service, shall have a great grace. They shall find the most sweet consolation of the Holy Ghost, who for love of Thee have cast away all carnal delight. They shall gain great freedom of mind, who for Thy name enter upon the narrow way and neglect all worldly care. O pleasant and delightful service of God, which makes a man truly free and holy! O sacred state of religious bondage, which makes men equal to angels, pleasing to God, terrible to the devils, and commendable to all the faithful! O service worthy to be embraced and always to be wished for, which leads to the supreme good and procures a joy that will never end!

Chasuble

Next, the priest puts on the chasuble. As he does so, he prays, "O Lord, Thou who hast said: 'My yoke is sweet and My burden light,' grant that I may carry this yoke and burden in such a manner as to obtain Thy grace." What this symbolizes may be known from the Ordination of a priest and from the missal. When the bishop places the folded chasuble on the back of a newly ordained priest, he says: "Receive the priestly garment, by which love is understood; for God is powerful to increase in you charity and a perfect work." Afterward, when fully unfolding the chasuble, he says: "With the garment of innocence may the Lord clothe thee."

So the chasuble signifies charity, without which the celebrant is like "sounding brass or a tinkling cymbal" (1 Cor. 13:1). It is worn over all the other vestments, as charity is above all the other virtues (cf. Col. 3:14). It hangs down in front and in back, symbolizing the two great parts of charity—love of God and love of neighbor (this is more evident with the Roman-style of chasuble, with its sides open, but it applies to the Gothic or semi-Gothic style too).

The chasuble is decorated in many ways, with various Christian symbols. But there are two symbols that almost all traditional chasubles have: on the front is a single vertical bar and on the back a cross. The bar in front represents the pillar that our good Lord faced as He was scourged. The cross on the back, often fashioned as a Latin cross (the vertical bar longer than the horizontal) depicts Christ's Cross, or the ancient Y-shaped cross, which depicts the way our Lord's hands and arms would have been seen by us as He hung on the Cross. The pillar and the cross are the two principal instruments of the Passion, so they have precedence over other symbols of the Passion.

When the priest ascends the altar for the faithful, with the cross on his back, it is like Christ carrying His Cross for us as He goes about the altar accomplishing salvation. It also represents a kind of target, such that when Our Lord walked among us, there was much murmuring about Him behind His back by His own, and much hatred from the Romans. Just so, the priest must follow in the footsteps of his Master, and experience the same thing, and bear the murmuring of his flock and the mockery and hatred of the world.

But this is the price of love. At the heart of a vocation to the priesthood is the service of God and sacrifice to God. To become a holocaust of love in the service of God and for the salvation of men is assuredly difficult and painful to nature; therefore, the genuine life of a priest is and ever will be a yoke and a burden. But divine grace and love help to make this yoke easy and this burden light. Grace alone carries every burden without being burdened; it alone makes sweet and pleasant to the taste all that is bitter. The chasuble is worn during the Sacrifice of the Mass; the altar is the furnace of divine love, and it is there that the Lord enkindles the divine fire of love on the earth, that at least some sparks of divine love may penetrate our cold hearts and inflame them with the ardor of that love.

Biretta

The last thing the priest puts on is the biretta, which has four corners. This signifies that the priest should preach the gospel to the four corners of the earth, "teaching all nations" (Mt. 28:19). There are three tabs on it to represent the Holy Trinity, which is the highest and greatest of our doctrines. So the biretta is physically above all the other vestments, as the dogma of the Trinity is above all other dogmas. You might have noticed that the priest puts on the biretta holding only the middle tab. And when the servers hand the biretta to the priest, they hand it is such a way that the priest may take it by the middle tab. This middle tab represents Christ, the Second Person of the Trinity, as it is only through Him, only by virtue of His Incarnation, that we can grasp the truth of the Trinity.

VESTMENTS AND THE POWERS OF THE PRIEST

To summarize all the vestments together, consider that:

1. Six powers of the priesthood are represented by these six vestments: to say Mass, bless, command, preach, baptize, and forgive sins.

2. Bishops have nine vestments, since they are of greater rank or perfection than priests. They wear the sandals, veil, tunic, dalmatic, ring, gloves, crosier, pectoral cross, and miter, since there are nine powers given to a bishop: to ordain, confirm, consecrate

bishops, consecrate churches, degrade the unworthy, call synods, consecrate the holy oils, rule a diocese, and bless vestments and holy vessels used in the service of the altar.

3. The vestments are a visible fulfillment of the famous admonition of St. Paul: "Put ye on the armor of God, that you may be able to stand against the deceits of the devil. Stand therefore having your loins girt about with truth, and having on the breastplate of justice. And your feet shod with the preparation of the gospel of peace; in all things take the shield of faith wherewith you may be able to extinguish all the fiery darts of the most wicked one. And take unto you the helmet of salvation, and the sword of the spirit, which is the word of God" (Eph. 6:11-17).

Color

There are five basic colors that are used for the liturgy: white (or gold for solemnities), red, green, purple, and black (though in some dioceses blue is used for Our Lady). Colors are important since they are produced by the varied refraction of the rays of light and, like light itself, stand in an intimate and mysterious relation to the inner spiritual life of man. Light and color, among all visible material things, are the nearest to the spiritual.

White is the color of light and represents radiant purity, innocence, and holiness as well as heavenly joy, bliss, and transfiguration. Thus, all the joyful and glorious mysteries are celebrated in white or in gold.

Red is the strongest and most gorgeous of the colors. It is the color of the most glaring light—fire. It represents the ardent, consuming fire of love that the Holy Ghost enkindles in the heart (Rom. 5:5) and is emblematic of the generous conquering love that yields up in martyrdom the greatest and dearest of all earthly blessings—namely, life itself—and triumphs in death. "Love is as strong as death, as hard as hell; the lamps thereof are fire and flames, many waters cannot quench it" (Cant. 8:6).

Green is a medium between the strong and weak colors; it is the most refreshing and soothing of colors to the eye. Like the spring, when nature awakens and develops new life and growth, green is a symbol of hope.

Purple is a subdued color. In nature purple is often concealed, and it is hard to detect sometimes when you are in the woods or even in the fields, so it's an ideal symbol of unpretentious humility, of holy retirement, and of well-tempered sorrow. The source of this laudable sorrow is the soul's being obliged to remain far from the Lord, in a world foreign to her. "Who shall deliver me from the body of this death?" (Rom. 7:24). Therefore, we see purple especially in Advent (when we are longing for the Incarnation) and Lent (when we are longing for the Resurrection).

Black is the opposite of white; it is the color of extinct life, the absence of joy; the inside of the tomb. It is used for the funeral Mass, since we do not know whether the faithful departed have been admitted into eternal light or whether they must abide for a while in darkness and the shadow of death (Is. 9:2).

I WILL GO UNTO THE ALTAR OF GOD

THE TIME FOR THE MASS IS, of course, determined by the needs of the faithful. But what is preferred may be seen in a good monastery, where the monks celebrate the Sacrifice during the day. "Normally, Mass must be celebrated in the day, and not at night, because Christ himself is present in the sacrament, who said, *I must work the works of him that sent me, whilst it is day: the night cometh, when no man can work. As long as I am in the world, I am the light of the world*. Again, in celebrating this mystery, we represent our Lord's passion: and since his passion was performed from the third hour to the ninth hour, this sacrament is normally performed in the Church in a solemn way during the period of the day" (St. Thomas Aquinas).

Processions in the Mass

The Mass begins with a procession. Processions are ancient in origin. The greatest procession in our spiritual history is probably the Hebrews' forty years of wandering in the desert. During the Babylonian exile, the Jews made their pilgrimage from distant lands to Mount Zion and understood their ascent to the Holy Mountain (Jerusalem) as a procession of prayer.

All the Jewish models of procession were filled with new meaning in the two great processions of the New Testament: Our Lord's triumphal entry into Jerusalem on Palm Sunday, and the *Via Dolorosa* of Good Friday. So every procession in our beautiful liturgy is at once glorious and painful, joyful and sad. We glory in the arrival of our King, in the person of the celebrant, but are pained by the suffering He had to undergo so that we might be redeemed. This is why the priest processes with his head bowed slightly, with his eyes downcast, and does so for the processions in both Low and High Masses. A mere child instinctively knows that this demeanor is proper to a procession. This demeanor may also be called *solemnity*, appropriate for the dignity of the King, Who is at the same time a Suffering Servant.

Five processions are used in the Mass: the processional, the Gospel procession, the Offertory procession, the Communion procession, and the recessional. These processions are all a manifestation of Christ, like the five times He appeared to His apostles after His Resurrection.

The faithful may walk behind Christ in a Eucharistic procession or walk up solemnly to the Communion rail to meet or receive Him. That solemn, prayerful walking can sanctify us. But we do not have to do the walking, we can simply unite our minds and hearts in prayer with what is happening at the altar.

THE PROCESSIONAL

After he is fully vested, the priest enters the church, in different ways, depending on whether he is to celebrate a Low Mass or a High Mass. In either case, an entrance bell is rung. You'll often see two of them in a church: one is on the wall near the sacristy, for the entrance at a Low Mass, and the other is at the entrance to the church from the narthex, for the signaling of the beginning of a High Mass. The entrance bell often has three small bells to it, to remind us that all is for the glory of the Holy Trinity; that the Father, Son, and Holy Ghost are calling us to worship.

"The priest comes forth from the holy chamber, clad in sacred vestments, and approaches the altar, to show that Christ, the hope of the nations, came forth from his secret dwelling in the heavens, clothed in holy flesh drawn from the spotless Virgin, and entered into this world" (Durandus). In the Solemn High Mass, first in line in the procession is the thurifer with the incense, then the crucifer with the processional cross, then torchbearers, acolytes, and the subdeacon and the deacon, who proceed slightly ahead of the priest. They hold the priest's cope at the front at the beginning of the Mass, but at the end they process in single file in front of him.

The subdeacon and the deacon represent several things. First, they represent the Law and the prophets of the Old Testament when they process in single file and thus are before Christ, Whom the priest represents. Second, when they stand on either side of the priest, they stand for Moses (who represents the Law, which is the greatest part of the Old Testament, and thus his position is on the right of the priest) and Elias (who represents the prophets, and his position is on the left of the priest) as they ministered to Christ on Mount Tabor, in the glory of the Transfiguration. Third, they represent the Testaments. The deacon represents the New Testament, and the subdeacon represents the Old Testament. In all the ceremonies, the priest is between them, as Christ is the end of the Old Testament and the beginning of the New. All the other ministers go before the priest, to prepare the way "before his face" (Lk. 10:1).

The assistant priest (if one is used) goes last before the celebrant to call to mind St. John the Baptist, who was the last of the prophets to come before the Lord to prepare His way.

The procession to the altar signifies that we are in procession to our home in heaven, like the Hebrews being led by Moses to the Promised Land in the Old Testament.

Candles are used in the procession on either side of the crucifix, like the pillar of fire that went before the Hebrews to guide them at night in their forty-year exodus from Egypt (Ex. 13:21). With them went Aaron, the high priest of the Lord, and Moses with his rod. (When the bishop processes in, he has his crosier, which in the New Law is used in place of Moses' rod.) The candles remind us of the admonition of the Lord, "Let your loins be girt and lamps burning in your hands" (Lk. 12:35). Just so, the candles are in our hands, and the ministers have put on their cinctures.

Incense is used in the procession too; it symbolizes the *shekinah* (the pillar of cloud) that hid the Hebrews from their enemies during the day.

The Purification and the Asperges

If the procession is simple—going to the altar directly from the sacristy—the priest and acolytes purify themselves with holy water first, saying the ancient prayer: "Thou shalt sprinkle me with hyssop, O Lord, and I shall be cleansed; Thou shalt wash me, and I shall be whiter than snow" (cf. Ps. 50:9). It is called a purification because the devout use of holy water removes all venial sin.

Under the Old Law, lepers were healed by being sprinkled with the blood of the sacrifices of the Temple, using a branch of hyssop.

This little plant that grows out of the cracks of rocks in the Holy Land represents the humility of Christ (Who is the rock that followed the Jews in the desert [cf. 1 Cor. 10:4]); the ancient practice for the lepers applies to us, since it is His blood that cleanses us from the leprosy of our souls.

"If the blood of goats and of oxen, and the ashes of a heifer being sprinkled, sanctify such as are defiled to the cleansing of the flesh . . ." (Heb. 9:13). "Cleansing of the flesh" is understood here to mean the removal of venial sin. So is it that holy water, mixed with blessed salt and blessed with the prayers of the Church, cleanses the people from sin and temptation. And if the bitter waters of Jericho were healed by the salt thrown into them by the prophet Eliseus (4 Kings 2:21-22), then how much more should the sprinkling of holy water accomplish?

Salt signifies wisdom, that the people of the Church might receive wisdom and knowledge and be "the salt of the earth" (Mt. 5:13). Salt preserves from corruption and so symbolizes the people's preservation from sin. But it is more than a symbol; the salt is blessed in order that the water will accomplish this cleansing of sin. This is directly connected to the reason why holy water is used against devils; when it is blessed, power is put into it, and part of the blessing is also an exorcism.

If the ceremony is solemn, then we call this cleansing the *Asperges*, which occurs on the principle Mass of a parish on Sundays (it is not used at other Masses, even if they are High Masses); it is to remind all of the vows of Baptism—to renounce the works of darkness and shun sin.

Notice the connection between the *Asperges* and the renewing of the Covenant. The ancient covenants in Asia Minor consisted of three parts: defining the terms of the covenant, making a solemn vow, and then sealing the covenant by cutting a bull in half and walking through the halves. The last part was deadly serious to them;

it meant that once it was done, the covenant was permanent and could be ended only by the death of one of the parties. And if one broke his word regarding the covenant, then the bull constituted a kind of curse: "Then may what happened to this bull happen to me."

So when God chose the Hebrews to be His people and led them to Mount Sinai through Moses, He spoke to them through this mysterious yet familiar language and symbolism. The terms were set (ten of them on two stone tablets), the promises made, but instead of by walking through the halves of a bull, the covenant was sealed by Moses' taking a branch of hyssop and sprinkling the blood over the people. Once that was done, the covenant (or Old Testament) was permanent. But since a covenant can be broken only by death, and since God cannot die and the Hebrews would not perish (God promised this to them), the covenant cannot be broken; it can only be fulfilled.

Our entrance into the New Covenant or Testament is like this, in the sacrament of Baptism with the setting of the terms (instructions), the promises ("Do you renounce Satan?"), and the pouring of water. Once we have entered into the New Testament, it cannot be broken; it can only be fulfilled in heaven or remain eternally unfulfilled in hell.

The text for the *Asperges* is from the fiftieth psalm. Consider for a moment what a Carthusian monk said about this moment in the Mass:

> In using hyssop to purify his sinful soul, David thus acknowledged his sin, and humbled himself because of it. His humility united him to the humble Savior in Whom he placed his trust. And in that union, our Savior communicates His Blood to him, touches his wounds with It, causes It to flow through his very veins, and so restores him to a purity which is His very own—the divine purity, purer far than any earthly purity: the immaculate whiteness of Him Whom the Fathers of the Church call "the First Virgin";

and of which the radiance even of snow is but a distant and, as it were, frigid image. "Thou shalt wash me, and I shall be whiter than snow." Notice that David the sinner does not sprinkle himself with hyssop; he does not purify himself—only God can do that. The work of regeneration is not ours; it is the work of the Holy Ghost within us.

Water was used as a sign of ancient hospitality. The guest or traveler in the Middle East was received at the door, where his feet were washed by the host or by a servant before bread was broken. In that area's hot, dusty clime, this was a great refreshment; a cool, soothing act of friendship to the guest weary of the world. We are travelers who have come to rest for a while from the weariness of life, that we might break the Bread of Life in friendship with our Savior.

Lastly, holy water is also a sacramental; it protects us like the blood on the door from the angel of death, for the destroying angel in our case is not a good angel, but the devil, the enemy of our souls. Devils lust for churches and those who go into them. It may seem strange, since they despise us so much, as to why they would lust in this way, but holy things are like rich treasures—the latter attract thieves; the former, demons.

During Paschal time, the *Vidi Aquam* is used in place of the *Asperges* to honor the Resurrection. The verses are taken from the vision of the prophet Ezekiel, who saw the city of God built upon the mountain—that is, the Church of God, that city built upon the mountain that cannot be hidden (cf. Mt. 5:14). The waters coming from the side of the Temple, as seen by the prophet, prefigured the waters of baptism coming from the side of the dead Christ, which was opened by the spear of Longinus (cf. Jn. 19:34; Ez. 47).

Once the *Asperges* is finished, the priest walks to the sedile to take off the cope and put on the maniple and the chasuble. It will strike the first-time visitor to our liturgy that a number of things are going on at the same time. It is a rather circular liturgy in that sense. The choir is singing the Introit, the servers are helping the priest, the faithful are opening their missals.

This is in contrast to the Mass of Paul VI, which is a very linear rite. In the *Novus Ordo*, one action begins, and the whole community is supposed to focus on that action. That action stops, and another one begins. Out of the twenty-nine rites of the Church, the Mass of Paul VI is the only rite that does this. All the ancient liturgies have several things going on simultaneously.

This circular approach lends itself to the community's praying in common and the individual's praying alone at the same time. There are those who say they are cramped by prayer in common and prefer to pray alone. Nonsense. The soldier who marches with his comrades is not cramped; the violinist in the orchestra is not cramped by his fellow musicians; the player on the football team is not cramped by his teammates; on the contrary, each is carried by the others. Prayer in common is not a question of restraint but of voluntary union made by the adherence of our hearts to the Sacred Heart. The Mass is an excellent antidote to the individualism of our times. It reinforces the worship of the individual with companionship. Collective prayer roots out the egoism of the individual.

CANDLES

Light is strictly prescribed for the celebration of Holy Mass. There is no legislation about electric light (a church can use as much as it wants and of whatever kind), but there is plenty about the candles on the altar. A burning candle on an altar is intended to represent Christ. The flame above it represents His Divinity; the candle itself, His humanity; and the wick, His soul.

Beeswax has been used from the earliest times, not just because of its good smell but because it comes from working bees, which from ancient times were seen as a type of virginity (they don't mate) and because the wax is formed from flowers. The flower is like the womb of the Blessed Virgin Mary.

The liturgical use of light does not have its origin in the mere dispelling of darkness (though it does just that), nor should it be seen primarily as a reminder of the Masses that had to be celebrated in the darkness of the catacombs during the time of persecution (though it does that too). Instead, the primary reason for the use of candles may be found in the prayers for Candlemas Day, on which the Church implores God "to grant that as the candles lighted with visible fire dispel the darkness of night, so in like manner our hearts, enlightened by invisible fire, that is, by the resplendent light of the Holy Ghost, may be delivered from all blindness of sin and with the purified eyes of the spirit be enabled to perceive what is pleasing to Him and conducive to our salvation, in order that, after the dark and dangerous combats of this earthly life, we may come to the possession of immortal light."

The reason may also be seen from the blessing of the New Fire on Holy Saturday, when the Church prays to the "Eternal Light and Creator of all light," that He would bless this light, "that we may be inflamed with love and be enlightened by the fire of the divine brightness." This is painfully brought home to us with the solemn extinguishing of light during Tenebrae, when light after light is extinguished, and darkness reigns in the church, for each Office of Matins for the Triduum.

Candlelight symbolizes the divine nature and essence, for "God is light and in Him there is no darkness" (1 Jn. 1:5). Christ is "Light from Light," as we say in the Creed. He is "the brightness of His Father's glory" (Heb. 1:3). He is "a light to the revelation of the Gentiles, and the glory of the people Israel" (Lk. 2:32). The passages that refer to God and light are many; good light enlightens the eyes and renders the things of this world visible, and the truth of faith shows us a new, more beautiful, and supernatural world; gives us insight into the most profound mysteries of God; and unveils the beauty and the splendor of the kingdom of grace, which is infinitely more marvelous than all the grandeur of the world of stars.

I say "good light," though this is hard to define. Supper can look good and tasty if the light is good. I suppose that's why a classy restaurant uses candlelight, or as close as they can get to it. Candlelight changes everything at a meal. It even makes us look good, whereas fluorescent light brings out every flaw and washes out color. I was told once that the reason why only fluorescent light is used in fast-food restaurants is because the light adds a certain tension to the atmosphere, which causes the customer to eat more rapidly, thus enabling the place to sell more food. If that is true, it seems foolish to use that light for the Mass.

The flame of light is mysterious (this can be experienced profoundly at the Easter Vigil, when only candlelight is used for the first part of the liturgy), pure, beautiful, radiant, and full of brightness and warmth. Divine grace is also a mystery, and it removes the stains of sin from the soul and imparts purity, beauty, and radiance; it fills the understanding with knowledge and wisdom, the will with power and strength, the heart with love and joy.

Unbleached wax is used for these candles at the altar, since these represent the Church Militant, or the living. We do not see each other as we truly are here on earth. But when we die, we are as we were born, and so unbleached candles are used near the coffin of the departed. It is as if they burn with a different flame than the ones on the altar, signifying the phrase in the Preface of the Dead in the Requiem, "Life has changed; it has not been taken away." So the unbleached candles represent the Church Suffering, which is in purgatory.

Distinctions of the rank of the celebrant are made with the addition of a separate candle for a Pontifical High Mass, four candles for a Pontifical Low Mass, and two candles for an ordinary priest to celebrate a Low Mass.

One other candle may be used in the celebration of Mass, and that is the Consecration Candle. The rubrics for the 1962 Mass actually prescribe it. It is lit and placed at the altar before the Consecration, to symbolize the Real Presence, as on the road to Emmaus, when the disciples recognized Christ at the breaking of the bread.

VEILING

The priest has arrived at the altar veiled with vestments from head to toe. But a bishop is even more veiled, in that he has special shoes, gloves, and even buskins to veil the ends of his trousers! His acolytes use special humeral veils (*humerus* means "shoulder" in Latin, so a humeral veil is one that goes over the shoulders) to carry or hold his miter or crosier.

Veiling has secular uses too. For example, at an important supper, the servants wait on the tables with gloved hands. This is not to hide their hands—everyone already knows what a hand looks like—but to show the importance of the occasion, so we can say that veiling (all of it, such as veiling the tables with white cloths or the wine glasses with the napkins) serves to *reveal* the significance of the supper, not to hide it. This is an important principle to grasp.

The unveiling of a thing is just as significant as the veiling, if not more so. Going back to the veiled hands for a moment, we know that their unveiling was an ancient sign of reverence. Eventually taking the gauntlet off and showing the empty hand (to see that there was no weapon in it) became a great sign of peace, from which comes the gesture of a handshake. To this day it is a mark of courtesy to remove gloves before shaking hands.

So when a bishop celebrates a Pontifical High Mass, you will see his acolytes gathered around him with their veils, like the archangels in the Apocalypse using three pairs of wings to hide their hands, feet, and faces. The throne of the bishop is symbolic of the throne of God, Who shares His dignity and life with His friends—who are all near Him.

The chalice is veiled too. Whether the priest carries it in for a Low Mass, or whether it is already on the altar for a High Mass, it is veiled like a miniature tabernacle—that is, the Ark of the Covenant. This veiled sacrificial gift is also symbolic of Christ prior to His Crucifixion, when He is not yet the Sign of Contradiction lifted up on the Cross. It also represents the clothed Christ, waiting to be stripped of His garments.

The priest's whole body veils the action at the altar; it serves as a kind of iconostasis. Certain actions and gestures are deliberately veiled. Even the doors of a church serve as a veil, though more so in former times; that is, they were entrusted to the *Ostiarius* (the doorkeeper, or the minor order of porter), who stood in the narthex and was in charge of opening the doors to the faithful and closing them to the uninitiated.

Penitents also stood in the narthex, and the priest would absolve them using a long, narrow staff called a narthex (also called a *vindicta*). Just as in the Roman Empire a praetor freed a slave by touching him with a staff of this kind, so the confessor touched the sinner to free him from the slavery of sin. In later centuries it was no longer possible to ascertain the fitness of the members of the congregation to participate in the celebration, nor was it necessary to protect the mysteries from profanation, since the Roman persecutions had subsided (though in our times profanation is increasing).

The Canon of the Mass is veiled in silence. Latin is a veil over the whole sacrifice. Women veil their heads, the tabernacle is veiled, the altar is veiled. Consider the veiling of images during Lent. Some call it a fasting of the eyes, but that is not the intent. The practice comes from the finding of the Cross by St. Helena. After the Cross had been found, it was wrapped in cloths but then unpacked in a solemn ritual so it could be shown to the faithful (this ritual remains in our liturgy on Good Friday during the unveiling of the cross). Two deacons stood guard with candles to make sure that no one stole a splinter from it; now it is two acolytes who hold the candles. The veiling of the cross is not to withdraw it from sight; it is instead to treat it as if it were the real Cross; to drive home the point that there was a real death on a real piece of wood in the shape of a cross, at a real place at a precise time in history, even to the time of day.

Of course, the Enlightenment sees all this as obscurantism. Illuminism puts forward the idea of a bright light shooing away all the bad things. "Fides" (faith) in the Baroque allegories is a woman with her veil drawn down over her eyes, head downcast—a willing and deliberate blindness. The Roman tribune Gnaeus Pompeius was an Enlightenment man in this sense. He once visited the Temple of Solomon and pulled aside the veil—a sacrilege that scandalized the Levites. When he saw nothing behind the veil, he snorted with a great sense of triumph. He could not see that the veil itself was the message; the curtain contained the message; it *revealed* the sanctuary.

Just so, the gloved hand of the server, the veiled chalice, and the woman's head veiled—these hide nothing. Everyone one knows what a woman's head looks like. Everyone knows what a chalice looks like. No, the purpose of the veil on a woman's head is to reveal who she truly is. The vestments on the priest are not to hide him; they reveal who he is.

As Martin Mosebach observes, we see three traditions woven together with the veil:

1. The Temple of Solomon with its veil in front of the Holy of Holies; the invisible God remained hidden inside the Holy of Holies.

2. The Epiphany, or the manifestation of Our Lord.

3. The Holy Sepulcher: the Sepulcher is where the Mass was first
celebrated; the niche in the cave where Jesus was laid served
as the altar. Those in the antechamber could hear the voice of
the priest but could not see him. The Consecration that took
place there unites the sacrifice of Golgotha and the moment
of the Resurrection. For the Resurrection is also a kind of transubstantiation—the greatest step and change a substance can
undergo—from death to life. In utter seclusion, without human
witnesses, this mystery took place.

A place to begin understanding the veil is in the book of Genesis.
Adam and Eve discovered their nakedness after the Fall. They had
suffered a terrible loss and put on clothes to try to regain some of
the radiance, some of the dignity that had been theirs before the
Fall. Veiling then becomes a visible sign of the grace and holiness
that has become invisible to human eyes. Veiling in the liturgy is not
intended to withdraw an object from view, or make a mystery of it
or to conceal its presence (though it might seem to do these things).
The appearance of veiled things is common knowledge anyway.
Everyone knew that there was nothing behind the curtain in the
Temple. The outward appearance of sacred things tells us little about
their inward nature. It is the veil that tells us. Consider that the Host
itself is a veil. By visible beauty, may we be led to invisible beauty.

PRAYING *AD DEUM*

When the priest has arrived at the altar, he does not greet the people;
he speaks to God on behalf of the people. To do so with his back to
God would be strange, to say the least. So the position of the priest
remains *ad Deum* ("toward God") for the duration of the Mass,
except for certain occasions I will speak of later.

"Now that the priest is occupied at the altar, it is more fitting
for him to remain as he is than to look behind him, for thus he

expresses the inner devotion with which he offers the sacrifice. The ploughman must not turn and look back when he is performing his worthy action. Nor would it be right for one who wishes to praise our Lord to turn his back to him, and his breast to servants" (Amalarius).

The customary Jewish way to attend a banquet was for everyone to be facing the same direction, at a long, low table, to enable the servants to attend to those dining. This was most likely how the Last Supper was celebrated.

For their formal worship, the Jews always worshipped toward the holy city of Jerusalem, whence their aid from on high would come. From the earliest days of the Church, Christians prayed facing east—the direction from which the Savior would come again. Another reason to pray facing east is that the sun rises there, and the sun is symbolic of the Son of God.

As the Most Rev. Edward Slattery of Tulsa pointed out, there are many problems with celebrating Holy Mass facing the people. First, it is a serious rupture with the Church's ancient tradition. Secondly, it gives the appearance that the priest and the people are engaged in a conversation about God, rather than the worship of God. And thirdly, it places an inordinate importance on the personality of the celebrant by placing him on a stage.

Cardinal Ratzinger said in the *Ratzinger Report* that when the priest and the people face each other to worship, there is a poor symbol of the Church. It is as though the Church is looking at herself—the assembly looking into a mirror. The better image of the Church is to have the whole assembly focused on one single point outside herself—namely, God.

There is an essential truth expressed by celebrating Mass *ad Deum* as opposed to *ad populum* ("toward the people"). At Mass, Christ joins us to Himself as He offers Himself in sacrifice to the Father for the world's redemption. Like Christ, we offer ourselves to the Father because we have become members of His Body through Baptism. All the faithful share in this offering (the lifting up of hearts at the Offertory, for example), though in a different way from that of the priest. Christ is the head of the Church, and the faithful are the members. So the priest acts *in persona Christi* ("in the person of Christ")—symbolic of the Head and members of the body of the Church facing the Father.

If possible, the Mass should be celebrated facing east. This position is called *ad orientem* ("toward the east"). St. Robert Bellarmine says, "When our Lord died on the Cross, he was looking towards the west. So we pray facing east, as if to look at the face of the Crucified. And since he *ascends above the heaven of heavens to the east*, we, so to speak, accompany him as he ascends by our prayers and petitions. And finally, it is believed that he will come from the east in judgment: *For as lightning cometh out of the east and appeareth even into the west, so shall also the coming of the Son of man be."*

Some early churches did not face east because they had been pagan temples that had been taken over by the Church, and the congregation did not have the money to rebuild them. We have a similar situation here at OLMC: our church does not face east, but we do not have the means to reorient the church. This is why the phrase *ad Deum* is useful.

When see the priest facing God with the people at Mass, you see adherence to Apostolic Tradition. This continuity is a guardian against making the Mass into a personal project; it does not allow a priest or a liturgical committee to refashion the Mass into their idea of what most pleases them about worship.

Celebrating the Mass toward God reveals the very nature of the Mass. It is worship. I recently saw a picture of an evangelical megachurch. Everything about it was symbolic of teaching. The pastor was sitting on the stage in comfortable, casual clothes with a boom mic, teleprompters, large television screens to show his face, ranks of computers in the foreground to coordinate the broadcast, et cetera. Symbolically, the whole thing communicated a lecture or a show but not worship. I would even go so far as to say that it communicated the pastor and not God.

But if the Eucharistic Sacrifice is offered to the one and triune God, how can this be communicated most fittingly? When we wish to speak to someone about something serious, we face him. Of course, when the priest instructs the faithful in a sermon during Mass, he leaves the altar and faces them. It would not be fitting for him to remain facing God while talking to them.

With that being said, there is an important distinction to be made between the exterior position of the priest and the people and their interior disposition. Listen to what Cardinal Estevez of the Congregation of Divine Worship once wrote about this.

> It is clear that the Eucharistic Sacrifice is offered to the one and triune God, and that the principal, eternal and high priest is Jesus Christ, Who acts through the ministry of the priest who visibly presides as His instrument. The liturgical assembly participates in the celebration in virtue of the common priesthood of the faithful which requires the ministry of the ordained priest to be exercised in the Eucharistic Synaxis. The physical position, especially with respect to the communication among the various members of the assembly, must be distinguished from the interior spiritual orientation of all. It would be a grave error to imagine that the principle orientation of the sacrificial action is toward the community.

So we must conclude that it is entirely possible to have a proper interior disposition of worship at a Mass in which the priest faces the faithful. And it is certainly possible to lack the proper disposition with the priest facing God. But I'm talking about a symbolic understanding of the Mass. And the better symbol is clearly *ad Deum*.

In an audience in 2005 Pope Benedict XVI said the following about the Mass: "A joyful celebration . . . includes, on the one hand, the adoring people and the liturgical assembly, and on the other, the Lord who returns and is present and active. . . . The heart of the liturgy is in this intersection between priests and faithful on one side, and the Lord and His might on the other."

Arrival at the Altar

When the priest arrives at the altar, all are standing. The faithful stand when the priest comes into the temple, to greet Christ, Who is represented by the celebrant. It is a mark of respect in our culture to stand to greet a superior; for example, members of Congress stand when the president walks in, and soldiers stand when a superior officer walks in.

In ancient Judaism "to stand" meant "to pray." And the Hebrews had to eat their first Paschal lamb (Ex. 12:11) standing, before heading off for the Promised Land.

In the early Church there were no pews or chairs; everyone stood for Mass. Kneeling was not used as it is today. St. Irenaeus (second century) saw standing as a symbol of the Resurrection, by which, through the grace of Christ, we have been freed from sin and death.

The celestial liturgy is also celebrated with the faithful standing. "After this I saw a great multitude, which no man could number, of all nations and tribes and peoples and tongues, standing before the throne and in sight of the Lamb, clothed with white robes, and palms in their hands" (Apoc. 7:9).

After handing his biretta to the acolyte, the priest and the acolytes genuflect, and for the Low Mass, the priest goes up to place his chalice on the altar and to open the missal. I love this removal of the biretta; it is a gentle mark of human respect to the Lord for the priest to take off his hat. In fact, that is one great reason for the priest to wear this special hat—so that he has something to take off in respect.

The priest ascends to the altar in silence in recognition of being in the presence of God. Things must be set in a certain way before we can approach Him. Externally this is true, but even more so of our interior. "Be still and know that I am God" the psalm says (Ps. 45:11).

The priest walks up three steps; this is symbolic of Christ and of Moses. Moses went up the mountain on behalf of the people since they could not go up; he had to do so on their behalf. This prefigured Christ's going up the hill of Calvary to do something that no other man could do. The acolytes remain in their places, and the priest ascends to intercede for the faithful to the Father.

Things have to be different on the mountain of the Lord (referred to as Mount Sion in Psalm 42). This is why Discalced Carmelite nuns, for example, do not wear shoes. It is not just a penance (though in the wintertime it is penitential); it is because they live on the holy mountain of Carmel, the mountain where God dwells; they never go back down.

The silence that the priest maintains here and in different places in the Sacred Liturgy is not an absence of sound. It has no gaps; it is a single great canticle, and the silence acts as an acoustic veil over the whole liturgy to reveal what the liturgy is. The Gregorian Rite has no artificial introduction of silence into the liturgy by the addition of pauses. When silence is at the beck and call of the celebrant, as opposed to the rite, the silence of the priest becomes the whole congregation waiting for him, wondering what is going to happen next. The silence in the Gregorian Rite is given as an integral part of the Mass, determined by the Church through two thousand years of development. And what often seems like silence in our rite is not quite silence; it is rather the priest praying to God in a low voice.

The altar is covered with three cloths. All accounts of the Resurrection mention the folded cloths in the Holy Sepulcher. As it says in the Easter Sequence: "I saw the tomb wherein the living one had lain, I saw His glory as He rose again; napkin and linen clothes, and angels twain."

When he arrives at the top step near the mensa, and after placing the veiled chalice on the corporal and putting the burse to the left, leaning on the gradine, he immediately walks to his right and opens the missal. Placed on a small wooden stand (or a golden one on a higher class of feast day, or perhaps covered with a cloth of the color of the particular feast), the missal seems to wait for the priest to open it.

I should point out that the rubrics actually specify a *sussinus* (cushion) for the missal to rest on. The cushion was used because in the East the ancient monarch received guests on a cushioned divan; there he pronounced law; there he was the visible monarch. The cushion is the representation of the divan of Solomon. But it has become customary to use a solid stand, if nothing else because it is hard for young altar boys to move the missal around in the Mass unless they have a stand.

In a traditional missal you will see seven ribbons used to mark various places. This is because the missal represents for us the Book of the Seven Seals mentioned in the book of the Apocalypse (cf. Apoc. 5:1). Only the Lamb was found worthy to open the book, so the acolytes do not open it, but only the priest, who represents Christ. This is why, at the beginning of a Low Mass, the back of the book always faces away from the tabernacle, and the opening faces the tabernacle, pointing toward Christ. When the missal is open before a High Mass, it symbolizes Christ as the Way, the Truth, and the Life. The more solemn stand represents Christ, Who is the Stand that holds open the Book of Life.

This rather simple but solemn opening of the missal is done in silence, as the opening of the book was done in the celestial liturgy. "And when he had opened the seventh seal, there was silence in heaven, as it were for half an hour" (Apoc. 8:1). Of course, we don't wait the half hour but use this silence as a representation.

In the traditional missal we see an attempt to pack the entire fullness of the Catholic Faith and practice into one book. Holy

Scripture is set in context (for instance, the way in which the Old and New Testaments are arranged to explain one another reciprocally); the tradition of everything from saints to vestments; and finally the revelation of the sacraments—Christ's healing and blessing presence mediated through the Church. The missal should therefore be beautiful, even gorgeous, because it represents all these splendid gifts.

When the priest comes back down to the footpace to begin the Prayers at the Foot of the Altar (or, in the High Mass, a second genuflection), we are reminded of Christ, "who bowed the heavens and came down" (Ps. 17:10).

Everything is now ready to begin the solemn preparation for the Mass. Even the sacred space in which it is celebrated is carefully prepared, right down to the lights used. This space is a manifestation of the inner power of the Catholic Mass, in that it seems to be almost indifferent to conditions of space (as a chaplain in the navy, I said Mass in many place that could hardly be called sacred), and yet it has produced masterpieces of architecture and art such as no other of man's ideas has been able to produce. When we say "sacred space," however, keep in mind that one of the most revolutionary innovations of the Church was the departure from a *cultus* of place-worship; holy mountains, sacred oaks or rivers, or even the Temple in Jerusalem. Worship can take place wherever a holy people are gathered before God. "For you are the temple of the living God; as God saith: I will dwell in them, and walk among them; and they shall be my people" (2 Cor. 6:16).

And for the things to be used, and even the space itself, there is one great principle to be followed—namely, that nothing broken, damaged, or inferior should be offered to God. Only the best should be given to Him in the Sacred Liturgy. Therefore the pastor must see to it that damaged things be repaired; that an excellent chalice, missal, vestments, and so forth are used, according the means of his parish. Even the very building of the church should be the very best that we can offer. The celebrant, clergy ministers, faithful; the whole assembly should be well arranged and outfitted, like a ship headed east on a diplomatic mission to its God.

ARRIVAL AT THE FOOTPACE

After the priest has come down from the altar, he and the servers genuflect. Whenever the priest descends from the altar, one of the things he represents is fallen man. When he ascends to the altar, he represents man redeemed by Christ. That is one reason why the three steps are so important for the Mass: there are three stages of the interior life that all must proceed through to enter heaven (St. John of the Cross calls them the Purgative, Illuminative, and the Unitive stages); so there often three steps from the footpace to the altar, or three steps from the nave to the altar.

A genuflection is made once the priest is at the footpace, and he remains standing while the servers and the faithful kneel. Things must be done the same way each time, since "the liturgy does not live off sympathetic surprises, of captivating discoveries, but of solemn repetitions" (Cardinal Ratzinger, *Entretiens sur la Foi*). God does not change, and He is not capricious. The liturgy ought to reflect this.

The genuflection is itself an act of humility and worship. It says to God, "I need You to lift me up." The root of kneeling as integral to worship may be found in St. John's account of the healing of the blind man: "And he fell down and worshipped him" (Lk. 9:38). This is recorded again and again in Scripture when suddenly someone recognizes the divinity of Christ.

Kneeling also has an ancient root in the imperial epiphany, in which the emperor was manifested in all his glory to the court. They waited in the court in expectation, and when a large curtain was drawn aside, all knelt in *prokynesis* (touching the forehead to the ground). We see something similar to the opening and the closing of the tabernacle. These ceremonies were added to the liturgy because the early Church (beginning with Constantine) knew that the whole liturgy was an epiphany of the Lord.

The early Christians stood during the liturgy to express that they were celebrating a liturgical sacrifice; a sacrificial meal (thus not reclining). It often happens that contemporary worshippers stand to express the opposite—that they are most decidedly *not* participating in a sacrifice. Kneeling speaks an unmistakable language that standing does not.

THE SIGN OF THE CROSS

The priest begins the solemn preparation for the Mass by making the Sign of the Cross. Notice that the words of the Sign are grammatically incorrect; "Name" is singular, and "Father, Son, and Holy Ghost" is plural. But if the priest said, "In the *Names* of the Father, Son, and Holy Ghost" to make it correct, he would commit a heresy. The Name of God refers to His essence, which is one. There cannot be more than one essence. Similar mistakes of grammar occur several times in the Mass, since the language of man will always fall short of the mystery.

In making the Sign of the Cross, the priest, with his hand flat, touches his forehead, then his chest, then his left shoulder, then his right shoulder. The movement from left to right is always a sign of the blessing of God in our liturgy.

The Sign of the Cross is an essential prayer of a Catholic, because we go to heaven by the Cross and by no other path. St. Patrick of Ireland made the Sign of the Cross hundreds of times a day. It must be made well; St. Bernadette of Soubirous made it so well that others, upon seeing her make it, learned much about how to pray well (she learned how to make it from the Blessed Virgin of Lourdes, so no wonder she made it so well).

PRAYERS AT THE FOOT OF THE ALTAR

The priest then begins these prayers: "I will go unto the altar of God," and the server responds, "Unto God who giveth joy to my youth" (Ps. 42:4). This begins a confession to God, which is necessary to do before the Mass can begin. As Job said, "If I would justify myself, my own mouth shall condemn me. If I would shew myself innocent, He shall prove me wicked" (Job 9:20). We were born with a conscience, so we have a deep need to confess our guilt. Yet at the same time we have a deep need to justify ourselves. The confessions on pop-psychology TV shows are largely made to justify. "I take full responsibility for my actions. Therefore I will not resign, and I expect you to vote for me in the next election," says the politician. This is only slightly better than the self-exploitation on the reality shows. Something is missing from these confessions. God is missing.

"There is an invisible and heavenly altar, which the unjust can never approach. No one comes to that heavenly altar but he who comes to this altar with care. He will find his life there, if at this altar, he *distinguishes his cause*" (St. Augustine).

"Unto God": this is God's altar. Men can spend their whole lives searching for love and acceptance, but only God can fulfill this; not even a beloved spouse can do it.

"Who giveth joy to my youth." *Youth* here refers not to a man's age, but to the soul. God is the one who scrapes off the barnacles, the detritus of life's sins and mistakes, and the garbage collected in the soul. His grace makes the soul young again; young in the sense of a restored innocence.

Besides referring to restored innocence, the term *youth* in the Forty-Second Psalm is to be understood as the supernatural and spiritual new life obtained by regeneration in the grace of the Holy Ghost. By grace, the old man of sin (Rom. 6:6) is destroyed in us and the newness of life in the Holy Ghost is given in its place (Col. 3:9).

So whoever approaches the altar as a spiritually newborn child—that is, full of holy simplicity, innocence, and purity of mind—will find that his youthfulness of spirit (that is, his fervor and cheerfulness in the service of God) or his young (that is, his still tender and weak) life of grace daily grows and waxes strong under the blessed influence of the Holy Sacrifice of the Mass.

In the literal sense of the psalm, David, still a young man when he wrote it, expresses astonishment that his soul is sad. We can sympathize with his sadness—he had been driven from Jerusalem by the revolt of his son Absalom and was grievously harassed by his enemies. Absalom had usurped the throne, so David asks God to judge him (David) and not the people. This is not pride (as though he were pouting, "Hey, I'm the king!"), since David knew that he was anointed for his task and Absalom was not. It separates him from Absalom, who was seeking to overthrow the authority of God, but only God can distinguish between what the human failure of David is and what the authority in him is, by virtue of his office. So his hope is not in his own strength, but in the strength of God.

His separation from the holy tabernacle in Jerusalem distresses him most of all, and it appears to him as a punishment of God, so he sorrowfully longs to return to the sanctuary of the Lord; there he will glorify God by sacrifices of praise and thanksgiving. In conclusion he encourages himself and cheers himself by rousing his hope in God. This is why the Forty-Second Psalm is not used for Requiem Masses or for Passiontide; this good cheer is not appropriate for those times, since we ought to weep with those who weep and mourn with those who mourn (cf. Rom. 12:15).

In the fuller sense of Scripture, we contrast ourselves with others in this psalm: "Judge me, O God, and distinguish my cause from the nation that is not holy: deliver me from the unjust and deceitful man. For thou art God my strength: why hast thou cast me off?" The answer is: because of sin. There is a law of sin in my members.

Who among us wants to be perceived like this? The sins we know that others can see inspire a certain kind of zeal within our souls for the removal of those sins. As to the ones that we are sure that others cannot see—with these we are more indulgent. But God sees everything.

So David says, "Judge me." Judge my cause because "You see everything." Here David is like a child who takes a flower to his mother to make up for a slight. The flower is not worth much of anything, but the gesture is, and the mother appreciates it. It is as though David is saying, like St. Peter, "Lord, you know everything; you know that I love you" (cf. Jn. 21:17).

The Discalced Carmelites have in their rule that the prioress is supposed to ask a sister who is dying if she is ready to go the Judgment. When St. Thérèse of the Child Jesus was asked this, she responded that indeed she was ready. Her reason was not like that of most people; reception of Extreme Unction, the Brown Scapular, a good confession, et cetera. She said she was ready because "I always sought humility of heart, and I never sought anything but the truth." What a magnificent answer!

"Send forth Thy light and Thy truth": this truth is so very painful at times to our fallen nature. But it is the same truth that heals the nature. It is His light, His truth, and it exposes everything. Is it not supremely difficult to change, to detach ourselves from what we like, or from what we are used to, and do that which is better or nobler? *Better* here means more grounded in the truth of God, more faithful to our tradition. It is that truth which will set us free.

"And I will go in unto the altar of God": David (or the priest or the faithful who assist at the Mass) recognizes the truth and that he will also be able to go to the altar. There is no reason for any of us to be cast down—no reason except our own refusal to receive what God has given us. He will not refuse to give. So we remind ourselves to hope in Him.

Looking at the psalm in the fuller sense of Scripture with Christ, and not us, at the center of it, we see the whole story of David and Absalom as the story of the Passion. Judas is Absalom. As David wanted to return to Jerusalem to offer the sacrifice, so Christ wanted to go to His altar, which was on the hill of Calvary. The wicked and deceitful man is our fallen human nature.

Notice that for the recital of this psalm the priest looks straight ahead. He has the liberty to close his eyes, or look at the tabernacle or the crucifix or the altar, but he should fix his eyes on one object and stay with it.

The priest says this psalm aloud. There are three levels of voice that are used in the Rite of St. Gregory: *vox clara, vox media, vox secreta* (the clear, middle, and secret voice). Three different voices, three different bows of the head, three different bows of the body: the whole rite honors the Holy Trinity.

Immediately after the conclusion of the Forty-Second Psalm, the celebrant says, "Our help is in the name of the Lord, who made heaven and earth" (Ps. 123:8). He makes the Sign of the Cross while doing so, which is a transition to what follows. Our misery is so great, that we cannot even think anything conducive to our own salvation, and without the grace of the Holy Ghost we cannot even pronounce worthily the Holy Name (cf. 2 Cor. 3:5). Since the *Adiutorium* ("our help") is a transition, it follows that only God can address our misery, that we may with confidence expect favor and pardon, "because with the Lord there is mercy and with Him plentiful redemption" (Ps. 129:7).

THE CONFITEOR

The priest then begins the Confiteor. He confesses his sins first, before the altar boys, who confess it on behalf of the faithful, since "the just is first accuser of himself" (Prov. 18:17). He accuses himself since "all have sinned and do need the glory of God." He does not accuse himself of any particular sin, lest he scandalize or discourage the faithful, but he does not need to, since this is not sacramental confession, in which the penitent must say the sin in kind and number.

"Before the priest or bishop ascends the steps of the altar and performs his sacred office, he takes thought for himself and bows low before the altar, to symbolize how Christ emptied himself, when he bowed the heavens and came down, taking the form of a servant. And considering how Solomon said, *The just man in the beginning is the accuser of himself,* he makes confession to those about him" (Durandus).

The priest ought to be adorned with blamelessness, purity, and sanctity of life. But despite his careful preparation, he knows and feels keenly that he is still far removed from such sanctity. The dignity, knowledge, and fullness of grace bestowed upon him also aggravate in him slight sins and infidelities of which he may be guilty in the service of God. Even light faults and negligences become grave evils in his eyes, when he weighs them in the scales of the sanctuary, since even "for sins forgiven he is not without fear" (Ecclus. 5:5). So he has every reason to make a public confession of guilt, to approach the altar only in a spirit of deep sorrow and compunction, and to implore heavenly and earthly intercession.

Standing before the altar, he strikes his breast like the publican, who stood in the Temple striking his breast and saying, "O God, be merciful to me a sinner" (Lk. 18:13). He claims that he has sinned exceedingly, in thought, word, and deed, but most of all for the things he has done. The sins of omission are included in the sorrow for the sins of deed.

The Confiteor is divided clearly into two parts, as it contains an acknowledgment of sin as well as a petition to the blessed in purgatory and heaven and the faithful present at the Mass to intercede on our behalf to God. In every Mass the intercession of the saints is repeatedly invoked, and God is petitioned for grace with confidence in their prayers and merits.

As St. Bonaventure put it:

> God has wished that we should pray to the saints and they should pray for us, in order that the faint-hearted may gain confidence to receive through worthy intercessors that which they do not dare ask of themselves or could not obtain by their own prayers; and so that humility may be preserved in those who pray, the dignity of the saints be made manifest, and finally, that in all the members of the body of Christ love and unity many be revealed, so that the lower creatures may confidently look up to those higher placed and implore their assistance, and these latter in return may in all love and kindness condescend unto them. (*Breviloquium*, V.10)

The saints are petitioned in the order of their hierarchy. It may seem odd that St. Joseph is not mentioned, given that many theologians (such as Suarez) think that he excelled all the other saints after Our Lady in holiness. The likely reason he is not mentioned here is that devotion to him grew only gradually (today he is the patron of the Universal Church) and that his not being mentioned harmonized with his mysteriously hidden and retired life. A pope could have inserted his name into the Confiteor, of course (as religious insert the name of their founder), but St. John XXIII inserted his name into the Canon, which is a higher prayer than the Confiteor.

The position of the body of the priest corresponds to the meaning of the Confiteor and to the interior disposition that should be adopted for this prayer. The profound inclination of the body, the joining of the hands, and the striking of the breast indicate a poor sinner who, laden with sin and full of compunction, stands before His Judge to implore grace and mercy. The priest does not presume to lift his eyes to heaven, but in confusion and profoundly inclined, he casts his eyes to the ground, since he is but dust and ashes.

The joining of the hands indicates recollection of mind and a spirit of devotion, a surrendering of oneself to God and a repose in God, a mistrust of one's own strength and a confident supplication for grace and mercy.

The striking of the breast three times indicates sorrow and displeasure for sins committed, since the heart concealed within the breast has to do with the cause of sin (the worst kind—the kind we freely choose) and should therefore be bruised and humbled and broken, so that God might create a new clean heart within us. We remember too that the striking of the breast is in imitation of the publican who was standing outside the Temple and whose prayer was acceptable to the Father, thus mentioned in praise by Christ.

The breast is struck three times, indicating the three kinds of sin (in thought, word, and deed—deed including the sins of omission), and our sorrow above all for the evil things that we have willfully chosen to do.

Then the servers repeat the Confiteor and ask for mercy for the priest. The servers say the Confiteor on behalf of the faithful (unless it is a Dialogue Mass, in which the faithful say all the parts of the acolytes). Like the priest, they are quite conscious of their misery and their sin. And like the priest, they too are not without fear even for sins forgiven. Both priest and faithful must live with this fear, by giving God their sins and living in trust of Him. The man who does not fear God is a fool; the man who thinks God is not merciful is ignorant. We need both the fear of Him and the trust in His mercy.

All this is in imitation of the Savior, who confessed for us. "I confess to thee, O Father, Lord of heaven and earth . . ." (Mt. 11:25). Priest and acolytes are bowed low in this sense, to indicate the great burden of Christ in the Garden of Olives as He took upon Himself the sins of the world. If there is a better description of the nature of that burden and the confession of our sins to the Father than the sermon of Bl. John Henry Newman called "On the Mental Sufferings of Our Lord," I do not know of it.

ABSOLUTION

After the servers repeat the Confiteor, the priest intercedes for the faithful and pronounces the absolution. This is not a sacramental absolution such as we receive in the confessional; it is rather an intercession. Notice that the priest asks Almighty God for "pardon, absolution, and remission" of sins. *Indulgentiam* (pardon) refers to intercession for the full remission of all our sins. *Absolutionem* (absolution) refers to intercession for the absolution of guilt—a gnawing and sometimes debilitating effect of sin. *Remissionem* (remission) refers to intercession against the punishment due to sin. The Sign of the Cross is made along with these intercessions, since it is only Christ's atoning sacrificial death that makes these three graces possible.

Once the priest has given the absolution, he bows slightly. Notice again that the priest bows in three ways in the Mass: once profoundly for the Confiteor, once midway for the adoration of the Trinity, and once slightly to express confidence and reverence. He then begins a short series of versicles (you will see this abbreviated in your missal as "V.") and responsories (abbreviated as "R.") which begin with the notion of God's being turned toward us. God turns away from us when we sin; He does not watch cruelty or perversion like a voyeur. But He turns favorably toward us even if we are ugly with sin but repentant and have acknowledged our guilt. When He turns to us we find peace, joy, and felicity in Him.

Dominus Vobiscum and the
Gifts of the Holy Ghost

Next, the priest says the famous "*Dominus vobiscum*" to the faithful, and the response comes back to him: "*Et cum spiritu tuo.*" For a long time the English translation of this in the Ordinary Form of the Roman Rite omitted the reference to a man's spirit—a very unfortunate omission and a very bad translation. I am happy to know that this has been restored in the new English translation.

St. Albert gives good reasons for referring to the spirit:

> We should consider why the people answer the priest in a different manner from that in which they were greeted. For they do not say, "May the Lord be with you", or something similar, but "and with thy spirit". There are three reasons for this. The first is that the priest, when he stands at the altar, must be entirely in the spirit. The second is that the spirit of man frequently goes astray. The third is that what happens at the altar is clearly a work done by spiritual power. So the one who stands at the altar must be nothing but spirit, and must think nothing of the body or of the cares of this world.

This is a very ancient greeting. St. Peter Damien pointed out that "this form of greeting was not instituted recently by the powers of human thought. Rather, it comes from the ancient authority of the sacred word. In the book of Ruth, when Booz greeted the reapers, he said to them, *Dominus vobiscum.*" And Durandus mentions that "Booz became a type of Christ, by taking Ruth the foreign woman, the Moabitess, to be his wife." So the ancient greeting prefigures Christ.

Remember that at this point the Mass has not yet begun. These prayers said at the foot of the altar are a solemn, public preparation for the Mass. And since the priest is about to ascend to the altar, we recall Our Lord departing from His apostles at His Ascension. The priest climbs the steps to the altar, going up, going away from the congregation, yet does not leave the flock behind. He takes the faithful with him; he takes their sins with him to ask forgiveness of them; he takes their needs with him, to plead them before God; above all, he takes their offering of love and gratitude. So this *Dominus Vobiscum* is like a goodbye, but a goodbye like no other. Christ departs from us to come much closer to us in Holy Communion.

Seven is often referred to as the number of the Holy Ghost. Seven times will the priest greet the faithful during the Mass with the *Dominus Vobiscum*. There are nine of these greetings in all between the procession and recession of the celebrant: one at the prayers of the foot of the altar, which we just saw (the Mass has not yet begun), one after the Mass is completed with the praying of the Last Gospel (which serves as an official thanksgiving for the Mass), and seven during the Mass.

At each salutation of the priest during the Mass, he prays that the faithful might receive a particular gift of the Holy Ghost, because it is that gift which will be most needed in order to participate in the Mass. The faithful respond through the server that the priest might receive an outpouring of the same gift, since it is that gift which he most needs to pray the Mass well. I am astounded at the intelligence of this arrangement—that the Church (guided by the Sanctifier) would have arranged these so perfectly, so brilliantly.

Wisdom

The first salutation during the Mass is after the Gloria; priest and faithful pray for the gift of wisdom, which they will need to benefit from the Collect and the Epistle that follow. Wisdom is the first and highest among the seven gifts of the Holy Ghost. It leads the souls of those who have it to see things from God's perspective. Wisdom is fullness of knowledge through affinity for the divine, as when a person comes to know Christ's Passion through suffering. It is also love, which inspires contemplative reflection on what we believe and directs the mind to judge according to its precepts. The gift of Wisdom supplements the virtue of faith and shields us against folly.

The virtue of charity is part of wisdom; it inspires contemplative reflection on the divine mysteries, enjoys thinking about them, and directs the mind to judge all things according to their right principles. This is very useful when we try to pray the Mass, given that our neighbor in the pew next to us might not be praying in a way that we find conducive to recollection.

Wisdom is distinct from faith. Faith is assent to the defined articles of Catholic belief, but wisdom goes further to a certain divine penetration of these truths.

Understanding

The second salutation is before the Gospel, when we pray for the gift of understanding. This gives to the mind of those who have it a charisma for apprehending Christ's public revelation easily and profoundly, very useful for the Gospel and the sermon that might follow it.

More specifically, the gift of understanding helps those who have it to penetrate to the heart of revealed truth even when they do not fully understand its entire meaning. It gives great confidence in the revealed Word of God and leads those who have it to reach true conclusions from revealed principles.

Counsel

The third salutation is before the Offertory. In this we pray for the gift of counsel, which makes us prefer the joys of sacrifice to the pleasures of the world, after the example of Christ by His immolation (the process of sacrificing) for us at the Last Supper. It is in the perfect place, given the nature of the Offertory.

The gift of counsel perfects in those who have it the virtue of prudence. It enables them to judge promptly and rightly, as by supernatural intuition, what should be done in difficult situations. So when we bring our crosses to the altar, in order to lift them up to God in union with His Son in the Offertory, to judge what should be offered is a work for which we need that great gift of counsel.

Fortitude

The fourth salutation is at the beginning of the Preface to the Canon. Here we pray for the gift of fortitude, which gives to those who receive it a strong spirit of resolution and firmness of mind and will to persevere with a quiet faith in God's providence that overcomes all obstacles. It also gives courage to persist in the practice of virtue despite trials, illness, persecution, or external failure. A Catholic who becomes fervent in God's service will soon be condemned by the world, but the gift of fortitude will sustain him as he carries the cross.

We see immediately how appropriate it is to pray for fortitude at the Preface, since the Canon is par excellence the prayer of the Cross. There is no cross given by God to His children that is not personally designed for their path to heaven. And everyone who receives the cross will need fortitude to carry it. It is too heavy to carry on our own, and it must be this way, lest the carrying of the cross become another human accomplishment and a source of pride.

Knowledge

The fifth salutation is given in a unique way, just before the *Agnus Dei*. The priest prays that the peace of the Lord would be with the faithful always. Here we pray for the gift of knowledge. This gift enables us to evaluate created things at their true worth—namely, in their relation to God. The gift of knowledge unmasks the pretense of creatures, reveals their emptiness, and points out their only true purpose as instruments in the service of God. It shows us the loving care of God, even in adversity, and directs us to glorify Him in every circumstance of life. Guided by its light, we put first things first and prize the friendship of God beyond all else. This is the perfect gift to desire before the reception of Holy Communion. To be able to see clearly that the Eucharist is above every other thing on this earth will prevent a bad Communion in the negative sense and, in the positive sense, will enable us to esteem Christ's friendship above all (especially in preference to human respect).

Piety

The sixth salutation is for the gift of piety, for which we pray just after receiving Holy Communion. This gift perfects the virtue of justice toward God and infuses in us an instinctive love for Him and devotion to those who are consecrated to Him. And since we owe Him thanksgiving in justice, we see the perfection of this gift being prayed for after Communion.

The gift of piety is essential for growth in the interior life in that it enables us to see God not merely as a just and terrible Judge but also as a loving Father (cf. Rom. 8:14).

Fear of the Lord

Just before the dismissal of the Mass, the *Ite Missa Est*, the priest and the faithful pray in the seventh salutation for the gift of fear of the Lord. This gift confirms in those who have it the theological virtue of hope and infuses profound respect for God's glory and selfless love for God. It protects from sin through dread of offending God. Here we are not praying for servile fear—the fear of mere punishment for doing what is wrong—but the fear of hurting someone we love.

This is a perfect gift to pray for with the dismissal; as we leave the Mass, we pray for each other to fear falling back into sin after having been given the greatest gift of holiness and life that the Father could possibly give us—namely, His Son.

Notice that during the Mass five times the priest will turn to the faithful and give the salutation. These five times commemorate the five apparitions of Christ after His Resurrection, so the Mass commemorates not only the death of the Lord, but also that fact that He is risen from the dead.

All seven gifts of the Holy Ghost are prayed for during the Mass because they are being poured into sinful souls, and receiving one gift without the others would pose dangers to a soul. For instance, if one received wisdom—and was able to start to see things as God sees them—he might fall into pride and mistake the view of God as his own. This would block him from receiving the next gift, understanding. Understanding gives the ability to understand public revelation, and thus checks the potential pride that can be the seedbed of false private revelation.

Understanding gives great confidence in the revealed Word of God, but that confidence—if left alone—could degenerate into a kind of blindness in the application of Scripture to daily life.

The gift of counsel prevents this by giving one a profound grasp of what is right and what is wrong. But the good counsel of what must be done and what must be avoided is not enough. One must act on that counsel, and thus he needs the gift of fortitude, which enables him to fight the good fight.

Men who fight for the Faith or for God, however, can become blind to what is truly good, so those with great fortitude can tear up the wheat with the cockle (cf. Mt. 13:24-30) and damage the good things God has planted. They need a gift to check the inordinate desire to destroy or attack what is evil, and that is the gift of knowledge, which prizes the friendship of God above all else, even above attacking what is against God.

But men who might have great knowledge of God, can become cold with knowledge and simply accumulate facts about God without giving their hearts to Him. To check this potential fault God gives the gift of piety. This gives one a filial affection for God as our most loving Father, and inspires him to love and respect for God's sake persons and things consecrated to Him, as well as those who are vested with His authority, His Blessed Mother and the saints, the Church and her visible Head, one's parents and superiors, one's country and its rulers.

But what if one has too much respect and love for superiors and falls into the danger of the worship of a personality? For that danger, God grants us the gift of fear of the Lord, which checks human respect and enables a person to respect his superior insofar as he is in union with God.

Each time we attend Holy Mass, the laity pray for the priest, and the priest for the laity, that each of the gifts of the Holy Ghost would be given in perfect order, in just the right part of the Mass where they should be prayed for, and at the right time. What depth the Mass has! What intelligence it displays, and what great care God has for those who worship Him in this Mass!

WE BELIEVE UNTO JUSTICE

THE PRIEST ASCENDS TO THE ALTAR

THE PREPARATION FOR THE MASS done in the sacristy—from the preparation of the sacred vessels to the laying out of the vestments to the prayers that the priest says while vesting—represent the thirty hidden years of Our Lord in the home at Nazareth. When the priest enters the sanctuary, we can think of Christ entering the Garden of Olives, and His prayer to the Father in that garden is the priest praying the prayers at the foot of the altar. When the priest bows low for the Confiteor, we see Our Lord faint at the sight of the sins of the world. When the priest ascends to the altar to kiss it, we are reminded of our Lord as He received the kiss of Judas Iscariot, since all of us have given that kiss to the Lord by our sins.

While it is very doubtful that the Mass was ever organized with the thought of presenting the central events of Our Lord's life in chronological order, nonetheless it can be fruitful to our devotion to see in each liturgical action an event in His life, with each action a source of mercy, just as His entire life was and is a great, continual source of mercy. Just as it takes centuries of meditation and prayer to unlock the mysteries of Sacred Scripture, so it took centuries to unlock the wisdom and beauty of the Rite of St. Gregory.

When you see the priest going up to kiss the altar, you might notice that he always steps with his right foot first. As we've seen before, the right always has precedence over the left, even down to the right thumb going over the left; the movement from left to right is a liturgical sign of God's blessing.

As he goes up, the priest prays the *Aufer a nobis*. The reference to the Holy of Holies in that prayer indicates that the true Holy of Holies is now the New Covenant of grace. The high priest of the Old Covenant entered into it but once a year with the sacrificial blood of animals. One can only imagine what that day was like for pious Jews when the Temple still stood, but it should astound us even more that the true Holy of Holies of the New Covenant is open to us every day, even to the most humble priest. Here Christ offers Himself by His own hands, to gain for us admission into the final Holy of Holies, which is heaven.

When the priest arrives at the altar after the prayers at the foot have been said, he lays his folded hands on the altar and is careful to touch the front of the altar with the ends of his smallest fingers, so that the middle three are on top of the altar, and his thumbs crossed, right over left, on top of them. The two fingers in front of the altar and touching it represent the dual nature of Christ, true God and true man, as it is only by this union that we are able even to approach the altar. The six fingers on top of the altar signify the faithful, like the six candles for the High Mass; that their prayers, works, joys, and sufferings must be presented to the Father by the mediation of the celebrant. The crossed thumbs bind the priest's hands together to remind him that to the end of the Mass he is bound to follow the laws of the Church regarding the rubrics.

Some might see such binding as being oppressive—the strict rubrics somehow curtailing the freedom of the celebrant. But like the ice skater who achieves great freedom in her skating after being bound by endless hours of practice, so it is that many priests feel a great freedom in not having to construct or fabricate gestures or actions in the liturgy in order to keep the faithful interested. With strict rubrics, the priest and the faithful are freed from the burden of novelty and are free to pray.

Next the priest kisses the altar, praying the *Oramus te*; the corporal has been placed on the altar, leaving a space of about two inches from the edge for this kiss. "We pray thee, O Lord, by the merits of thy saints, whose relics are here present, and of all thy saints, that thou wouldst be indulgent to all my sins." This is in reference to the relics of the saints (martyrs) placed in the little tomb of the altar stone. The altar also signifies Christ, so the priest embraces Him by putting his hands outside the corporal, flat on the altar, and bowing low, he kisses the altar, according to the words of the Holy Ghost: "Let him kiss me with the kiss of his mouth" (Cant. 1:1).

But the altar also signifies the Church, made up of all the faithful: "If thou make an altar of stone unto me thou shalt not build it of hewn stone" (Ex. 20:25). It is built of the hearts of the faithful, so the kiss is to remind the priest that he is to dedicate his life to their service.

In the old Roman republic, it was customary to kiss images of the gods; to kiss the family table before the meal or the threshold of the temple of whatever god a man was going to worship. This act of reverence was an act of thanksgiving to the blessings of the gods or the blessings that came to the family from their table.

When a priest kisses the altar, he is doing several things at once:

1. He reverences the altar as the vessel that brings to us our crucified Lord.

2. He reverences the altar as Christ Himself, Who is the Cornerstone, the "stone rejected by the builders" (cf. Mt. 21:42), and as St. Paul says, the stone that followed the Hebrews in the Exodus, giving drink to all the Chosen People (cf. 1 Cor. 10:4).

3. As the number of martyrs grew in the Church, the relics of martyrs were placed in the altar (or altar stone if the altar was made of wood) in the middle, near the front ledge of the mensa. In fact, the old Code of Canon Law mandated the relics of martyrs in the mensa. So the prayer *Oramus te* was added to express our desire that God would look upon the merits of the martyrs so that we might receive forgiveness of our sins. At the same time, we think of Christ Himself kissing with love those martyrs, because of their sacrifices, and embracing His Bride, the Church. This kiss is repeated several times in the Mass, to express just how much love Christ lavishes on His Bride.

4. The priest is reminded once again of his own unworthiness, as he asks God to remit all his sins and all the punishment due to them. His confidence is based not on his own holiness, but on that of the martyrs.

5. The priest is reminded to lay down his very life for his flock, like his good Master.

The priest needs this reminder every single day. He needs the words of this prayer, needs to feel the cold stone of the altar through the linens, needs to genuflect and bow low and often to God, so that pride might be rooted out of his soul. He needs to kiss that cold altar to remember to love even the most unlovable of his flock. He needs a reminder not to be cold to them.

As the priest ascends to the altar and kisses it during the High Mass, Gregorian chant is being sung, but not as background music. The last thing the chant should be is background music or some kind of art music, as we hear when we are edified by a good concert. As Martin Mosebach puts it, "Chant is something which must be practiced one's whole life long. It does justice to every phrase; nothing is purely ornamental; syllables are neither skipped over nor stretched out for the sake of the melody, as is often the case in great compositions."

He points out further why vernacular hymns must not be used during the Mass:

> In liturgy which is governed by vernacular hymns, the believer is constantly moved from one style to another and so he has to deal with highly subjective poetry of varied levels. He is moved and stirred—but not by the thing itself, liturgy: he is moved and stirred by the express sentiments of the commentary upon it. By contrast, the bond that Gregorian chant weaves between liturgical action and song is so close that it is impossible to separate form and content. All the chants create a ladder of liturgical expression on which the movements, actions and the content of the prayers are brought into a perfect harmony.

The length of the Gregorian composition is in harmony with the time it takes to perform an action in the High Mass. For example, the Introit is about as long as it takes for the procession to go from the narthex to the altar and say the prayers at the foot.

After the priest has kissed the altar, he turns immediately to his right (right foot first) to go to the missal and read the Introit, if he is celebrating a Low Mass. This represents two things at once: first, for the worshipper who wants to see the Mass as the whole drama of the Passion, death, and Resurrection in detail, it represents Christ being lead as a prisoner to Annas the High Priest, and the reading of the Introit represents His being falsely accused by Annas. Second, for the worshipper who is praying the Mass with a less detailed allegorical remembrance, it represents Christ going to the Jews, since the Epistle side of the altar is the side on which the Old Testament is read or sung.

"And his own received him not" (John 1:11). So, as Christ is the stone rejected by the builders, the priest representing Christ turns his back on the Epistle side once the Epistle, Gradual, and Alleluia are said, and goes to the opposite side of the altar, which we call the Gospel side. This represents Christ bringing the Good News to the Gentiles. That procession is a bittersweet action: bitter in the rejection of the Messias by His own and His walking away from them; sweet in the joy that the Gospel is given to the Gentiles. But at the very end of Mass, the priest returns to the Epistle side to represent the Second Coming, for then there will be a large-scale conversion of the Jews to the Church, foretold by St. Paul in the Epistle to the Romans (11:25-26), which will take place at the consummation of the world.

THE IMPOSITION OF INCENSE

During the High Mass, the priest turns to his right (if he turns, it is always to the right for the reasons given earlier) to impose incense on the coals in the thurible. Once the incense is imposed and blessed, he turns back to incense the altar. He incenses the cross three times, making a genuflection before and after. Then he incenses the relics of the saints on each side of the tabernacle, the altar three times on the Epistle side, twice at the end, three times coming back, a genuflection in the middle, and three times over the mensa on the Gospel side, twice at the end, and three times coming back, the same as the

Epistle side. This is to make our church like the sanctuary seen by St. John in his vision of the heavenly liturgy: "Another angel came and stood before the altar, having a golden censer, and there was given him much incense, that he should offer of the prayers of the all the saints upon the golden altar which is before the throne of God. And the smoke of the incense of the prayers of all the saints ascended up before God from the hand of the angel" (Apoc. 8:3-4).

Thus, incense typifies the prayers of Christians ascending before God, and that Angel is Christ Our Lord, the Mediator between us and His Father; the thurible is the heart of man upright before God; the altar is His Church; the fire is charity; the smoke is the prayers of the people ascending to heaven. The ancient prayer of David is used for the incensing of the altar: "Let my prayer be directed, O Lord, as incense in thy sight; the lifting up of my hands as an evening sacrifice" (Ps. 140:2).

Incense is one of the gifts given to the newborn Savior by the wise men. It is an offering to be given only to the Divinity. Pagans realized this too, by the way, and we are reminded of the martyrdom of St. Agnes, who would not burn incense to a false god. So the altar is incensed not because we worship it, but insofar as it represents Christ; the relics because they are part of saints who once received the Body and Blood of Christ while living. The celebrant is incensed only insofar as he takes the place of Our Lord and represents Him and offers the Sacrifice in His Name and by His power (this is also connected to the fact that incense was burned in the presence of Roman aristocracy, who were connected to the emperor, who was eventually seen by pagans as divine). The ministers are incensed because they recall Him Who came in the form of a slave and was found as a man. The people are incensed because they are the temples of the Holy Ghost.

The word *incense* is from the Latin *incendere*, meaning to set on fire as in a sacrifice. Offering incense is an act of sacrifice, the giving of an expensive gift to God, like fresh flowers. When the faithful are incensed, it is at once a purification of them, protection of them, and an honoring of Christ, who is present within them.

This incensation marks the formal beginning of the High Mass. In the service of God given in the Temple of Solomon, the high priest could not begin the service without incense (cf. Lev. 16:12). Thus, at the beginning of the Mass the priest and the faithful are removed somewhat from this sin-tainted world and transported to an atmosphere of sanctity.

A good, honorable priest at my seminary, the late Fr. John Quinn, was to celebrate Mass, and I was the sacristan for it. I had not prepared for him yet, being new at the job, and when I asked if he wanted incense, he looked at me with a friendly reprimand, to which I replied, "I'll prepare the incense, Father."

I put one coal in and could feel his eyes on me, so I readied another one, and sensed his dissatisfaction. "Three coals, Father?" He responded with an effort of patience: "Mr. Jackson, beware the poverty of Judas!" After the first incensation of the altar, it was difficult to see him, given that he had dumped seven spoonfuls of incense onto the three coals. During his sermon, he addressed this and said, "Some have accused me of using so much incense that they cannot see the altar. This is not a problem, but an ideal! It is said in the Scriptures that the Lamb was seated on His throne surrounded by *multum incensum. Multum incensum*, gentlemen!"

When incense is imposed, the celebrant gently puts it over the coals in three small spoonfuls, one for each member of the Holy Trinity. The thurifer asks for a blessing, and the priest says, "Be thou blessed by Him in whose honor thou shalt burn." He then makes the Sign of the Cross over the now burning incense. This formula shows the principal object of the incensing—the glorification of God. While it marks the beginning of the Mass, it also marks the end of the prayers at the foot of the altar.

This is also known as the formal beginning of the Mass of the Catechumens, or the first part of the Mass. In the ancient Church, this first part was meant for all the faithful, but especially for those who were not yet fully initiated into the Faith. Catechumens would leave after the sermon for more instruction, while those who had been baptized and confirmed and had received Holy Communion stayed for the rest of the Mass. It would be an error, however, to think of the Mass of the Catechumens as simply an instruction; it is for worship above all. Three fundamentals of liturgical prayer may be found in it:

1. Reading, in which the Beloved (Christ) speaks to His Father, and also to His Spouse (the Church), and brings the Father and His Spouse joy in the sound of His voice.

2. Praise, in which the Spouse speaks of her Beloved and delights in saying all these things about Him.

3. Prayer, in which the Spouse, having found her Beloved, speaks to Him and shares with Him her desires, sorrows, and joys.

We see once again that this is not just some teaching, as is done in the sermon. This is a great conversation between the Beloved and His Father and His Spouse, and it ought to be elevated, noble, far beyond ordinary speech; and so it is done in Latin, and we are privileged to listen in and even take part in it.

THE INTROIT

After the priest has been incensed (in the High Mass he stands at the Epistle side), he turns to the missal to begin the Introit. In the Low Mass, he simply walks over to the missal and begins praying aloud the Introit, from the Latin "He comes in," because it is customary for the choir to sing it while the celebrant is entering the sanctuary in a High Mass. The Introit always recalls the desires of the saints of the Old Testament for the coming of the Lord, like Isaias crying out, "Send forth, O Lord, the lamb, the ruler of the earth" (Is. 16:1).

Some Sundays are named by the first words of the Introit. For example, *Laetare* Sunday and *Quasimodo* Sunday are so called from the first word of the liturgy on each of those days.

Notice in your missal that there is often a reference to a Station— "Station at the Church of St. Peter," for example (*Statio ad S. Petrum*). These words indicate the church in Rome where the Pope and the faithful would offer the Divine Sacrifice. There was a solemn procession to that church, and the procession stopped (*statio*) at the church of the saint whose feast it was. So, for the feast of St. Cecilia, for example, the procession might have gone from the Lateran to her basilica, and then Mass was celebrated. At the Lateran there would have been an assembly called a *Collecta* (we take our word *Collect* from it), then a procession with the cross at the head, with psalms sung and the Litany of the Saints. To this day, before the High Mass begins, the sacred ministers gather in formation with the cross facing them, waiting for the priest (and deacon and subdeacon if it is a Solemn High Mass) to join the formation. This waiting is called the *Statio*, which is done in the back of the parish hall on Sundays and great feasts.

I say formation (rather military in this case), since Tertullian points out that the word *statio* passed from the language of the military into the Church: the assemblies of the Christians came to be called *Stationes*, because they bore a certain resemblance to the sentinels of the Roman army. As "good soldiers of Jesus Christ," the faithful of those ancient times wished to protect themselves against the snares and assaults of the infernal adversary; and to this end they persevered in fasting, prayer, reading the recitation of the Psalms, and the celebration of Mass until 3:00 p.m. On some days of the year these Stations were penitential, such as during Advent,

Lent, and Ember days and on vigils, or at special times when there were chastisements going on, such as war, pestilence, or famine. There were also joyful Stations, such as those that fell on Sundays or on great feast days.

There were seven principal churches of Rome where the Stations were most frequent: St. John in the Lateran, St. Peter in the Vatican, St. Mary Major, St. Paul Outside the Walls, St. Lawrence Outside the Walls, the Holy Cross in Jerusalem, and St. Sebastian Outside the Walls.

The arrangement of the Stations was completed by St. Gregory the Great, and for the first time they were written into the Sacramentary, and later into the Missal. The present-day arrangement comes from St. Gregory, though a few churches received their Station days from later popes.

When the popes left Rome for Avignon (A.D. 1305-1309), they no longer took part in the Stations. But the Stations were still kept, and the relics of the saints on that particular day were venerated. Of all the penitential processions, the greatest was on St. Mark's day (April 25) and is simply called the Major Litanies. The Minor Litanies refers to the processions made through the fields and farms three days before the Ascension.

Going back to the Introit, we see that almost always a psalm is used, though in an abbreviated form, with a Gloria Patri and an Alleluia. In those Masses that do not have the Forty-Second Psalm at the foot of the altar, such as the Masses of Passiontide or a Requiem, the air of joy in the Gloria Patri and the Alleluia is removed, in order to indicate the sorrow, grief, and affliction of the assembly at the death of one of its members, or the death of its Savior.

On the rare occasion when there is no Introit, such as the Mass of Holy Saturday, the Blessing of the New Fire and the other prayers and procession take the place of it, since its great purpose is to prepare the way for the Sacrifice by presenting to the faithful the holy thoughts and good resolutions that are connected to the feast day. An example of this preparation or setting of a theme may be found in the Introit of the feast of St. Jerome Emiliani, who took wonderful care of the many orphans who were living on the streets of Venice and surviving off garbage. So the Introit of his feast is taken from the Lamentations: "My liver is poured out upon the earth, for destruction of the daughter of my people, when the child and the suckling fainted away in the streets of the city" (Lam. 2:11).

In every Introit, you will find an astounding connection between the life of the saint or the content of the feast and the liturgy of that day. The Introits are magnificent works of the art of prayer, to be treasured and prayed with attention and devotion.

Notice that the simple antiphon from the Psalms uses words given by the Holy Ghost Himself; no hymns are sung at this time. Hymns are wonderful compositions, but in the early Church, Gnostics, Arians, and Manicheans used hymns for a subtle indoctrination to heresy—something they could not accomplish through the Psalms. We might say the same for Protestantism. To this day there are hymns that carry an agenda, but the Psalms are immune to such manipulation.

The ancient rule as to what to sing was based on the missal; only that which was written and laid down in the missal could be sung. The development of organ Masses and orchestral Masses may be seen as a departure from the missal, and therefore they ought to be seen as lesser than Masses that use Gregorian chant to sing precisely what is in the missal. This is why we see even in the Second Vatican Council a description of Gregorian chant as having pride of place, then polyphony, with hymns in the last place.

In a Solemn High Pontifical Mass, an assistant priest used to use a small rod capped with a hand with its index finger extended to point to the Introit in the missal for the bishop. This same device was used by rabbis for reading the Torah; they could not touch the sacred text. The rod is no longer used, but the index finger of the master of ceremonies at a High Mass or the index finger of the assistant priest is. This is not because the bishop or the celebrant cannot find his way around the missal. In fact, the priest may have to gently correct the MC while the Mass is being celebrated, since often he is just learning the task. The reason for the pointing is because the celebrant—even if he is a bishop—must submit to the traditional order of prayer. The finger comes down to the page of the missal, symbolizing that the order of worship comes from above; it is not up to the celebrant to change it as he wishes.

The *bugia* (the small candlestick whose handle is held by an acolyte for a bishop) expresses something similar. There is usually plenty of light around to read the missal, and one candle does not compensate for its lack, so it is not just extra light. Rather, the light is to symbolize that the sacred texts are not self-explanatory (contrary to Protestant doctrines). The reader's intellect must be set alight if the texts are to be understood. The bishop must read the texts from the page even if he knows them by heart. The bishop is an "illuminated" person, not due to his scholarship, but because it is added to him from outside, as a gift from above; it is not something merited.

The light near the missal also means that the prayers of the missal cannot be understood as automatic formulae, carrying out the user's intentions like magic spells. The missal is a closed book unless it is read in the correct light, a light that cannot be manipulated.

During the Introit, if the priest reads the Holy Name, he bows his head profoundly toward the cross. If he reads the name of the Blessed Virgin, he bows his head midway but toward the missal. If he reads the name of the saint of the day, or the name of the pope, he bows his head slightly toward the missal. Three bows of the head, three bows of the body, three levels of volume are used to say the Mass properly; the Holy Trinity is subtly adored throughout the Mass.

Following the Introit are a few lines called the Versicle; usually taken from the Psalms. At the end, the celebrant says the doxology

"Glory be" and repeats the Introit as far as the Versicle. The Introit signifies the desires of our spiritual ancestors for the coming of the Lord, and as Christ came to glorify the Godhead by the mystery of the Incarnation, so the Introit is repeated to show that as the patriarchs and prophets desired His advent in the Incarnation, so we desire His advent in the Mass. The Introit antiphon is then said twice to signify the two advents of the Lord: His coming as a baby and His coming as a lion.

At the very beginning of the Introit, the celebrant crosses himself, for he is going to renew in the Mass (in a mystical manner) the Sacrifice of the Cross.

This part of the Mass contains three things: the Introit, the Versicle, and the Glory Be, for there are three kinds of offices that prefigured and personified Christ:

1. *Patriarchs.* The Introit relates to the patriarchs; they are first because it is they who first received revelation concerning the holy mysteries.

2. *Prophets.* The Versicle relates to the prophets, who saw in a clearer manner the times when Our Lord would fulfill the things revealed to the patriarchs.

3. *Apostles.* The Glory Be relates to them, for the mystery of the Trinity was revealed to them.

Another way to look at the Glory Be in the middle of the Introit is to see the whole Introit as an expression of the ardent longing that made "the clouds rain the just" (Is. 45:8). This psalmody is always preceded by the cross, since, from the first instant of His Incarnation, Christ saw the rods, the thorns, the blows, the nails (cf. *Mediator Dei* of Ven. Pius XII, which explains that Christ's human intellect was flooded with the Beatific Vision at the moment of his conception).

In Catholic art this is often painted as the Christ Child pressing to His heart a little crown of thorns. But the ones to whom this was first revealed were the angels, who in their astonishment gave praise to God for His wisdom. For this reason a Glory Be divides the Introit.

At the end of the doxology is the word *amen*. It is a Hebrew word meaning "firm" or "solid" and is the last word of the Bible (it closes the book of the Apocalypse). It was never translated into Latin, but the Hebrew is retained in the Mass because the Mass is the real presentation of the Sacrifice of Calvary, and its original proclamation—"Jesus of Nazareth, King of the Jews," abbreviated INRI—was in Latin, Greek, and Hebrew. Similarly the Kyrie was not translated into Latin but was left in the Greek.

Amen means several things; one is an affirmation—"It is true; I affirm it." St. Augustine said it is like signing a document. It also expresses a wish for a realization that depends on God alone: "So be it." It also expresses our consent to the object of the prayer. In the heavenly liturgy, the amen resounds without end. It is an eternal amen.

THE KYRIE

When the Introit is finished, the priest turns to his left to go to the center of the altar, to recite the Kyrie. This represents Christ being brought to Caiaphas and also St. Peter's triple denial of Our Lord.

The number of Kyries varied in the history of the liturgy, but by the eighth century they were fixed at nine, symbolic of the Trinity and the nine choirs of angels. The first three invocations are to the Father, the second three to the Son, and the third three to the Holy Ghost. Notice that the second set of invocations could have used the title "Lord" (*Kyrios*), but "Christ" is used to signify that He has a human nature, so we call on Him for mercy by the name by which He is known as a man.

The three Divine Persons are separately and consecutively invoked; the invocation of each is repeated exactly three times, to signify that with each Person the two others are at least virtually invoked, since by the fact of their mystical indwelling in one another, all three of the Divine Persons are and live eternally in one another.

This indwelling, by the way, is what we call Circuminsession in theology. Fr. John Hardon had a good definition of this: "Circuminsession is the mutual immanence of the three distinct persons of the Holy Trinity. The Father is entirely in the Son, likewise in the Holy Spirit; and so is the Son in the Father and the Holy Spirit; and the Holy Spirit in the Father and the Son. Circuminsession also identifies the mutual immanence of the two distinct natures in the one Person of Jesus Christ."

Nine times is mercy cried for, not just in unity with the nine choirs of angels, but also because there are nine kinds of sins committed by us: original, venial, and mortal; sins of thought, word, and deed; and sins of malice, weakness, and ignorance.

St. Albert the Great said of this:

> Now, "Lord" is a name of power, and power does three things. It avenges iniquity by just judgment. It restrains the evil will by its severity. It defends virtue and goodness by equitable laws. Therefore the faithful, who feel themselves to be guilty of iniquity, cry out a first time, *Kyrie, eleison,* calling upon the mercy of Our Lord, that they may not know the avenging sword. A second time the faithful cry out, *Kyrie, eleison,* for they know their wills to be rebellious, and they desire him to check their rebellion, yet in mercy, not in wrath and fury. Still a third time they cry out. For they feel that those things within them that agree to the law of God are not yet free, and so they say, *Kyrie, eleison,* that they may be made free.

The Kyrie is said alternately between priest and server in the Low Mass, but it is important for the faithful to be united *in heart* with the priest as opposed to saying the words only, since this cry of distress and appeal for help expresses our need to be saved. Salvation comes from Christ's sacrifice. The Kyrie expresses our desire to benefit the utmost from the Blood of Christ shed for us.

God pursued humanity, which from the time of Adam has tried to escape from the yoke of love and obedience. God embraces this guilty, fleeing humanity in infinite charity; the Word became flesh. So the prayer of mankind since its fall has become a profound sigh. "For we know that every creature groaneth, and travaileth in pain even till now" (Rom 8:22).

The Kyrie is the supplication of the blind man from Jericho ("Son of David, have pity on me" [Mk. 10:47]) and of the Canaanite woman ("Lord, Son of David, have mercy on me!" [Mt. 15:22]). It is said or sung at every Mass. It is part of what is called the Common of the Mass—that which is commonly said at every Mass. The Proper of the Mass comprises those parts that change for each Mass, such as the Epistle. The Common might engender complaint from those who easily tire of repetition in the liturgy. I guess they've never been in love. People in love never tire of repeating that they love each other, nor do they tire of hearing it.

The Kyrie is also a fitting preface for the Gloria. Cardinal Wiseman once wrote, "The Kyrie—that cry for mercy which is to be found in every liturgy of East and West—seems introduced as if to give grander effect to the outburst of joy and praise which succeeds it in the Gloria; it is a deepening of our humiliation, that our triumph may the better be felt."

And Fr. Nicholas Gihr had a wonderful thing to say on the fittingness of the Kyrie for our souls:

> As long as we children of Eve are constrained to remain in this vale of tears weeping and mourning, in exile and misery, no prayer is so necessary, none so befitting our condition as the

Kyrie, this heartfelt appeal, this humble cry for mercy to the triune God, Who is compassionate and merciful, long suffering and plenteous in mercy (Ps. 102:8). "Man born of woman, living for a short time, is filled with many miseries" (Job 14:1), "all his days are full of sorrows and miseries" (Eccles. 2:23): who can enumerate them—the sins, the temptations, the dangers, the defects, the weaknesses, the sufferings, the wants, the diseases, the cares, the adversities, the hardships and the tribulations that here below surround man and oppress his heart? Freedom and redemption, protection and assistance, consolation and refreshment the poor man finds only with God, Who is good and whose mercy endureth forever (Ps. 117:1). "As a father has compassion on them that fear Him; for He knoweth our frame and He remembereth that we are dust" (Ps. 102:13-14). "The mercy of God will follow us all the days of our life" (Ps.22: 6): and like unto an ever visible star, a never-setting star in the heavens, it sheds its gentle and consoling rays upon us, in the morning as well as in the evening of life. But in order that the plenitude of Divine Mercy may descend upon us, the cry of the Kyrie must proceed from a heart penetrated with a lively sense of its poverty and misery.

As to the length of the Proper of the Mass, it is based on the Solemn High Mass, such that the time the celebrant needs to move from the sedile to the altar, or for him to complete the incensation of the altar, matches the length of time it takes to sing the appropriate part of the Mass in Gregorian Chant.

The Gloria

Once the Kyrie is finished, we are ready for the Gloria, if the Mass calls for one (normally at least a third-class feast does). The Gloria is a doxology (*doxa* in Greek means "glory" or "honor," so a doxology is a word or prayer to glorify). In the early Church, there was a fair number of spontaneous prayers. Many doxologies and invocations (such as can be found in the epistles of St. Paul) were gradually composed by combining these acclamations into one. Soon the Church learned how improper spontaneous prayer can be in the liturgy, and wisely chose the best prayers for her highest act of worship of our God. The Gloria is sometimes called the greater doxology, in comparison with the lesser doxology, the Gloria Patri.

The word *gloria* is of uncertain origin but is used in Latin to translate a Hebrew word meaning "brightness" or "splendor." The first part of this great hymn was sung by angels to shepherds to tell them of the birth of the Messias. No one really knows who completed the hymn, except that it was originally sung in Greek; tradition has it that the version we use was arranged by St. Hilary of Poitiers.

The celebrant says the hymn even if the choir sings it, for he is taking the place of the angel of the great counsel: "For behold I bring you tidings of great joy" (Lk. 2:10). He recites the Gloria as a preparation for the coming of the Lord in the Mass. He stands in the middle of the altar to recite this hymn, for as the Epistle side signifies the Old Testament, and the Gospel side the New Testament, the Nativity occurs between the Testaments, and Christ is the Mediator between God and man. Also, as Durandus pointed out, the priest stands at the middle of the altar for the Gloria to show that the Messiah was born "when all things were in the midst of silence."

While the priest recites the Gloria, he stands erect at the middle of the altar with his hands joined. At the first line of it, he unfolds his hands, raises them slightly in a kind of circular motion, and folds them again. This is an ancient gesture meant to signify an invocation of the angels that they might assist in our prayer.

The Church never wearies of praising and magnifying God, in union with the celestial liturgy, which St. John heard in his vision;

"Let us be glad and rejoice and give glory to Him, the Lord our God, the Almighty" (cf. Apoc. 19:6-7). In the Gloria, the canticle of praise first heard on the plains of Bethlehem, all creation should unite. The stars twinkle, the flowers bloom, the ocean is agitated, the birds sing; but more precious is the praise that man consciously and freely offers to God. This praise of joy expresses heavenly joy. As Fr. Matthias Scheeben once put it, "The greatest happiness of the blessed does not spring from the joy over their possession of the highest Good, but consists in the joy experienced over the happiness and glory which God possesses, and one's own perfection also rejoices the spirit still more, because it is pleasing to God and tends to His honor, rather than because that perfection is pleasing to self and redounds to one's own honor." Our faces light up when we see a beautiful rainbow (or at least they should) or a work of art or when we hear a moving story about some virtuous person. But nothing pleases and delights the loving soul quite like the consideration of the infinite majesty, beauty, goodness, holiness, wisdom, power, and mercy of God.

St. Philip Neri celebrated a Low Mass at a very early hour on the day of his death, which was the feast of Corpus Christi. At the Gloria, he was suddenly rapt in ecstasy and began to sing the Gloria in a clear loud voice from beginning to end, full of devotion and jubilation, as though he had already departed this world and had begun to rejoice among the choirs of angels in the next world.

Blessed Hyacinth Cormier said that "we should not seek in the Gloria a logical progression of ideas. It is, rather, an impulsive succession of acclamations and words of praise, that spring forth unplanned from the soul. Faith, the freedom of prayer, and a love that knows how to weave all things together: these are the only rules."

When the Gloria is finished, the priest kisses the altar, turns to the faithful, and says the *Dominus Vobiscum*. This was the salute of the angel to Gideon the Judge (Jdg. 6:12), and of Asa and of Booz to the reapers; for Booz espousing Ruth was a figure of Christ espousing the Church (Ruth 2:6). Literally this means "The Lord is with you." It is in the present tense, because individually every man who has been baptized carries the living presence of the Lord in his soul ("and with thy spirit"), and it is true collectively because "where two or three are gathered in my name there am I in the midst of them" (Mt. 18:20).

The bishop does not say this greeting when he celebrates Mass, but says, "Pax vobiscum," since he signifies more perfectly Christ Our Lord, Who after His Resurrection said to the disciples, "Peace be to you" (Lk. 24:36).

When the celebrant turns around, he always turns to his right and returns the same way, like the angel who sat at the right-hand side of the sepulcher of the risen Lord, since Christ was then in the other world beyond this world of suffering. So the right signifies the world of glory, and the faithful are reminded by this gesture to seek the things above.

But when the priest turns all the way around (he does this once, when he says "Pray, brethren, that my sacrifice and yours . . .") before the Preface, we see him in accord with the Psalmist: "I have gone round, and I have offered up in his tabernacle a sacrifice of jubilation" (Ps. 26:6).

The priest turns slightly to the cross and bows when he says, "Oremus" ("Let us pray"). This is to recognize that Christ is the Mediator between God and man. He was the angel St. John saw standing before the throne of God, offering the prayers of the saints to the Father (Apoc. 8:3-4).

THE COLLECT

After the Gloria, the priest kisses the altar, which is a symbol of Christ as the Head of the Church and the elect as His members. Since the priest stands at the altar as a mediator between heaven and earth, he first salutes with the altar-kiss the Church Triumphant, to express our love and reverence for the souls in heaven, and then by the *Dominus Vobiscum* he addresses the Church Militant in words that call down upon the gathered faithful salvation and blessing. He next returns to the Epistle side, bows his head to the cross, and says, "Oremus," praying for the Church Suffering, and begins the Collect. The call to pray together (*oremus*) shows how important it is to pray with the priest by following along with the missal. The best and the most profitable participation in the Holy Sacrifice consists in the faithful present at the Mass following the priest step by step, jointly praying and offering with him.

St. Albert gives a good reason as to why it is called the Collect. "The prayer is called the 'Collect', either because the priest, who knows the secrets of the people, collects these secretes and offers them to our Lord, or because it is made for the people, who are collected in the communion of our Lord. For the work of God is always to collect, as the work of the devils is to disperse."

The Collect is said at the corner of the altar like the prayers of the Old Law: "For Aaron shall pray upon the horns thereof" (Ex. 30:10). The Collect is the same as the one prayed with each hour of the Divine Office each day. Together with the Secret and the Postcommunion, they are the key elements of the Proper—that part of the liturgy that changes each day. They are always of an uneven number. Recall that the number one tells us of one God, one Church, one Baptism; three teaches us the Holy Trinity and the three prayers offered by Christ in the garden; five teaches us the five holy wounds; seven teaches us the seven gifts of the Holy Ghost and the seven sacraments. As neither God nor His Church can be equally divided (this part is God, that part is human), so an uneven number cannot be equally divided, and thus better represents the unity of the Bride and her divine Spouse.

The prayers are directed to the Father, and sometimes to the Son, but not to the Holy Ghost, for He is in the world as the Paraclete (a Greek word for advocate) and serves as our Comforter. When prayer is directed to the Father, the prayer ends with "Through Christ our Lord. Amen." We say this because "no man cometh to the Father but through me" (Jn. 14:6) When the prayer is directed to God the Son, the ending is: "Who liveth and reigneth God forever and ever. Amen."

Standing at the altar, the celebrant lifts up his hands in prayer, according to the words of the Apostle, "Lift up the hands which hang down" (Heb. 12:12). The custom is ancient; it comes from the original tabernacle and the Temple, for when Israel fought against Amalec, Moses went up into the mountain: "And when Moses lifted up his hands Israel overcame: but if he let them down a little Amalec overcame.... And Aaron and Hur stayed up his hands on both sides" (Ex. 17:11-12). Again, when Solomon built the Temple, during the dedication he "stood before the altar of the Lord in the sight of the assembly of Israel, and spread forth his hands toward heaven, and said: the Lord God of Israel, there is no God like thee, in heaven above or on the earth" (3 Kgs. 8:22-23).

The priest's lifting up his hands has a profound human significance, as when a child reaches for his mother, or a friend sees an old friend, or a soldier puts his hands up as he surrenders: "All my life I will bless you, in your name I lift up my hands" (Ps. 62:5). David expresses praise in the line "I stretch out my hands; like thirsty ground I yearn for you" (Ps. 142:6). These gestures prefigure Christ's hands spread out on the Cross, when He offered the sacrifice of Himself. These hand gestures of the priest are always done modestly, just like the glances to the cross or the folding of his hands.

All Collects are constructed according to a certain plan: God is first addressed by His name (O God), then a clause of praise (who art, who hast, et cetera), a request (grant us), and the conclusion, which is always through Christ Our Lord. These prayers are a preparation for sacrifice, not explanations for the benefit of the congregation, nor are they a kind of "warming up" for the latter.

Orations (the Collect is an oration) are at the level of classic generality, for they are the Church's public prayer for all people, yet their substance is such that the individual silent reader can be deeply struck by them. St. Thomas points out that the orations have four parts, and this can be seen by looking at the Collect for Easter Friday:

1. *Oratio* (oration), which is the elevation of the soul to God: "Almighty and eternal God . . ."

2. *Gratiarum actio* (the act of giving thanks), which is a thanksgiving for a good that has been received: ". . . who in the Paschal mystery instituted the covenant, whereby you forgave mankind . . ."

3. *Postulatio* (petition): ". . . grant that what we outwardly celebrate we may follow in our deeds."

4. *Obsecratio* (entreaty): "Through our Lord Jesus Christ . . ."

The priest does not say, "I beseech Thee" in the Collect, but is always speaking on behalf of the faithful and says, "We beseech Thee." This way of speaking was very familiar in ancient times and in our times is somewhat like an attorney speaking to a judge on behalf of his client. But it is more like the bearer (courier) of a letter (in ancient times that was the only way you could send a letter). Thus, the language is as though the writer of the letter is saying, "Through this bearer I greet you."

Again, the Collects are almost always addressed to the Father. He is the first Person of the Blessed Trinity, and as such He is (in a manner) the original source not only of the divine nature that from all eternity He imparts to the Son and with the Son to the Holy Ghost, but of all created things.

Prayer is beneficial only when it rests on the bedrock of truth. This does not mean just being free from error—it means that prayer ought to spring from truth or dogma, *dogma* being another word for truth. Dogmatic thought releases prayer from any slavery to individual caprice and from the uncertainty and sluggishness that follow in the wake of emotion.

Various individual truths of revelation hold a special attraction for certain temperaments and conditions to which they respond. Thus it is that some of the faithful have a special affinity for particular mysteries of faith—this person attracted to the Visitation, that person to the Passion. There are even religious orders that are centered on one aspect of the Faith and are known by that aspect—the Visitation nuns, say, or the Passionists. This is another indication of how grace builds on nature. So, if prayer stresses one mystery of faith in an exclusive manner, it will satisfy only those of that temperament. Therefore any prayer meant for the corporate body must have the fullness of religious truth.

This is the genius of the *Lex Orandi* (the "Law of Prayer") in the Roman Rite, seen easily in the Collects. This law condenses into prayer the whole of religious truth. Prayer in common will be most fruitful, therefore, if it does not concentrate on some particular portion of dogma, but as far as possible the whole of divine teaching. But while thought is emphasized, there is no frigid domination of reason. The Collects are permeated by warmth of feeling. Liturgical emotion as a rule is subdued and controlled, to be sure, but it smolders like the fiery heart of a volcano whose summit stands out clear against the sky.

If emotion were not restrained in liturgical prayer, people would either take it seriously and would feel obliged to force themselves into an emotion that is not really theirs, or they would lapse into indifference; insulating themselves from the value of the prayer, and consequently the Word would be depreciated. So if prayer is to be fruitful for a corporate body, it must be intense, but at the same time tranquil in tone. This notion is summed up in one of the antiphons for Lauds: "Let us joyfully taste of the sober drunkenness of the Spirit." There is no danger to spiritual modesty, so that we can pour out our hearts and still feel that nothing has been dragged into the light that should remain hidden.

The prayer of the Collects is also very cautious, in that they do not rashly utter things like vows, and they are not full of permanent repudiations of sin, or an all-embracing consecration of one's entire being, utter contempt for the world, promises of exclusive love and so on. These are present as ideas, but as a humble plea that the suppliant may have similar sentiments or to encourage the suppliant to ponder their goodness and nobility. If there were strong vows given on a regular basis, then the people who made them would quickly discover that they are very difficult and perhaps impossible to keep. Then people would develop artificial sentiments—forcing intentions that remain beyond their ability. Or they would take the words as merely passing recommendations about a line of conduct that would be nice to have but not real. In this sense Christ taught us about our prayer when He said, "Let your yea be yea, and your nay be nay" (Mt. 5:37). Thus, the liturgy solves the problem of providing a constant incentive to the highest moral aims, while at the same time remaining true and lofty, and satisfying everyday needs.

Gratia supponit naturam—liturgical prayer takes nature for granted (sometimes that excellent phrase of St. Thomas is translated as "grace builds on nature," but literally we could say grace *supposes* nature). Because of this, the liturgy needs a good culture. Grace needs real beauty to take root. It hardly grows at all in a soil of ugliness. But if, for example, the language in culture becomes degraded, base, or perverted, there is a danger of the cultural element of prayer becoming coarse, with a clumsy and monotonous imagery, and its ideas become empty and tedious, the emotion paltry and artificial and insipid. I remember a priest once complaining about "the insipid picnic music of modern liturgy" (he was an accomplished pianist) being an extremely poor soil for the seed of the Faith.

The Catholic liturgy is not concerned with the individual's reverence and worship for God. It is not concerned with the awakening, formation, and sanctification of the individual soul as such. It does not even concern itself with collective groups such as this monastery or that parish. In the liturgy God is to be honored by the body of the faithful—the whole Church—and the faithful derive sanctification from this act of worship. Here we see how sharply it differs from Protestant worship, which is predominantly individualistic. The individual Catholic, by his absorption into the higher unity, finds both liberty and discipline. *Gratia supponit naturam*—it originates in the twofold nature of man, who is both social and solitary.

But side by side with the strictly ritual is popular devotion, which has a more strongly personal element. These devotions vary from country to country and are more suited to an individual congregation. A parade in honor of St. Anthony of Padua with firecrackers thrown in front of the Blessed Sacrament in Padua is quite fitting (firecrackers were the poor man's twenty-one-gun salute). But it may not be fitting in Littleton, Colorado.

The Epistle

After the Collect comes the Epistle. It is introduced briefly, where the priest simply says, "A reading from the Book of . . . " He lays his hands on the missal as he reads in the Low Mass, but if the Epistle is sung, the subdeacon holds the missal away from the altar.

The Mass follows the old synagogue service in its structure. After some prayers, the rabbi would read from the Law and the Prophets, and then psalms were sung, and an explanation or sermon would follow. We know Our Lord gave the commentary on the readings on more than one occasion. But why use the Scriptures, and not the readings from the Fathers of the Church (which was done in many churches long ago)? Fr. Gihr has a good answer:

> The Church with predilection and preference employs in her liturgy Scriptural words, because they are especially holy and venerable, efficacious and full of grace: they are indeed, the words of God— words that have the Holy Ghost for their author. The words are supernatural, heavenly and divine. In the readings now following we have the word of God, by which He speaks to us and instructs us in all doctrine and truth—"The Spirit searcheth all things; yea, the deep things of God" (I Cor. 2:10); hence the writings inspired by Him are of wonderful depth and inexhaustibleness, full of spirit and power, full of light and life. They teach the science of the Saints and show unto us the kingdom of God. In the midst of a world fallen away from Christianity and hostile to the Church, amid all the sufferings and persecutions that oppress us, amid the storms that rage around us, the imperishable word of God, which does not pass away, though even heaven and earth should pass away, encourages and raises us up and imparts life eternal to all who receive it with faith and docility.

The Epistle is generally taken from the New Testament and in times of penance the Old Testament, such as on Ember days. It is always sung by the subdeacon at the Solemn High Mass, for the subdeacon represents not only St. John the Baptist, but his carrying with him the Old Testament, which prepared the world for the coming of Christ. He faces the altar on the Epistle side, since the altar signifies Christ and since the entire Old Testament looked with great longing for the Messias.

The Epistle, whether from the Old or the New Testament, is read facing the east. Like the eyes of St. John the Baptist, who looked for the Redeemer, so the priest fixes his eyes on the Messias, who is the "True Orient, or the orient from on high."

In the Solemn High Mass the subdeacon chants the Epistle and not the celebrant. But before he does so, he does not receive a blessing from the priest, as the deacon does. There is a good reason for this, as explained by St. Albert the Great. "The subdeacon declares the doctrine of the imperfect. And since this doctrine was represented by the preaching of John the Baptist, at a time when Christ was still hidden, the subdeacon does not seek a blessing from the bishop or the priest." Note that is was common to think of the blessing in medieval times as a kind of perfection.

The subdeacon is accompanied by the master of ceremonies, but no other acolytes. Again, St. Albert the Great gives the reason: "He goes with but one acolyte, for they were few who followed the preaching of John and of the law and the prophets."

He chants the Epistle facing the altar, for as Durandus notes, "The face of the one who reads the epistle must be turned to the altar, because the preaching of John directed himself and others towards Christ, whom the altar represents." St. John the Baptist is the voice of one crying in the wilderness; so the subdeacon sings alone and is escorted to his place without acolytes, since the Baptist was alone, and without escort to face Herod. There are no candles around the subdeacon because, as we hear in the Last Gospel about the Baptist, "he was not the light" (Jn. 1:8).

When the Epistle begins, notice how sober the presentation of it is. There is no greeting of the people, no prayer for purification, and no solemn escort to the place where it is read. The subdeacon simply sings, "*Lectio* . . . [A reading from . . .]" This is because the subdeacon represents the Baptist, who led the most pure of lives and spoke most plainly and alone when he preached.

The faithful remain seated for the Epistle like "them that sit in darkness and the shadow of death" (Isa. 9:2), awaiting Christ, Who is the Light. Being seated also represents the attitude of St. Mary Cleopas, who sits at the feet of Christ as one receiving teaching with docility.

In the early Church the Epistles were sung at the limits of the sanctuary (which represents heaven) and of the nave (which represents earth), on an elevated area or platform called the ambo, to symbolize that the Word of God descends from heaven to earth, like a pre-incarnation. To this day the subdeacon goes back a little from the altar, not quite near the altar and not quite near the nave. This too represents well the Baptist, who is between the Testaments.

There are a limited number of readings or Epistles used in the Gregorian Rite, and this is for good reasons. Dr. Peter Kwasniewski pointed out in an article for the website New Liturgical Movement that "the goal of liturgy is not to make us familiar with Scripture in the manner of a Bible study—which, of course, ought to be taking place outside of Mass—but to give us the right formation of mind with regard to the realities of our faith. The fundamental elements of faith need to be inculcated week after week, day after day; and thus it is pedagogically most appropriate to have certain readings repeated annually, e.g., the Epistle and Gospel for the various Sundays after Pentecost, the readings for Easter Week, the readings for certain categories of saints. In this way, the Christian people are formed by the proclamation of fundamental texts throughout the cycle of the year, rather than being carried off each day into new regions of text, especially some of the drier historical narratives or longer passages of the Prophets, from which it may be hard to profit except by extra-liturgical study."

As to increasing the number of readings of Scripture in the old Mass, he goes on to say:

> The entire liturgy is knit together as a seamless garment: the prayers honor and invoke the saint; the readings extol the virtues

of the saint, who is put forward as our example and teacher; the Eucharistic sacrifice manifestly links the Church Triumphant, represented by the lists of saints in the Roman Canon, to all of us pilgrims in the Church Militant. The whole liturgy acquires a unity of sanctification, showing us both the primordial Way of sanctity—Jesus in the Holy Eucharist—and the models of sanctity achieved, the saints.

There could be a more ample distribution of pertinent readings for martyrs, virgins, popes, confessors, doctors, etc. Even with such a distribution, however, the profound unity of the liturgy will be perfectly maintained whenever the fitting harmony of prayers, antiphons, readings, and Ordinary is respected throughout. Specific propers and readings could be appointed for certain saints, emphasizing the contemplative vocation of one or the missionary vocation of another; but again, all with a view towards the integrity of the liturgy as a coming together of the communion of saints to celebrate victory already accomplished and victory yet to be achieved.

There is nothing wrong with a wider selection from Scripture per se, provided it carefully observes the liturgical laws summarized above. The problem is rather with a free-floating (i.e., largely sanctoral-independent) rationalistic sequence of Scripture readings that accomplishes little in the way of deep instruction and illumination of the mystery of the Saints, God's "chosen ones," to whom we are to conform ourselves as we strive to be conformed by grace to the ultimate Holy One of God, Jesus Christ.

At the end of the Epistle, the subdeacon goes to the middle of the sanctuary to genuflect, as he did at the beginning before singing the Epistle. This shows that Christ is the source of the Old Testament, for "in the beginning was the Word" (Jn. 1:1). Then the subdeacon goes to the corner of the altar to receive a blessing, showing that Christ blesses all the goodness of the Old Testament, even though He was rejected by Israel. We do not see this blessing in the Low Mass, but remember that the paradigm of the Mass is the Solemn High Mass, and not the Low Mass. In return for this blessing, the subdeacon kisses the back of the right hand of the celebrant, signifying those Jews who did believe and who did love the Savior, starting with the Baptist. This blessing has another meaning. "When he returns to the priest, he kisses his right hand, to show that he does not attribute his advance in virtue to himself, but to God. *The right hand of the Lord hath exalted me: the right hand of the Lord hath wrought strength*" (St. Albert).

At the end of the Epistle, the phrase *Deo Gratias* ("Thanks be to God") is announced. The first reason for this is simply to thank God for the instruction we have received through the mouth of His messenger. We thank Him because we have just received a letter from heaven, as from a good Friend. These letters water our hearts, where the Divine seed was planted.

But there is another sense in which this phrase is used, which goes back to the time of persecution in the Roman Empire. The *Ostiarius* (the minor order of porter) or doorkeeper had the tough job of trying to recognize Christians who were trying to get into Mass. The watchword often given was *Deo Gratias*. So no matter how difficult the story that is depicted in the reading, no matter how strong the persecution, it is still the watchword; that is, the Epistle might be about St. Paul being shipwrecked or beaten, or St. Peter arrested and thrown into prison, but we still say, "Thanks be to God," since there is nothing outside the providence of God. True, at the time when these terrible events occurred, it would not have been easy to say this. But now we can even rejoice in the imprisonment of St. Paul, as he rejoiced, since in many ways his imprisonment meant our freedom.

The readings are repeated in a one-year cycle. The first Gospel was written in about A.D. 50. This indicates that the message of the Gospel had been preached and known to the faithful for about twenty years before the first Gospel was even introduced. This is part of oral tradition. In societies in which literacy was limited and the circulation of written texts uncommon, memory and tradition were all important. A specific pattern of words was used (thus the importance of reading just one translation), so that the faithful could learn the story. We still find this custom among preliterate children; once they hear a fairy tale they want to hear it again in exactly the same words. They will object to the slightest change of the story. We should too, being the children of the Most High. We should insist on fidelity to the text, and that the subdeacon or the celebrant would read or sing it just as it is.

I suppose someone could object to this line of thought, and say that our society is not oral and that we are not preliterate children. True enough. However, we need to hear these texts over and over, since repetition is the mother of all learning. And as St. Augustine said, we need to hear a parable a minimum of forty times before we can start to understand it. That is independent of our literacy or lack thereof.

In the ancient synagogue service, readings were done first from the Law, and then the prophets, arranged in a cycle. Now they are taken from any part of the Old or New Testaments, except the Gospels. They are almost always from an Apostle, which is why we call it the Epistle (*epistola* in Latin means "letter"), given that their testimony comes down to us by means of letters. If the text is from the Old Testament, it was chosen by the Church as an illustration of the New Testament. The Church regards the entire Old Testament in light of the New Testament; as a foundation for the New Testament.

When the Epistle is read at the Low Mass, the presentation must not be given in a way that looks only to the understanding of the faithful. It must be stylized in the same way as the Oration or Collect. The reader must never inject his own sentiments or even convictions (no matter how right) into the sacred text, but must present it with strict objectivity, with reverence, as if he were reverently presenting the text both to God and to the faithful on a plate of gold. This is best accomplished by chanting the Epistle.

The Gradual

The celebrant then reads the Gradual (from the Latin word *gradus*, meaning "step"), for it tells of the grades or steps of virtue we must acquire in our journey through this life. Historically it comes from the Gradual Psalms; those Psalms that were sung on the steps going up into the Temple in the times of the kings of Israel. The Gradual is another legacy from the synagogue service, in which the readings were followed by the chanting of psalms. The psalms were originally sung by two cantors from a marble pulpit called an ambo, with steps leading up to it as a reminder of the Jews going up the steps of the Temple. But as we came out of persecution, our churches naturally became more beautiful and ornate, with more singers assisting (chant sounding much better that way) until the chanting was wholly taken over by the schola (choir).

The Graduals were originally composed of complete psalms, and they always have a profound connection to what was in the Epistle or what will be in the Gospel. They give expression to the celebration of the liturgical year or feast, which began at the Introit. They do this like a red cord holding together several medals; it binds together the two readings (Epistle and Gospel). In the Epistle, God descends to us, speaks to us, makes known His mysteries, and exhorts or gives admonition, but in the Gradual we respond by soaring up to God, by praising, thanking, loving, admiring, or lamenting or rejoicing, depending on the content of the reading and what the feast day is and what will be sung in the Gospel.

Take, for example, the feast of the Holy Innocents. In the Epistle, St. John relates how in a vision he beheld and heard singing before the throne of God all the chaste souls that were purchased from among men, as the firstfruits unto God and the Lamb, and they sang a new canticle that no one else can sing. And the Gospel for the feast narrates in touching simplicity how these tender and unspotted little victims were cruelly murdered for the Infant Jesus. Between these readings is the Gradual, which is always in a Versicle and Responsory:

℣. "Our soul hath been delivered as a sparrow out of the snare of the fowlers."

℞. "The snare is broken, and we are delivered: our help is in the name of the Lord, who made heaven and earth."

This Gradual is a perfect response of the Church to the glory of the feast day, to the justice that is deservedly given to the Innocents (it is not only mercy here we speak of; it is very just to give them heaven), and to God in praise for how He delivered them.

Take another example: the feast of the Holy Angels. The Epistle describes the protecting care of the holy angels, as well as the veneration that we owe to them. And in the Gospel for the feast, Our Lord shows what a frightful sin it is to scandalize little children. Between the readings is the Gradual:

℣. He hath given His angels charge over thee, to keep thee in all thy ways.

℞. In their hands they shall bear thee up, lest thou dash thy foot against a stone.

The very word *scandal* is from the Latin and means a stone in the path upon which we can stumble.

Since the Graduals are the response to the preaching of St. John the Baptist (who is represented by the subdeacon), it is fitting that they are the most difficult parts of the Mass to sing in Gregorian chant and so are sung not by the congregation but by the schola. This technical difficulty is understandable in itself, but in a fuller sense it is a symbol of the idea that in order to hear the Baptist's preaching of repentance, and in order to hear the Gospel properly and observe the New Law ("Love one another as I have loved"), great effort will be required. "One cannot love the good God even a little, except by the sweat of his brow," said St. Vincent de Paul. It takes real effort even to see the connections between the reading and the Gospel, and sometimes great effort to praise God as opposed to whining about His decrees.

THE ALLELUIA

The Gradual is followed by the Alleluia, since "they who sow in tears shall reap in joy" (Ps. 125:5). When sung in Gregorian Chant, the Alleluia seems to float, to go on and on even on a single note. "We prolong indefinitely the heavenly song, that the ecstatic soul may fly toward those blessed regions where life shall have no end, the light no cloud, and happiness be unmixed with sorrow" (St. Gregory the Great).

This Hebrew word *alleluia* expresses the unutterable joys of heaven, which "eye hath not seen or ear heard, nor hath it entered into the heart of man, what things God has in store for them that love him" (1 Cor. 2:9).

This is one difficult word to translate! Literally the word is a transliteration of two Hebrew words that mean "Praise God." But there is much more to it than just that transliteration. Pope Innocent III said it meant "Ye children, praise the Lord." St. Augustine at first thought it meant "O Lord, save me" and later said it was a praise that words cannot translate. St. Jerome thought it meant "Sing the praises of the Lord." St. Gregory the Great wrote that it meant "Light, life, and salvation." The reason for these very different interpretations is that the word is made up of Hebrew abbreviations, or pieces of words, and it is so hard to translate because it stands for many things at once. So it is left in the Hebrew.

The Alleluia is an exclamation of joy that in Gregorian chant imitates the reaction that the blessed will have when they enter heaven and see God. Our mouths will be open, and I suspect we will be able to manage only one syllable of joy for the first twenty or thirty million years of our life in heaven. So it is that in some Alleluias, just the first letter can take a whole minute to sing; this represents the ineffability of God, transcending all words. But time is rather lost in chant—these chants are like the time in heaven as opposed to the time on earth.

To enter into this time properly, it is wise for the priest to remove his watch (one might say this goes for the faithful too!) and simply enter the mysteries with his mind and heart concentrating on doing his duty reverently. One way to ensure irreverence is to take pains to complete the Mass in twenty minutes—with a sermon. This is possible, I've heard, but it seems to me that the only way to do so is for the priest to slop his way through the Mass, slurring the words and making the crosses so fast that they are indistinguishable from a nervous twitch.

The Major Alleluia (when there is no Gradual or Tract) is used for the season of Eastertide, and it too has two Versicles but without any Responsory. The Gradual is retained during Easter Week but is omitted on the Saturday before Low Sunday, but after that two Alleluias are sung, followed by two verses, each with an Alleluia. This symbolizes the singing of the Alleluia without measure to note that salvation has been purchased for us, and the way to eternal joys is open.

But the reason the Gradual is still in Easter Week is because the reference to the faithful was almost exclusively to the newly baptized, who had risen to new life on Holy Saturday. During the whole week there were more instructions for them, and they wore white robes the whole time. The white robes were laid aside at the conclusion of the week, as was the Gradual. The Gradual lies midway, if you will, between the mournful Tract and the exultant Alleluia; it denotes the laborious and difficult pilgrimage of the children of God to heaven. So at times the Gradual is put aside and gives place entirely to the Tract, when our grief of soul has reached its depths, such as on Good Friday.

At other times the Gradual is replaced by the Alleluia to show how the soul forgets the earth for a while and rejoices with the blessed in heaven. So using the Gradual during Easter Week showed the neophytes that for the whole term of their earthly existence, they must grow from virtue to virtue, in the midst of labors and even combats. But the date of their arrival at the New Jerusalem was signified by the end of the Gradual ("the strife is done"), which occurred on the octave day of their baptisms.

This is similar to the season of Septuagesima. The medieval Doctors saw Septuagesima to Easter as representative of the seventy years of captivity of the Jews in Babylon, where they sat on the banks of the rivers of that kingdom and wept, longing for their home in Sion. For all these days the Alleluia is silent. The weeks of Septuagesima and Quadragesima (Lent) equal seventy days.

THE TRACT

Tract is a musical term that relates to the mode of singing and not to the contents. There was a peculiar way of singing it in which a cantor sang all the verses without any assistance from the choir and did so in a slow, protracted manner, uniformly and measured. The word is from the Latin and means "drawn out" or "stretched."

St. Albert the Great elaborates:

> On days set aside for penance, the Gradual is followed by the Tract.
> For so great is the weight of the iniquity that sin lays upon us, that

we are scarce drawn toward goodness even by force. Therefore, the spouse in the Canticle of Canticles cries in lamentation, *Draw me after thee.* And since this takes place with the help of penitential works, the Tract is sung with long drawn out notes that sound mournful and severe. And it often has several verses, since a man must be drawn to penance in many ways before sin is finally destroyed. He must desist from the act of sin, and pluck from his will the roots of sin, and blot out the remnants of a long habit of sin. By all these verses, then, we must be drawn as along a rough way.

In times of penance the Tract follows the Gradual. The Tract calls to our minds those times when for seventy years the Israelites dwelt in captivity on the rivers of Assyria, and wept for the deliverance of Israel (Ez. 1:3).

Take, for example, the Tracts on the Mondays, Wednesdays, and Fridays of Lent—days in the early Church that were set aside for the strictest penance and for those doing public penance. You will see two Versicles, but no Responsories, since there was no response of a choir.

℣. O Lord, deal not with us according to our sins: nor reward us according to our iniquities.

℣. Remember not, O Lord, our former iniquities: let Thy mercies speedily prevent us, for we are become exceedingly poor.

℣. (Genuflect) Help us O God, our Savior: and for the glory of Thy name, O Lord, deliver us; and forgive us our sins for Thy name's sake.

On certain days the mournful melody of the Tract is continued in a prolonged canticle called the Sequence. The Sequences are poems of the highest quality, composed in the Middle Ages, mostly by monks. They were very numerous, but only five have been retained in the 1962 missal: *Victimae Paschali Laudes* (Easter), *Veni*

Sancte Spiritus (Pentecost), *Lauda Sion* (Corpus Christi), *Stabat Mater* (Our Lady of Sorrows), and *Dies Irae* (the Requiem Mass). They are called Sequences because they follow (are sequential to) the Alleluia. And the *Stabat Mater* is used devotionally for the Stations of the Cross.

The first of these is attributed to Notker the Stammerer, a Benedictine monk of St. Gall in Switzerland (a wonderful place to visit, by the way). During his time the whole Church felt that his equal was not to be found; that he was a vessel of the Holy Ghost and favored by God with the gift of divine praise for the edification of the faithful.

The *Dies Irae* is considered by many to be the most magnificent hymn ever composed for the Church. It is a perfect work of art.

Fr. Gihr sums up the Gradual, Tract, and Alleluia with the Sequences: "If we compare the varied form and composition of the chant intervening between the Epistle and Gospel, we cannot but admire with what refined delicacy the Church understands how to indicate and set forth the manifold dispositions and shades of the soul's interior life, from the most profound sorrow to the height of joy—as is evident from the contents as well as from the form and melody of the pieces of chant chosen by her. And thus the soul becomes ever more worthily prepared and disposed to receive the word of God, now about to be announced in the Gospel."

The Gospel

After the Alleluia or Tract, the priest goes to the center of the altar; it is time for Christ to bring the Good News to the Gentiles. As Christ's first mission was to Capharnaum, a city in which there were many Gentiles, He needed to prepare for it, as it would cost Him dearly. So He prayed and fasted for forty days in the desert. The priest praying in silence in the middle of the altar recalls this recollection, and his bowing low symbolizes the great weight or burden of that forty-day fast.

Two prayers are said by the priest at this time to ask for purity of heart in order to announce the Gospel worthily. *Purity* means single-hearted or not complex. The priest constantly prays for purity even back in the sacristy, not only to avoid sexual impurity but to concentrate on doing his job well and not be worried about the thurible's chain being broken, or the MC standing in the wrong place, or have his mind on the upcoming sermon or crying children or an acolyte's hair catching on fire or anything except this Gospel, as if it were the only thing in the world at that time that really mattered.

The Fathers of the Church frequently said that the Gospel should be received with a similar purity as when we receive the Holy Eucharist. Wisdom does not enter into an unclean soul, nor does it dwell in a body subject to sin (Wis 1:4). The prayer for purification, then, has its foundation in the life of St. Isaias the prophet. In a vision, he beheld the glory of the Lord and confessed his sinfulness and unworthiness. Then a seraph took from the altar of incense in heaven a live coal and touched it to the lips of the prophet, and the coal burned away the prophet's defilement. Then the angel said, "Behold! this hath touched thy lips, and thy iniquities shall be taken away, and thy sin shall be cleansed." Only then did St. Isaias say, "Lo, here am I, send me!" (Is. 6). The live coal is a symbol of grace and its efficacy. Grace is like a spiritual fire that burns away earthly impurity.

Before the Gospel is sung or read, the missal is transferred from the Epistle side of the altar to the Gospel side. There is great depth to this liturgical action, for in either the Low Mass, in which the server transfers the missal, or the Solemn High Mass, in which there is much ceremony involved, the transfer represents both the sadness of the Word being taken from the Jews and the joy of its being given to the Gentiles. But there should be no gloating on our part. Rather we should feel a salutary fear since we are no better than the Jews.

When a people close their mind and heart to the Gospel, it will be given to another people. The same goes for an individual.

In the Solemn High Mass the deacon takes the Evangelarium from the master of ceremonies and, walking up to the right of the celebrant, lays the book on the altar and kneels to pray for the purification of his lips and of his soul. This placing of the book on the altar signifies the identity of the Word with Christ, Who is sacrificed, laid on the altar for our salvation. Then the celebrant blesses him, since the Savior blessed the apostles before they went to proclaim the gospel to every creature. The deacon asks the priest for the blessing, signifying that no one can preach who is not commissioned to do so by the Church.

I should note here that the word *gospel* comes from the Old English, from *god* ("good") and *spel* ("story" or "message"). It is a translation from the Greek *euangelion,* "a reward for bringing good news." And what good news it is: sin blotted out, heaven opened even to Gentiles, the devil chained, and the human race restored to its original inheritance!

The celebrant always blesses the deacon with his right hand, and the deacon kisses the celebrant's hand after the blessing. The right hand here signifies the other world of glory and of happiness, where the angel sat at the right hand side of the tomb when the Lord had risen and passed into that other world of happiness and of glory. The blessing is most necessary, since it is not possible to announce the Gospel, unless sent by Christ, Whom the celebrant represents. "How shall they preach unless they be sent?" (Rom. 10:15). The blessing also takes place at the right of the celebrant, which signifies that the deacon proclaims the Gospel with the same authority as the priest.

The deacon then takes the Evangelarium from the altar, which remind us that the Gospels come directly from Christ. When the Church authorized the printing of an Evangelarium, every effort was made to stress the importance of the text, such as the use of very stately uncials long after they had gone out of common use, with richly decorated miniatures within the letters. The covers for it are made of gold, or ivory or silver, or beautifully decorated leather. It should be a beautiful book, different from others.

This taking of the Evangelarium from the altar was prefigured by Moses' taking the tables of stone from the hands of the Lord on Mount Sinai. The Gospel is also taken from the altar to represent the New Law coming from the Jewish Temple, for "the law shall go forth from Sion, and the word of the Lord from Jerusalem" (Mic. 4.2). As Moses went up the mountain to receive the Law, so the deacon goes up to the altar to receive the New Law in the Gospels.

The deacon takes the book in his hands, with the Gospels raised high, like Moses coming down from Sinai with the stone tablets of the Old Law. In the Evangelarium are the contents of the New Law, which may be understood especially in the Beatitudes.

The procession then goes two by two, to symbolize the first missionary journey of the apostles, who were sent by Our Lord in pairs to preach the gospel. The acolytes hold two candles on either side of the book, and these signify the truths of both the Old and New Testaments, which enlighten the souls of men. Notice that in every procession of the clergy, the highest ranking member comes last. And every procession in ancient times (and in our own as well) showed great honor to a visiting dignitary or to the passing of an important person.

The place of the proclamation is ideally outside the sanctuary and in the nave. I say ideally since the Good News is being brought to the Gentiles, who are outside of the Holy Land. The subdeacon goes first since he represents St. John the Baptist, who went before the New Testament. The deacon places the book in the hands of the subdeacon, who holds it up for the deacon to sing. The subdeacon in this position also signifies the Jewish people, to whom revelation was first given and who therefore held the revelation of God for the Gentile nations. The holding of the Evangelarium for the deacon—where a man becomes a book-rest and his forehead a throne—signifies the renunciation of will, the indebtedness of man for the Gospel, and his loving submission to it.

The Gospel is sung facing north. The north stands for the cold, in the sense of the devil's attempt to freeze and dry up the godly qualities of the faithful by the coldness of infidelity. Lucifer said of himself, "I will place my seat in the north, and I will be like the Most High" (Is. 14:13-14). There is another reference to the north that explains this facing: "From the north shall an evil break forth upon all the inhabitants of the land" (Jer. 1:14). The deacon does not turn around to face the faithful, since Christ is the living Word, and He is right in front of the deacon. Besides, the singing or reading of the Gospel during the Mass is not just another instruction. It is the worship of God.

The deacon then prays for the faithful that the Lord might grace them with the gift of understanding, and they respond in prayer that He might bless the deacon with the same. The people rise to stand for the Gospel to show, as Pope Anastasias explained, that they are willing to stand up for Christ and defend Him, and even die for Him if necessary. This is also to show the old world shaking off the dust of the tomb (those who sit in the shadow of death, as we learned about being seated for the Epistle) and raised to life by the word of Jesus Christ. It also represents the other miracles of His ministry: the sick healed and raised and walking, the dead raised to life, the crowd leaving all to follow Him. We are like Lazarus in the tomb, to whom Christ says, "Arise" (cf. 2 Esdras 10:4).

The faithful stand to receive the Good News, for as St. Francis de Sales points out, "When the Gospel is to be read at Mass, stand up to show that you are ready and equipped to walk on the way that the Gospel commands. To stir your devotion, you can say as you do so, *Jesus Christ was made obedient unto death, even the death of the cross.*"

The deacon begins, "A continuation of the Holy Gospel . . ." The reason he says "a continuation" is because in the early Church a whole book of the Gospel was read straight through in daily portions. After the celebrant considered that a sufficient amount had been read that day, he would signal the lector to stop. At the words "A continuation of the Holy Gospel . . ." the deacon makes the Sign of the Cross with his thumb over the text of the Gospel, to signify where the blessing comes from, and a triple Sign over the forehead, lips, and heart:

+ *Over the forehead*, that our intellect might be blessed, and that we would understand what we hear. This is also to remind us of what St. Paul said, "God forbid that I should glory save in the cross of Jesus Christ" (Gal. 6:14).

+ *Over the lips*, that our speech would be blessed, that we would give this Good News to all we meet, and that we might confess Christ, for "with the mouth confession is made unto salvation" (Rom. 10:10).

+ *Over the heart*, since "with the heart we believe unto justice" (Rom. 10:10).

Then, taking the thurible from the MC, the deacon incenses the Gospel three times, which is called the triple perfume of St. Mary Magdalen. The Magdalen wished to honor Christ at the house of Simon the Pharisee, at the house of Simon the Leper, and at the Holy Sepulcher, with expensive perfumed oil. Christ said of her, "Wheresoever this gospel shall be preached in the whole world, that also which she hath done shall be told in memory of her" (Mt. 26:13). So the deacon incenses the Evangelarium three times to remember the honor done to Him by the Magdalen.

The entirety of the Gospels is not found in the Missal, only extracts. It is always an invitation to the faithful to go deeper into the Gospel (and into the Epistles), so that they might know the context of the reading better and learn more of the mystery.

But it takes forty readings before one begins to understand a single parable, according to St. Augustine. So the Church selects a number of these readings, and starting at the age of listening (say, around the age of reason), one will have heard them forty times by about age forty-seven, and then it's time to start over. Repetition is the mother of all learning, as the ancient saw goes, but we shall probably not hear the parable in the Mass more than a few times in our lives, if we hear it only at Mass.

When the Gospel is finished in the Low Mass, the acolyte answers for the people, "*Laus tibi, Christe!*" ("Praise to Thee, O Christ!"), and at the same time, the priest kisses the initial words of the Gospel, over which the Sign of the Cross had been made, and says, "By the virtue of the words of the Gospel may our sins be blotted out." This little prayer indicates that the Gospel may be understood as a sacramental, effecting the remission of venial sins.

In the Solemn High Mass the Evangelarium is brought up by the deacon for the priest to venerate.

> When the Gospel has been read, the deacon gives the Gospel-book to the subdeacon to carry, to show that the latter has now been instructed. They return in procession to the giver of sanctity, to show that all good things must be referred to God.
>
> *Canst thou send lightning bolts, and will they go, and will they return and say to thee: Here we are?* (Job 38:35). Those who proclaim the Gospel are lightning bolts who shine by their good examples and thunder with their words and return to our Lord when they thank Him for the progress they make. And the giver of sanctity kisses the book that he may say with the Apostle, *I am delighted with the law of God, according to the inward man* (Rom. 7:22). Thus ends the reading of the holy Gospel, which is salvation for us, and defense against the devil. (St. Albert)

The kiss at the end is done to ask pardon for all the offenses we have made against the Word and is also an act of thanksgiving, which expresses the burning in our hearts when we hear the Gospel. For after

Christ opened the meaning of the Scripture to His disciples on the road to Emmaus, they said "Was not our heart burning within us whilst he spoke in the way and opened to us the scriptures?" (Lk. 24:32).

THE SERMON

After the Gospel is completed, the priest places his maniple on the altar before he goes to the pulpit to preach (that is, if he preaches). Recall that the maniple is taken off as a sign to the faithful that the Mass is to be interrupted. The priest places the maniple on the altar, since the altar is used as a receptacle for a bishop's vestments; he always vests from an altar and not from a vesting table, which signifies that all his authority comes from the altar, from Christ. Some priests lay the maniple on the missal, which is a custom well established and therefore legitimate, but I think the better custom is to put it on the altar, since the missal is not really used as a receptacle for vestments, but the altar is.

The basis for giving the sermon at this point may be found in the Gospel according to St. Luke:

> And He came to Nazareth, where he was brought up: and he went into the synagogue, according to his custom, on the Sabbath day: and he rose up to read. And the book of Isaias the prophet was delivered unto him. And as he unfolded the book, he found the place where it was written: The spirit of the Lord is upon me. Wherefore he hath anointed me to preach the gospel to the poor: he hath sent me to heal the contrite of heart, to preach deliverance to the captives and sight to the blind, to set at liberty them that are bruised, to preach the acceptable year of the Lord and the day of reward. And when he had folded the book, he restored it to the minister and sat down. And the eyes of all in the synagogue were fixed on him. And he began to say to them: This day is fulfilled this scripture in your ears. (Lk. 4:16-21)

The priest may give a sermon, a homily, or a ferverino. A sermon is preaching on a particular subject; a homily is an explanation of a text of Scripture; and a ferverino is a passionate encouragement to some virtue or to stir up the faithful on some point of devotion. In the Rite of St. Gregory, it is customary to deliver a sermon or a homily on a Sunday, and ferverinos are given on special occasions or at a daily Mass, when there is little time.

The priest is required to preach on Sundays and Holy Days of Obligation, and it is something he ought to do for certain other occasions. But in the Gregorian Rite it is not done every day. It is essential in a parish, since St. Paul said, "How shall they believe in him whom they have not heard; and how shall they hear without a preacher?" (Rom. 10:14) But practically speaking it cannot be done every day. The basic rule for preaching is one hour of preparation for each minute of preaching. The parish priest does not have the time, then, to compose a three minute sermon for each day. There are canned sermons that one can buy, of course—"homily helps" and "homily hints" aplenty. But if the priest avails himself of these, then he will cut himself off from one of the primary sources of his own growth and sanctification, which is the hard work of preparing a sermon.

It is even harder to preach the sermon, since no matter how hard the preacher prepares and delivers, there are always those in the flock who turn away from their pastor, and who will not even look at him, contrary to the words in the passage above: "the eyes of all the synagogue were fixed on him." But this is part of the cross of being a priest, since the servant is not greater than the Master, and when Our Lord tried to preach to the crowds, or to Pharisees or Sadducees or even His own hand-picked followers, He was not listened to with any devotion by some. Some did not even open their eyes when He was trying to speak to them. And some listened only to hear something to hold against Him if they listened at all.

As Dom Mark Kirby, O.S.B., noted, however:

Holy Mass celebrated worthily, reverently, and carefully is itself the most convincing of sermons. The priest who stands before the altar in a holy fear, and who serves the Lord in reverence and with love, will touch more hearts than the most eloquent of preachers. At the altar a priest preaches with his whole being. He enters into the sanctuary not to be seen, but to see, and in seeing the radiance of the glory of the Lord concealed in the Mysteries of His Body and Blood, he becomes to all a sign of His real presence and a witness of His glory, and this more perfectly than Moses when he descended from the holy mountain transfigured by the divine brightness.

THE LIFE OF THE WORLD TO COME

THE CREED

THE NICENE CREED FOLLOWS THE GOSPEL (or the sermon, if there is one), which represents the public ministry of Christ. When the sick are healed and the dead raised and sinners forgiven, the Enemy is furious, and he seeks to lash out against the Messiah. But he cannot do so now, since Christ is raised gloriously to His throne in heaven. The word of the humble workman of Nazareth has transformed the world; it has abolished slavery, exalted poverty, consoled sorrow, consecrated sacrifice. So the Enemy tries to attack the Body of Christ here on earth, through the spread of false doctrine. The Church responds by boldly by saying aloud the Creed, or better yet singing it triumphally, since Christ has conquered the Prince of this world.

There are a number of creeds written for the Church. The oldest is the Apostles' Creed, which is used in the sacrament of Baptism. The Athanasian Creed is used in conjunction with the Minor Orders on the way to priesthood and also on certain days in the Divine Office. The Nicene Creed is used for the Mass; it seems it was inserted into the Mass by the order of Charlemagne at his imperial chapel. As the universal Church saw the wisdom of this, it became standard throughout the Gregorian Rite. Although the Athanasian and Nicene Creeds are fuller explanations of the Creed, there is but one Creed; there is but one Faith.

Imagine our life without the Faith! What a sad, dark picture we are without light from a higher world! The Faith brings to man consolation, instruction, warning, confidence, fortitude, and self-denial on his journey through life; it inspires him with courage and hope in death; it accompanies him beyond the tomb to blissful immortality. It is to man a heavenly, brilliant star that serves as an unfailing guide on this dangerous passage to his true home. It is to him like an angel, who supports him in his arms, a strong defense and refuge in every danger.

In Latin the Creed is called a *symbolum fidei* ("sign of faith") from the Greek *sunbolos*, "a sign of recognition." The Creed was used in ancient times like a password used by soldiers.

Not all Masses have the Creed; but when it is recited, it is for three reasons:

1. A feast day has a historical foundation or a dogmatic subject is contained in the Creed.

2. Because the Creed designates doctrine, it is recited on the feasts of the principal teachers of doctrine, the apostles.

3. The Creed can enhance the exterior splendor of the feast, according to what the popes or councils of an age wish to extol.

As he intones the Creed, he raises his arms and lowers them, invoking the angels to assist in the proclamation of the Faith. For good reason, the Creed is intoned by the celebrant, who stands for Christ. "The giver of sanctity begins the creed to show that faith is a gift from God and that from God through the givers of sanctity, good things flow in an orderly way through the various ranks of the Church to the people. As the psalmist says, *Like the precious ointment on the head, that ran down upon the beard, the beard of Aaron, which ran down the skirt of his garments*" (St. Albert).

During the Creed, the priest's hands are joined before his breast, which corresponds to humble homage and abandonment of oneself to the absolute truth and veracity of God, and with perfect submission of will and understanding to the infinite majesty of God.

The Creed is like a response to the Gospel. *Credo* means "I believe." Christ has proclaimed the truth, and all the faithful say they believe it with the Creed.

Why do we say we believe *in* God? When we behold nature, the sun with its revolutions and the stars with theirs, the night and the day, we cannot help recognizing that Someone has provided this order. We call this a rational truth. If a man failed to come to such a conclusion, he would be on a par with beasts, to which understanding has not been given, since they are irrational creatures. But to know God as the Holy Trinity means that He has told it to us. The moment I state my belief in Him, I leap up from myself and go to Him, which is another reason we stand quickly for the beginning of the Creed.

At the words "*et homo factus est*" ("and He became man"), all bow while genuflecting (a kind of lowering of ourselves) to adore the Savior, since He lowered Himself in order to become man. Those particular words are written in large block letters on the altar card to remind the priest that he is to say them more slowly than the rest of the Creed, because of their importance. This is reflected too in many of the great musical compositions of the Creed, beginning with chant, which slows down at these words. That same style of writing on the altar cards is found for the words of Consecration, and in the Last Gospel, "*et verbum caro factum est.*"

At the end of the Creed the priest and the faithful make the Sign of the Cross when the words "and the life of the world to come" are sung. Here the Sign acts as a shield against the adversaries of the Faith, and at the same time we are reminded that the only way to arrive safely at that life of the world to come is by the royal road of the Cross. The way of suffering in this perishable life leads to the home of imperishable joys.

When the Creed is finished, the celebrant kisses the altar and turns to greet the faithful. As the altar represents Christ, and as the greeting is to send the Holy Ghost to the congregation, the kiss thus represents the Holy Ghost coming from the Father and the Son, just as we proclaim in the Creed.

During the solemn high Mass, the priest goes to sit after he has recited the Creed, and the choir is still chanting. The deacon bows to the priest and goes up to spread the corporal on the altar. The corporal is ideally made of white linen. "*They took the body of Jesus and bound it in linen cloths.* Hence has come down the custom of the Church, of consecrating Our Lord's body not on silk or gold, but in a clean linen cloth" (St. Bede the Venerable).

Next, the priest turns to pray the *Dominus Vobiscum* and *Oremus*—an invitation to pray and also a command to do so, though now it is prayed especially for the baptized, since only they can actually participate in the Sacrifice. In this salutation we pray for the gift of counsel, which makes us prefer the joys of sacrifice to the pleasures of the world, after the example of Christ by His immolation (the process of sacrificing) for us at the Last Supper. It is in the perfect place, given the nature of the Offertory.

The Mass of the Catechumens ends at this point. In the early Church, a deacon would call on all the unbaptized or the excommunicated to withdraw. Anyone could come and pray and be instructed and thus actively participate in the Mass. But only the baptized could actually participate and offer sacrifice.

THE OFFERTORY

Then begins the Offertory, which is sung with a verse or verses that were chanted in a shortened form of a procession in which gifts were brought up. This was done at every Mass, but we see it now only occasionally; at Candlemas for example, which is the traditional occasion to bring up all the candles to be used at an altar for a year's time so that they can be blessed. Another example is the offering of candles in procession to the bishop by those being ordained in the Minor Orders or the priesthood.

The collection takes place at this time (if there is one), and the intention is to give something in return to the Lord for what He has given us and is about to give us in Holy Communion. Although the collection is of material goods for the maintenance of the church or for the poor or for the diocese, it is not part of the Sacred Liturgy. A collection is not essential to the Mass and, outside of Sundays, is taken only occasionally.

In the Solemn High Mass, we see the procession in a short form, in which the gifts are still brought to the altar, but the Church saw over the years that the greatest gifts were the sacred vessels and the bread and wine. The gesture of giving other gifts such as livestock in the first century was appreciated but over time became unmanageable due to the sheer numbers.

The gifts (meaning the bread in a ciborium and the water and wine in the cruets) are completely covered by the humeral veil and are placed on the credence table on the Epistle side of the altar. The unveiling of the gifts in the Byzantine rite of Mass is more solemn than in our rite. In it, the gifts are brought through the church with incense and candles, and the faithful bow or fall to the ground. This is because the unveiling symbolizes the terrible moment of the stripping of Our Lord's garments. We do not do this because in our rite the bread and wine are not considered worthy of veneration until they have been sacrificed and thus become Our Lord.

Even in the Low Mass, the priest's taking the veil off the chalice and handing it to the acolyte represents the stripping of the garments. Sometimes when I celebrate Mass, this comes to mind, and I find it a difficult thing to do, but at the same time I am glad His garments were stripped. I would never be able to be truly detached from the things of this world, unless He had suffered that indignity.

When the celebrant prays the *Dominus Vobiscum* of the Offertory, the deacon and the subdeacon stand behind the celebrant in a line, so that the subdeacon is on the floor, and the deacon one step below the celebrant, who is on the platform at the altar. The subdeacon represents the Old Testament and the Jews, who by the Law and the Prophecy came only near the great Sacrifice; the deacon represents the New Testament, the Gospel, and the apostles, who came higher and nearer to the perfect Man, Jesus Christ, figured by the celebrant, who is closest to the altar.

"The priest turns to the people and then back to the altar, because Christ, when He lived there below, turned sometimes from prayer to preaching, and sometimes from preaching back to prayer" (Durandus).

When the priest prays, "*Oremus*," the deacon makes a genuflection and goes to the side of the celebrant to wait for the gifts. The subdeacon takes the gifts, which are completely covered by the humeral veil, and brings them up to the altar. As the subdeacon here represents the Old Testament, so the veiled gifts represent the mysteries and ceremonies of the Mass that were veiled and foretold in the sacrifices and ceremonies of the Old Testament.

The Offertory prayers have great signification—that is, they clearly signify what is happening and what is about to happen. This clarity or signification is not dismissive of mystery, but it brings it into better focus.

The Offering of the Bread

The first of the gifts to be offered to the Father is the bread. The Fathers of the Church spoke often of the one bread made up of many grains gathered together from all the shocks. To provide this bread, the grains had to be crushed in the mill, and for the wine to be used in the Mass, the grapes gathered from many vines had to be pressed in the winepress to yield the wine. This represents the spirit of unity of a parish or a religious community, which cannot be acquired except by a continual crushing and pressing of selfishness, the party spirit, the cliques, the little rivalries, the jealousies and envies, the critical and disparaging outlook, and the focus on what is wrong.

In the High Mass the paten with the large altar bread is handed to the priest. He takes the paten in both hands, holds it at eye level, lifts up his eyes briefly to heaven ("and raising His eyes to heaven, blessed, as He gave thanks . . ."), and quickly lowers them. This action is harmonized with the prayer wherein he is reminded of his unworthiness and is humbly offering up the bread for his own innumerable sins. This prayer is called the *Suscipe Sancte Pater*.

The first person singular is used here since the celebrant is not just praying for himself but interceding for the faithful so that they might have grace to make their offering with fitting devotion. This prayer is an anticipation of the Canon. *Immaculate Host* refers in advance to what is not yet on the altar. It also has the meaning of the bread that has been specially made and reserved (set aside for no other purpose), which will be transubstantiated into the Body of Christ. The general doctrine of the Mass is present here: the one who offers, to whom, with what, for what end, for whose benefit— all this is to be found in this prayer.

The bread to be used in the Sacrifice is brought to the altar on the paten, as was done in the Jewish ceremonies of the Loaves of Proposition. The Lord commanded Moses that he should make twelve loaves of bread and put them on a clean table: "And each Sabbath they should be before the Lord. And they shall be Aaron's and his sons', that they may eat them in the holy places" (Lev. 24:8-9). These loaves were also called the priests' bread, for the priests alone could prepare it and eat it; it was called the proposition bread since it was placed on the Table of Proposition in twelve loaves, to represent each of the tribes of Israel.

Great care was taken to prepare the bread used for the Mass. St. Gregory the Great mentions that it was twisted like a braid and wound into a circle of four inches in diameter. Later it was a small round loaf divided into four parts by a cross-notch (*panis quadratus*) with an XP (chi-rho) stamped on it. Monastic custom by the Middle Ages was to select the wheat kernel by kernel, and only those monks who were at least a deacon could bake it, and they had to be in amice and alb. All the baking was done in silence, except for the singing of certain psalms.

The bread itself is called a Host when it has been offered, from the Latin *hostia*, meaning a sacrificial victim that was being slaughtered. Until it has been offered, it is referred to as altar bread. To this day the bread to be used must be made of wheaten flour that has been mixed with natural water and baked in fire, and it must be pure (no additives), whole, and fresh. The bread must be unleavened. This is because the Eucharist was instituted on the Pasch, "the first day of Unleavened Bread." It is generally admitted that this is the kind of bread Our Lord used for the Last Supper. Medieval thought saw leaven as a symbol of impurity, inasmuch as its fermentation works decomposition or decay in bread, but unleavened bread has no such change. It also saw a connection with the admonition of St. Paul: "Purge out the old leaven, that you may be a new paste, as you are unleavened. For Christ our pasch is sacrificed. Therefore, let us feast, not with the old leaven, nor with the leaven of malice and wickedness: but with the unleavened bread of sincerity and truth" (1 Cor. 5:7-8).

Our Lord identified what this was and spoke of three kinds of leaven: the leaven of the Pharisees, which is hypocrisy and consists in honoring God with mere lip service; the leaven of the Sadducees, who denied the life of the world to come, which is a lack of faith; and the leaven of Herod, who rendered unto Caesar the things that are God's.

We should consider that leaven grows only in a lukewarm environment. And we ought to shudder to hear the warning of Christ recorded in the book of the Apocalypse: "But because thou art lukewarm, and neither cold nor hot, I will begin to vomit thee out of my mouth" (Apoc. 3:16). So we purge out the old leaven by going to confession and ridding ourselves of the horror of lukewarmness and mortal sin.

Once the prayer is finished, the celebrant makes with the paten and bread (now referred to as the Host, since it has been offered) a small Sign of the Cross over the place where the Host is to be laid on the corporal. This action shows that the Sacrifice made on the Cross is the same Sacrifice made on the altar.

In the Old Testament the gesture of laying the bread on the altar is seen as a source of sanctification (cf. Ex. 29:37), but further ceremonies in the rites of the ancient Temple will bring the offering to a more perfect state. All those Jewish ceremonies prefigure the Mass.

The paten is then half hidden under the corporal at the center and to the right of the corporal for the Low Mass. At the High Mass the deacon gives it to the subdeacon, and covers it with the humeral veil, which the subdeacon is wearing, and the subdeacon keeps it aloft in front of his eyes until the end of the Our Father. It recalls the hiding of the apostles during the Savior's Passion, as He foretold: "All you shall be scandalized in me this night, for it is written: I will strike the shepherd and the sheep of the flock shall be dispersed" (Mt. 26:31).

It also tells of the identity of Christ, which was hidden during the Passion. The pagans were blind in that they could not recognize His connection with God, with the exception of the centurion who realized Christ was the Son of God. His disciples were blind to His kingship, with the exception of His mother and St. Dismas. And the Jews were blind to His being the Messiah, with the exception of Nicodemus the Pharisee. The hidden paten at the Low Mass reminds us of all the blind witnesses. In the High Mass, the subdeacon acts as a witness, but holds the hidden paten in front of his eyes, so that he cannot see the sacrifice. This represents Christ's own people, the pagans, and the Jews who did not see their Savior on the Cross. The subdeacon represents the Old Testament especially and thus stands for the Jews in a special way.

But at the end of the Our Father, when the priest sings, "Forgive us our trespasses," the subdeacon comes up, the paten is unveiled, and the humeral veil is put aside. It is an intensely beautiful ceremony, which represents that the prayer of Christ on the Cross for forgiveness was certainly for the Jews, and this forgiveness will open their eyes at the end of the world, so that they will see Christ as the Lord and convert and complete the Church, which is not whole without them. It is that same prayer of forgiveness that enables us and pagans to see; our blindness is taken away by Our Lord's prayer to the Father, which is graciously bestowed on us by the Sanctifier.

The Commixture

After the Host is offered, the priest goes to the Epistle side for the mixture of water and wine in the chalice. The wine to be used must be pressed from ripe grapes, fully fermented, not soured or settled or artificially composed. There are no directives as to its color or taste. If a red wine is used, this presumes a fair amount of extra labor, in keeping the altar cloths and linens white and without wine stains. Often in a parish, the workers needed to do this cleaning are not available, so a white wine is used out of consideration for them.

Having a little water in the chalice was a Jewish liturgical custom. It was even done in normal daily life; in France one still finds wine served with a little water in restaurants, in case the customer wishes to dilute the wine slightly, or if children are learning to drink alcohol properly, they drink mostly water with a little wine mixed with it.

The meaning of the commixture is deep; it shows our sacrifice united with Christ's. As the water takes on the flavor, color, taste, and all things referring to the accidents of the wine, and does so without ceasing to be water, so we, by uniting ourselves to Christ, become like Him but retain our identities.

The drop of water (only a little is used) is blessed by the priest, since it represents the Church Militant, the living faithful of the Church. At a Requiem, however, the water is not blessed, since the prayer in that Mass is for the faithful departed. That drop of water recalls to our minds St. Isaias the Prophet: "Behold, the gentiles are as a drop in the bucket" (Is. 40:15).

If there are any drops of water on the sides of the chalice and not in the wine, the priest carefully wipes that part of the chalice. This is a symbol for those who are baptized and thus members of the Church, but who refuse union with the Lord. They cannot stay where they are; and this goes for all of us—either we advance in union with Christ or regress and stay away from Him. There is no standing still in the interior life.

We see in the commixture that as the wine receives the water, so Christ receives us and with us our sins, though this reception cannot take place if we are in mortal sin. This mixture which is now on the altar, ready to be offered, symbolizes the union of the faithful with Christ—a bond so strong it cannot be separated, no more than the water can be taken back out of the wine.

Very early in the Church the Gnostics began to doubt and attack the use of wine, and in their Masses they used only water. St. Cyprian summed up the error quite succinctly: "When someone offers only wine, then Christ begins to exist without us. When they offer only water, then we begin to exist without Christ." Much later, it was precisely this symbolism of the commixture that Martin Luther rejected because he saw in it the perfect work of God (the wine) being mixed with the work of man, which was impure and sinful (the water). He thought the separation should be absolute. Now he knows that he was wrong.

St. Cyprian goes on to say, "The divine Scriptures declare in the Apocalypse that the waters signify the peoples. So when water is mixed with wine in the chalice, the people are united to Christ. Therefore, in the sanctification of Our Lord's chalice, neither wine alone nor water alone may be offered. If only wine were offered, then would the blood of Christ be without us. If there were only water, the people would be without Christ."

St. Peter made it clear long ago: "By Christ he hath given us very great and precious promises, that by these we may be made partakers of the divine nature" (2 Pet. 1:4). Yes! Poor, frail, human nature, by the communication of heavenly gifts and graces, is elevated to a supernatural state, endowed with riches beyond imagination and clothed with incomparable glory. St. Agnes put it beautifully: "With sparkly and glittering gems hath He covered my breast, with golden garments hath He clothed me, with artistic and precious jewels hath He adorned me, and moreover, He hath shown me incomparable treasures, which are to be mine, if I remain true to Him."

The Offering of the Wine

For the offering of the wine, the priest is assisted by the deacon, who holds up the chalice with the priest. This is a relic from the times in which the chalice was particularly heavy, but that is not the reason we continue the practice. The prayer said at this moment is the *Offerimus*, which is in the plural as it is said by both priest and deacon, because it is in harmony with the prayer in the commixture, which speaks of the union of Christ and His faithful.

The design of the chalice can be quite varied, but it must be of precious metal. If a gold chalice is used, it signifies the treasures of wisdom that are hidden in Christ (cf. Col. 2:3). If a silver chalice is used, it signifies purity from sin. The design must have the cup, a node with which to grasp the chalice correctly, a stem that is a few inches long above and below the node (and thin enough so that the priest can use it with the canonical digits held together), and a solid base.

The significance of the chalice itself is described by St. Albert: "We use the chalice to stand for the tomb, the paten for the stone placed at the mouth of the tomb, the pall and corporal for the winding cloths in which Our Lord's body was wrapped by St. Joseph in his work of love."

The bread and wine are now on the corporal, blessed, set apart from profane use, and set aside for divine use, which is the very definition of the holy. It is now the time when the priest and the faithful should offer themselves with all they have. This self-offering was done symbolically in the commixture, but now it is to be made expressly for the purpose of awakening in the hearts of the worshippers sentiments of self-sacrifice.

In Spiritu Humilitatis

Once the chalice has been offered, the priest bows low for the prayer *In spiritu humilitatis*. It is a perfect expression of the meaning of the whole Offertory. It is taken from the book of the prophet Daniel, a reference to the three young men in the fiery furnace, who were unable to offer to God the sacrifices of the Law and so offered themselves in place of the victims that they lacked. "As gold in the furnace He hath received them" (Wis. 3:6). We too should offer ourselves as a holocaust in the furnace of our sufferings, persecutions, and temptations. And the way to offer ourselves is with hearts penetrated with penitential love and sorrow, a mind bowed down with compunction. "A sacrifice to God is an afflicted spirit; a contrite and humbled heart He does not despise" (Ps. 50:19).

There is no notion in this prayer of doubting God's acceptance of the Sacrifice, as St. Robert Bellarmine wrote: "The priest does not doubt whether the sacrifice of the Mass will be pleasing to God in itself, or insofar as it was instituted by Christ; but he doubts of his own interior dispositions. For this reason, he asks for humility and contrition, that he may so continue the sacrifice which he has begun that it may also please God insofar as he is offering it."

"During this holy function, we must offer ourselves with compunction of heart as a sacrifice; for when we commemorate the mystery of the Passion of Our Lord, we must imitate that which we celebrate. The Mass will be a sacrifice for us to God, when we have made an offering of ourselves. But we should, moreover, after retirement from prayer, endeavor as far as we are able with God's assistance, to keep our mind in recollection and renewed strength, so that passing thoughts may not distract it, nor vain joy find its way into the heart, and that thus our soul may not, by carelessness and fickleness, again lose the spirit of compunction it has required" (St. Gregory the Great, *Dialogues* 4.59).

It is a temptation for some clergy to emphasize the joyful, with much laughter, in worship. But having fun in the Sacrifice of the Mass is utterly foreign to what our ancestors did at the Mass on Calvary. When Our Lord breathed His last breath and darkness fell over Calvary and the whole area, the beholders were seized with such fear and sorrow that they returned to their homes striking their breasts (cf. Lk. 23:48). But everything that moves and affects the soul in joy or sorrow, prosperity or adversity, distress or death, ought to be placed consciously on the altar at this time, directly on the Heart of our Redeemer.

Veni Sanctificator

The priest then addresses the Holy Ghost directly with the prayer *Veni Sanctificator* ("Come, Sanctifier"), which is a great blessing over the gifts. When God is asked to bless the sacrifice, know that the Latin *benedicere* (from which we have our word *bless*) means to speak well, to say what is good. This can be done in many ways: if one already possesses the good that is said of him, then blessing means to praise or glorify the possessor. If a person or thing does not as yet possess the good, then blessing means wishing the person or thing a good. The blessing of God is efficacious and infallibly imparts good to the creature, though whether the creature accepts it is another matter. The liturgical blessing of the Church is also never without fruit (provided it is done correctly), but it is always a good wish. The faithful can also bless—that is, impart good by desire and prayer.

The proximate reason why the Holy Ghost is invoked here lies in the analogy that the Consecration bears to the Incarnation. The great similarity between the Holy Eucharist on the altar and the Incarnation in the womb of the Virgin is often commented upon by the Fathers. As these two great mysteries are works of divine love and holiness, so are they manifestations of the Holy Ghost, Who is infinite personal love and sanctity. All three of the Divine Persons accomplish the Consecration, but we ascribe the action particularly to the Sanctifier.

Mary once asked, "How shall this be done, because I know not man?" The archangel replied, "The Holy Ghost shall come upon thee, and the power of the Most High shall overshadow thee." If we ask, "How shall the bread become the Body of Christ and the wine, mingled with water, become the Blood of Christ?" The answer is: "The Holy Ghost shall overshadow each and shall effect what is beyond language and conception."

The Incensation of the Gifts

Once the invocation of the Holy Ghost upon the gifts is given, the priest turns to his right to put incense on the coals in the thurible. The first incensation in the High Mass comes before the Introit. The second is for the Gospel, the third is for the Offertory, the fourth is for the Blessed Sacrament. Incensation is always done in order; at the Offertory, first come the offerings, then the crucifix, the reliquaries, the altar, the celebrant, the deacon, the subdeacon, and then all the ministers, and finally the people.

The incense enhances prayer by the pleasant odor and signifies that the gifts are to be used only for God, or set aside for God. It also purifies prayer by softening the light and somewhat obscuring the priest and the altar, the effect of which detaches us from this world.

Although the gifts have reached a great height of sanctity in that they have been offered, there is still an element of the human in them that strikes us; that is, the wine represents Christ, and the water represents man. Just so, the weakness of the drop of water compared with the strength of the wine expresses the difference between God and man. We should be conscious of that difference at all times during the Mass. When we are weak, then we are strong (cf. 2 Cor. 12:10).

The other incensations are to signify that which already belongs to God. The faithful are incensed after being bowed to, just as in the medieval courts of Europe the king received a genuflection on the left knee, but nobility received a bow. The faithful are considered noble in the court of Christ by virtue of their baptism. They are the legal heirs of the kingdom, the sons and daughters of the Most High

God, and their being incensed is a reminder of this. St. Benedict used this idea to explain the long hours of the Benedictines in choir; a vocation to be a Benedictine monk was a vocation to serve at the royal court, a vocation to be a personal servant to His Majesty.

The priest incenses the gifts three times in the form of a Greek cross (in a Latin cross the vertical dimension is longer than the horizontal; in a Greek cross, the vertical and horizontal are the same length), to recall the Passion foreshadowed by St. Mary Magdalen. "This woman, in pouring this ointment upon my body has done it for my burial" (Mt. 26:12). Then, after the three crosses, the incense is moved above the gifts in three circles, signifying the triple crown the Savior received at His Ascension, as He was and is Priest, Prophet, and King. May we long to see Him that way in His true glory, with His crowns and surrounded by His friends.

Durandus says of this:

> The prayers of the saints bring us to an eternal crown through the burning charity of our Lord's passion, and so the priest swings the censer both in the shape of a cross and of a crown. He incenses the offerings with threefold swings to recall how Mary Magdalene thrice brought spices to anoint the body of Jesus. Once, when she anointed his feet at the house of Simon the Pharisee; once when she poured ointment upon his head in the house of Simon the Leper; and once when she went with spices to anoint Jesus after he had been placed in the tomb—for there the intention is counted for the deed.

The numbers are significant here. The points over which the thurible is passed over the gifts are nine in total. These signify the nine choirs of angels who assist us in taking our prayer to God and distributing His graces to us in return. The prayers that the priest says at this point are in perfect accord with this gesture and number. For the relics and the altar, the thurible is either passed in front of or over in twenty places. The prayers that are said at this point have to do with being kept in the grace that was just asked for in the incensation of the gifts. So our vigil here on earth is a period of waiting for the coming of the Savior. Thus the number twenty, since we find in Scripture that that number signifies waiting: Jacob waiting twenty years to get possession of his wives and property, Israel waiting twenty years for a deliverer from the oppression of Jabin, twenty for deliverance through Samson, twenty for the Ark at Kirjath-jearim, twenty for Solomon to complete the houses, et cetera.

The incense is blessed with a special prayer invoking St. Michael the Archangel. While the angel who holds the golden thurible in the celestial liturgy is not named (Apoc. 8:4), the Church came to the conclusion that St. Michael was the one holding it. This was the result of theological reflection and confirmation of it in private revelation.

The blessing is not given in the Requiem, since the Church no longer has jurisdiction over the souls in purgatory. She cannot bind them, nor can she loose them by her power as she can here on earth. She can help them with her intercession, however, in neighborly love of them. This love comes from God: the glowing coal and the rising smoke signify the fire of divine love that can burn in our hearts and is given back to Him in intercession for the faithful departed.

The Incensation of the Altar

The reason the altar is incensed at this time (not just the gifts and relics and faithful, and so forth), is made clear from the ancient Council of Rhotom. "At the time when the Gospel is finished, the Offering is incensed as a remembrance of the death of the Savior." That is, when the body of the dead Lord was placed in the tomb, before it was laid away, Joseph of Arimathea and Nicodemus the Pharisee and the holy women wrapped incense around it in the folds of the linens, after the manner of the Jews when burying their dead (cf. Lk. 23:56), thus, the incensing of the bread and wine soon to be changed into the Body and Blood of Christ, and the incensing of the altar, which represents Christ, is to honor Him Whom these typify and recall to our mind.

And Durandus says, "And he goes on to incense the altar on every side, since the fame of that deed has been spread throughout the Church, as our Lord himself foretold."

The Lavabo

Once the incensation is completed by the priest, he remains at the Epistle side of the altar to have his hands washed. In a Low Mass, the Lavabo, as it is called, has the water applied only to the canonical digits of the priest. In the High Mass, he washes his hands and not just the fingers. This is, of course, a practical necessity, since burnt incense tends to be sticky, and the hands should be clean to handle the chalice and the Body of the Lord. But there is a far greater reason for the Lavabo than just getting the hands clean.

"We did not set out for the church with defiled hands; this washing is a symbol that you ought to be pure from all sinful and unlawful deeds. For since the hands are a symbol of action, by washing them we represent the purity and blamelessness of our conduct. Or have you not heard how blessed David disclosed this mystery, saying, *I will wash my hands among the innocent; and will compass thy altar, O Lord*" (St. Cyril of Jerusalem).

Before Our Lord offered Himself in the bread and wine, He washed the feet of the apostles to show the purity needed for the sacrifice. This is done on Holy Thursday, but it is done symbolically at every Mass. Our Lord, before He gave the apostles His Body and Blood at the Last Supper, washed their feet, symbolizing among other things the purity that would be required to participate in the Supper. St. Thomas Aquinas says that the symbolism of washing feet would be a better or higher symbolism, but "it is sufficient to wash the hands; besides, it is more convenient, and it is enough to show perfect purity, especially as it is to our hands that all works are ascribed." And the washing of hands was a gesture of interior purification, even in ancient times for the Hebrews (cf. Ex. 30:19).

When the Paschal Supper, or Last Supper, was over, a hymn of thanksgiving was said, before Christ went to the Garden of Olives. The priest also ends the Offertory with a hymn, the *Lavabo Inter Innocentes*.

The Suscipe Sancta Trinitas and the Orate Fratres

Once the Lavabo is finished, the priest turns to go back to the center of the altar, which symbolizes Christ going immediately to the Garden of Olives after the Last Supper, to prepare for His death. The priest bows low to pray the *Suscipe Sancta Trinitas*; the bow tells us of the humbled Savior, Who bowed before the disciples to wash their feet at the Last Supper, but it is also symbolic of His agony in the garden, bent over with the weight of our sins. In the garden, after some time of prayer, He searched for Sts. Peter, James, and John, asking, "Could you not watch with me one hour? Watch ye and pray" (Mt. 26:40-41). For this, the priest interrupts his prayer, turns to the faithful, and says, "*Orate Fratres*" ("Pray, brethren") like the exhortation to the apostles in the garden. The *Orate Fratres* is not, in the context of the Mass, an accusation but is said with affectionate compassion, as Our Lord asked the three to pray with Him in the garden.

All through the Offertory, the prayers are especially about the Church Triumphant, but now the priest turns to the Church Militant, the *omnes circumstantium* (all those standing present, as the faithful are referred to in the Canon—a reference to how the faithful went to Mass in the early Church) and asks for their prayers. His calling the faithful *fratres* ("brethren") refers to the Church Militant as a kind of family.

The response expresses a wish that their sacrifice be received at the priest's hands for the glory of God, for the benefit of those present, and for the benefit of the whole Church. As he receives their prayers, the priest turns in a full circle to signify the reception of and then giving of their prayers to God in the Sacrifice.

This prayer is said when the presentation and arrangement of the gifts is complete. The nature of the prayer reminds the priest that he is a mediator and has an exalted role above the laity, as he has been chosen by God to be their mediator, keenly representing the One Mediator. Yet the priest asks that the faithful pray for his sacrifice, which is public self-accusation that he is in great need of them to do this work. This exalts the faithful and shows how important their role is in the Sacrifice and for the interior life of their priest.

You may have wondered why the priest starts out praying audibly and then goes back to silence beginning with this part of the Mass. Only seven times does he speak distinctly from the *Orate Fratres* to his reception of Communion. The reason he says these things out loud but briefly is because Our Lord spoke out loud but briefly seven times on the Cross. As the Passion of the Lord is primary in this part of the Mass, the great medieval commentators on the Liturgy see the Seven Last Words of Christ being expressed liturgically. The Seven Last Words are actually phrases that came out of the silence of the Passion so that all could hear; they are taken from three Gospels:

1. The first occasion of this audible speech is here at the *Orate Fratres*, which corresponds to Christ's first word: "Father, forgive them for they know not what they do" (Lk. 23:34). This is in accord with the plea that God would accept our sacrifice.

2. "Amen, I say to thee: this day thou shalt be with me in paradise" (Lk. 23:43). This is in harmony with the end of the Secret, which is always the phrase "world without end," said or sung distinctly

(*per omnia saecula saeculorum*), before beginning the Preface of the Mass, and of the song of the angels singing the Sanctus.

3. "Woman, behold thy son. To the disciple, Behold your mother" (cf. Jn. 19:26-27). This corresponds to third time the priest breaks silence, the *nobis quoque peccatoribus*: "to us sinners also, Thy servants hoping in the multitude of Thy mercies . . ." Even in His agony He gives us the gift of His most holy Mother, who intercedes for us so that we might receive a multitude of mercies.

4. "My God, my God, why hast thou forsaken me?" (Mk. 15:34) corresponds with the Pater Noster. As Christ cried out to His Father with great passion, so we cry out to the Father in the words that Jesus taught us.

5. "I thirst" (Jn. 19:28) corresponds with the *Pax Domini sit semper vobiscum*. That is, Our Lord has a great thirst for souls, for His friends. And He freely grants His peace to any who come to Him with a humbled and contrite heart—that is, His friends.

6. "It is consummated" (Jn. 19:30) is in accord with the singing of the Agnus Dei—of Christ, Who takes away the sins of the world. The consummation of the Sacrifice of Christ takes our sins away.

7. "Father, into thy hands I commend my spirit" (Lk. 23:46) is in accord with the *Domine non sum dingus*. The death of Christ was caused by our sins, so it is fitting to express our fundamental unworthiness to receive Him as a result. He gives Himself to the Father, and the Father gives Him to us.

The action of the priest while saying the *Orate Fratres* is to make a full circle. "On this occasion, after the priest has spoken these words, he completes the circle in turning back to the altar. For one psalm says, I have gone round and have offered up a sacrifice of jubilation. So he does indeed go round, as he prepares himself to sacrifice" (Durandus).

The Secret

After the *Orate Fratres* and its response is finished, the priest prays the Secret in silence. Some authors maintain that it is called the Secret because it is said silently. But this is unlikely, because many prayers are said silently and because at one time it was said aloud so that everyone could hear it. Most likely it is called the Secret because it was a prayer said *super secreta* ("above that which was set apart," from the Latin *secretus*, a participle of the verb *secernere*, meaning "to set apart").

With that being said, still, there is something hidden with the Secret. "There is a sign of this in the Book of Numbers, where Aaron and his priest sons alone must enter the tabernacle and sort and carry the things when the camp is to advance. None other of the people are allowed to see the things of the sanctuary before they have been wrapped up; and if they look out of curiosity, they must die. For many people despise holy things which are put publicly on display, and so they take from them an occasion of death; but if they had been covered and wrapped up and veiled from their sight, they would have revered them" (St. Albert).

And Amalarius says further, "Christ was the paschal lamb prepared for sacrifice, though this lay hid. It was concealed from the apostles; it was concealed from the others who believed; it was concealed from the people of the Jews, until the day of the Supper, when he manifested the passion more clearly. Therefore the priest speaks in secret until that day arrives."

All the Secrets allude to the offerings on the altar to be used in the sacrifice (those particularly on the corporal) and ask that by becoming

Christ they may avail for our salvation (*salvare*, "to preserve"). They speak particularly of oblations, offerings, the *superpositas*—that is collected together, almost heaped up, if you will, like the little pile of loaves brought by the faithful in ancient times at the Offertory.

All the Secrets harmonize perfectly with the Collects of the Mass in regard to their construction, number, succession, and concluding form. But they differ in that the Collects ask for some special grace regarding the mystery of the day, and the Secrets are oblation prayers, which ask that the gifts be blessed, dedicated, sanctified, and consecrated; and that the graces of the Sacrifice be bestowed on the Church. The Secret always ends with the phrase "world without end."

FOR GRACE WILL EVER BE GIVEN HIM
WHO DUTIFULLY RETURNS THANKS

The Preface

AFTER THE SECRET, which is symbolic of the Savior's time in the Garden of Olives, He now begins His Way of the Cross in the Preface. During the reception and carrying of His Cross, He received shouts of insult and blasphemies. The Preface is a reparation for this: the Church in our name thanks God for all the mercies we have received. The Preface also corresponds to Christ's giving thanks before the first Consecration in history, at the Last Supper.

The Roman Canon is one prayer, from the Preface to the *Per Ipsum*. The Preface is a solemn introduction to the Canon. Originally it was left for the celebrant to improvise. But improvisational prayer was eliminated rather quickly from the liturgy for obvious reasons, such as risk of the celebrant's saying something banal, stupid, or even heretical. By the third century, there were as many Prefaces as there were Masses. That is still the case with the Mozarabic and Ambrosian Rites. Today there are eighteen prefaces used in the 1962 Roman Missal.

The formula for the Preface is simple:

1. The versicles are a short dialogue between celebrant and people, and date from the second century. This calls to mind the ancient Jewish feasts of purifying the Temple: "All the priests made prayer, while the sacrifice was consuming, Jonathan beginning and the rest answering" (2 Mach. 1:23).

2. The motive of our praise is stated, which varies according to the feast. For example, "We give thanks unto thee, who dist set the salvation of mankind upon the tree of the Cross, so that whence came death thence also life might rise again" (Preface of the Passion). "For thy Son was lifted up into heaven, so that he might make us partakers of his godhead" (Preface of the Ascension).

3. The conclusion invokes the angels, who properly glorify God as He should be adored. How appropriate it is to invoke the angels in the Mass, given that St. Gregory of Nyssa said that the walls are white with angels at the Sacrifice!

The greatest of all the Prefaces is the *Exultet,* which is sung only once a year, at the Easter Vigil.

We may wonder with the first versicle—the *Dominus Vobiscum*—why the priest does not turn around to face the people. This is because the Preface is the fulfillment of Moses on Mount Sinai, where he entered into the holy cloud and began to commune face-to-face with the Lord. From the *Orate Fratres* to the *Ecce Agnus Dei*, the priest has eyes and mind directed only to the Sacrifice, and the faithful will see his face again only after the marvels of the Consecration and Communion have been completed, like the Hebrews seeing the face of Moses only after the Law had been given.

The imperative *sursum corda* is some rather curious Latin. Literally it means "Hearts up!" or "Hearts on high!" It reminds me of the drill instructor giving the order "Right face!" in no uncertain terms. And literally the faithful calmly respond, "We have hearts, and they are towards the Lord." This rather odd phrase refers to a certain mood that should begin every prayer, according to St. Cyprian—namely, that every fleshly and worldly thought should be put aside and the mind inclined solely to the Lord. Of all the times of the Mass when we should try to close our minds to distractions, this is the most important.

But if our mind is in heaven by thought, then our hearts should follow. That is, our desires and wants should be directed mainly to the next life. Ordinarily this is very difficult to do, but it should be done at least once a day at Holy Mass. The more estranged the soul becomes from frivolity and the distractions of the world, the more she can lift her mind and heart to heavenly things.

The priest's raising his hands at the *sursum corda* reminds us of the invitation of St. Jeremias the prophet: "Let us raise our hearts together with our hands to the Lord in heaven" (Lam. 3:41).

At the third versicle the priest enjoins the faithful, "Let us give thanks to the Lord God," while joining his hands before his breast and bowing his shoulders to the crucifix. This reminds him once again (he needs many such reminders to celebrate Mass well) of how dependent he is on the Sacrifice of the Cross for the grace to do what he is doing. He would not be giving thanks were it not for the Cross. He needs a noble heart to perform his duty, as do the faithful to perform theirs. Gratitude is the sign of a noble heart, and ingratitude is the mark of a mean soul. Fervent thanksgiving belongs to Christian perfection. The more devout and perfect the soul, the more it will be filled with the spirit of gratitude. The saints, when on earth, never wearied of thanking God, and unceasing thanksgiving is their blessed occupation in eternity.

Notice that thanksgiving is declared to be just (*justum*), right (*aequum*), and salutary (*salutare*). It is just because gratitude is closely allied to justice, which is the will and endeavor to repay, as far as possible, benefits received. It is God's will that we be just. "In all things give thanks; for this is the will of God in Christ Jesus" (1 Thess. 5:18). It is right to give Him thanks, in the sense of its being proper and becoming. After all, the Father is about to give us His only-begotten Son. It is salutary, in that it promotes our temporal and eternal welfare. Gratitude opens to us the treasures of divine liberality. Gratitude is supremely profitable to friendship, but ingratitude is like a scorching wind that dries up blessings.

Thomas à Kempis put this succinctly: "The gifts of grace cannot abound or flow in us, because we are ungrateful to the Giver; and because we do not return them all to the fountainhead. For grace will ever be given him who dutifully returns thanks. Be grateful then for the least, and thou shalt be worthy to receive greater things" (*Imit.* 2.10).

And how far should our thanksgiving go? How often should it be done? *Semper et ubique*, as it says in the Preface. Always and everywhere. There is no time or place in which we should not from the fullness of our hearts say, "Thanks be to God!"

But we are not equal to the task. We stammer like infants sometimes when we pray, and so we call upon the angels to praise God properly, and thus, at the conclusion of the Preface we sing the Sanctus—the song of the angels—and the priest prays it bowed low as the angels are bowed.

There is a range of ideas expressed in the Preface. One of them is a primitive consciousness that we owe God, our Creator and our Lord, adoration and praise. Another is that we have been elected, chosen by God, and that we can do nothing less than thank Him over and over again. *Thank* is from the same root in English as *think*. So it is proper that the Consecration be filled with a thoughtful remembrance of the Lord. But it is more than a thoughtful recalling of memories from the past; it is enveloped in prayer before God that is filled with gratitude. Above all we should remember that *the* thanksgiving of the Church (*eucharistia* in the Greek) is a remembrance of a Sacrifice already consummated, which brought us redemption: "Do this in memory of me."

The celebrant, standing at the altar with his face turned from the people and toward God, tells the faithful that he offers a sacrifice to God even if there is no one else to see it but God; that the assistance of the faithful is not necessary for the sacrifice; that he stands there as the chosen of the Lord, raised up from among men to plead their cause before the throne of grace and to offer a sacrifice to God.

At the end of the Preface is a glimpse of the kingdom of angels. Several choirs of angels are mentioned by name. The Dominations in a manner unknown to us adore the majesty of the Creator (*adorant dominationes*), in a way that no mortal is capable of doing. The Powers tremble in profound humility and reverential awe (*tremunt potestates*) before the grandeur of the Divine Majesty. The Seraphim are mentioned last, as they constitute the highest choir of the angelic kingdom and are emphatically called blessed (*beata seraphim*) because they above all burn and glow with an incomparable love of God.

The Sanctus

These exceedingly blessed hosts of heavenly spirits are eternally immersed in the loving and praising vision of the glory of God; they are never weary of celebrating and blessing the glory of their Creator. They invite and urge us to rise and lift our spirits above the lowliness of the earth and place our minds and hearts for a little while in the heights of the heavenly Jerusalem. We are aware of our lowliness, however, which is why we seek to join ourselves to the angels, who can praise better than we, and this joint praise of the human and the angelic is called the Sanctus.

The Sanctus was recorded by St. Isaias (6:3-4): "And the Seraphim cried one to another, and said: Holy, holy, holy, the Lord God of hosts, all the earth is full of Thy glory. And the lintels of the doors [of the Temple] were moved at the voice of him that cried, and the house was filled with smoke [that is, with the cloud of the glory of light]." St. John the Apostle also heard the celestial canticle (Apoc. 4:8).

The Sanctus recalls more than just the Seraphim, who sang this hymn, however; it is a reminder that the Church should take part in the heavenly singing. By the Middle Ages the clergy assisting in choir were the ones who sang it with the priest. In the High Mass we see the vestige of this practice, when as soon as the Sanctus begins, the deacon and the subdeacon walk up on each side of the priest to say the prayer with him. This also represents the Church Militant, Suffering, and Triumphant assisting the angels in their praise.

"*Sanctus* is said thrice, to express the mystery of the Trinity of persons. But to express the unity of the essence, *Dominus Deus* is said" (St. Antoninus).

The triple *holy* was also used by the children in the fiery furnace— Hananiah, Mishael, and Azariah—when they called out for mercy and protection (cf. Dan. 1-3). The Hebrew way to express "most holy" was by repeating *holy* three times.

Notice that in the Low Mass, there are three tones or voices used by the celebrant. During the Preface, he annunciates the prayer in a voice loud enough for the whole congregation to hear. At the Sanctus his voice is lowered so that only those in the front half of the nave can hear it. At the *Te Igitur* (the first word of the Canon proper), his voice is a whisper so that only the server can hear it.

This reminds us of the Day of Atonement (Yom Kippur) in the ancient Temple. Once a year the high priest would go into the Holy of Holies on this day to do several things. He would sprinkle the Mercy Seat (the place of the Lord's unseen presence) with the blood of two victims previously sacrificed and whisper the name of God three times to complete the cleansing of Israel and the Temple from sin. He would also whisper, "*Anna baShem Kappur Na*," meaning, "I beseech Thee on the Name make Thou atonement." God would then accept the offering and turn it into a sacrifice on the merit of His name. Then the high priest could go back to the people and declare, "Now the sanctuary is cleansed."

When you hear the phrase *Dominus Deus Sabaoth* (*sabaoth* means "host," as in an army) keep in mind that this is not calling God a god of war like the Roman god Mars, but it refers to the heavenly hosts, the angels and the saints, the whole multitude of creatures that God made in the six days of creation, who are like an army having one mission and arranged in a hierarchy of ranks.

In this beautiful hymn we celebrate the interior and eternal glory of God, which is invisible to us. This uncreated glory of the Lord of Hosts is unveiled, however, in the works of creation and redemption; for "heaven and earth" (*coeli et terra*), the sum of all creation, the visible and invisible world, bear witness to the glory of God. Heaven and earth are full of His glory—that is, of proofs of His power and greatness, of His goodness and mercy.

Going deeper into this great prayer, we see that it tells us of the three most holy Persons in the Holy Trinity, while the singular "Lord God of Hosts" tells us of the unity of one nature in God. Thus, we see in the Sanctus the two greatest mysteries of our Faith: the two natures of Christ united in one Person, and the three Persons united in one Godhead.

Added to the Sanctus was the exclamation from the Gospel, "Hosanna to the Son of David," from Christ's triumphal entry into

Jerusalem. The hosanna was the chant of the Hebrew children given to Christ when He rode into Jerusalem, but the Sign of the Cross is made with our prayer to remind us that the praise was short lived. Only five days after the hosannas were sung, the same crowd was shouting, "Crucify Him!" St. Augustine points out that the word *hosanna* is more an exclamation than a thing; a way to express great joy.

The original verse of the psalm from which the acclamation is taken (Ps. 117:25-26) is a bit different: "O Lord save me! O Lord, give me success! Blessed is he that cometh in the name of the Lord!" The first words of the psalm verse were sung by the congregation at the procession of the Feast of Tabernacles, and the last by the priest's choir when the faithful were entering the Temple. The liturgical text for the Mass is not taken directly from the psalm, then, but from the Gospel, as it refers to the Savior and to the fact that He is about to come to us on the altar.

But what a coming it is, for as Durandus points out, "The preface may also represent how Jesus went to the great upper room that had been made ready for the Passover, where he spoke much with the disciples and giving thanks, sang a hymn to God the Father. *And a hymn being said, they went out unto mount Olivet.*"

TE IGITUR

"When praise and thanksgiving have been made for the great grace of our redemption, then comes a silence on all the Church. The noise of words stops: the heart's devotion attends to God alone: and the priest, accompanied by the prayers and desires of all, begins to pour forth the prayer" (St. Remigius).

Te igitur formally begins the Canon, and the text has not been changed since the time of St. Gregory the Great (beginning of the seventh century) and only slightly since A.D. 400. In the early days of the Church it was called the Action, and in the Byzantine Rite it is called the Anaphora—the offering that is lifted up.

When the celebrant or MC turns the page of the missal to the beginning of the Canon, you might be able to see a large illustration, usually of the Crucifixion, and usually taking up an entire page of the missal. The illustration is always on the left and the text is on the right, since the text and actual prayer are more important than the illustration, and the right always takes precedence over the left in the Gregorian Rite. In ancient missals the *T* of the first word was written large and illuminated with various designs, but eventually the illumination took up the whole page.

This reminds us of the Hebrew letter *Tau*, which was also richly decorated and ornamented with various designs in Hebrew Scripture. It looks like a cross when written, and we should remember that those who belonged to God according to the Old Covenant once had the *Tau* marked on their foreheads. "Go through the midst of the city, through the midst of Jerusalem, and mark Tau upon the foreheads of the men that sigh and moan for all the abominations that are committed in the midst thereof" (Ez. 9:4).

The priest looks up to heaven when he says, "*Te*" ("You"), which reminds us of the way that Christ often spoke to His Father. "They took therefore the stone away. And Jesus lifting up his eyes, said: Father, I give thee thanks that thou hast heard me." (Jn. 11:41). It is a plea for acceptance. *Igitur* means "therefore," joining the Preface (wonderfully interrupted by the Sanctus) to the Canon. *Supplices* means "bowed down," so the priest bows low during this first sentence.

From this point onward, the priest uses the first person plural, speaking to God on behalf of all. This is the point that is especially the prayer of Christ the High Priest to the Father. As He often prayed to His Father in words most of the disciples could not hear, but a few of them (the evangelists) recorded, so the prayer of the priest is to the Father, and we are privileged to know what is being prayed, though we do not hear it. Christ prays like Anna praying in the Temple, which is a kind of precaution, lest by being heard often, it might be learned by bad men who would make a mockery of its holy words, as happened in ancient times. "Now Anna spoke in her heart, and only her lips moved: but her voice was not heard at all" (1 Kgs. 1:13).

That only the priest is speaking also reminds us of Moses, who would often pray alone on the mountaintop, conversing with God on behalf of the people, but the faithful not hearing what he said. That the priest speaks in the first person singular for the Consecration as with all the other sacraments reminds us of his being another Christ: "for this is *my* body . . ."

The chants of the Sanctus are followed by profound silence, the first time in the Mass for silence of this depth—silence from the priest and silence from the faithful. This calls to mind not only the high priest of old going into the Holy of Holies alone, but also that the carrying of the Cross has come to an end, and Christ is now nailed to it.

The silence of the whole congregation—even if there are priests in attendance or if a bishop is attending—humbles us, as it is symbolic of the fact that none of the apostles or disciples raised their voices in defense of Christ at any time during His Passion.

"And He was silent. And He opened not His mouth, but was led like a lamb to the slaughter" (Is. 53:7). He was silent with the mockery and beating at the house of Herod, silent at the scourging, silent in the praetorium under the rods and the thorns, silent on Calvary in response to the blasphemies. His silence teaches louder than words His pardon of injuries; His astounding forgiveness of the persecutions. During the six hours He was on the cross He prayed in silence, breaking it only for the Seven Last Words, treasured by the evangelists as the testament of His heart.

It is at this time that our hearts should be like the holy women of Jerusalem; like St. Veronica, who drew near to comfort Him with her famous cloth. Our cloth must be repentance and our appreciation and gratitude for His Passion.

The silence also harmonizes with the mystery of Transubstantiation, in which the material elements of the bread and wine are changed into the Body and Blood of Christ, without the senses perceiving it or the created mind able to comprehend it; the Real Presence and sacrificial life of the Savior under the sacramental species are concealed beyond all discernment. So the holy silence is quite suited to indicate and to recall the concealment and depth, the incomprehensibility and ineffableness of the wonderful mysteries enacted on the altar. "The Lord is in his holy temple; let all the earth keep silence before him!" (Hab. 2:20).

Dr. Joseph Shaw, in an article in *Latin Mass Magazine* (Summer 2013) has this to say about a silent canon, and indeed the silence of the whole Mass, as opposed to a Dialogue Mass:

> Non-verbal participation was moreover given a spiritual justification: Duffy (Eamon) quotes a Medieval commentator's explanation of the silent Canon, which has a more general application, as being *ne impediatur populus orare* (lest it impede the praying of the people). This tradition found a defender in Pope Pius XII, who strongly rebuked those who criticized forms of liturgical participation in which the Faithful do not follow the liturgy word for word.
>
> Two bad reasons for the twentieth century promotion of the Dialogue Mass were criticized by Pope Pius XII in his great encyclical *Mediator Dei* (1947). The first is the suggestion that the liturgy needs an outward, social aspect if it is to be a truly public act; the second was the decline of the Solemn Mass. Against the first, which had perhaps been encouraged by the febrile atmosphere of the First World War and its aftermath, when the Dialogue Mass was spreading, Pius XII emphasized the intrinsically social nature of the liturgy. Against the second he condemned the tendency to see the Dialogue Mass as a substitute for the Solemn Mass.
>
> In the case of the Low Mass, the silence or near-silence of the church, while the priest and the server alone maintain the sacred

dialogue within the sanctuary, communicates profoundly the mysterious and other-worldly nature of the liturgy, even to those unfamiliar with it. This was noted by the playwright Oscar Wilde:

> When one contemplates all this from the point of view of Art alone one cannot but be grateful that the supreme office of the Church should be the playing of the tragedy, without the shedding of blood, the mystical presentation by means of dialogue and costume and gesture even of the Passion of her Lord, and it is always a source of pleasure and awe to me to remember that the ultimate survival of the Greek Chorus, lost elsewhere to art, is to be found in the servitor answering the priest at Mass.

Blessed John Paul II also emphasized the value of silent participation in the liturgy:

> Yet active participation does not preclude the active passivity of silence, stillness and listening: indeed, it demands it. Worshippers are not passive, for instance, when listening to the homily, or following the prayers of the celebrant, and the chants and music of the liturgy. These are experiences of silence and stillness, but they are in their own way profoundly active. In a culture which neither favours nor fosters meditative quiet, the art of interior listening is learned only with difficulty. Here we see how the liturgy, though it must always be properly inculturated, must also be counter-cultural.

The priest at the altar is the representative and image of the praying and sacrificing Savior. Now, as on the Mount of Olives and on the Cross, Jesus prayed not only in loud tones but also in a low voice and in the silence of His heart to His Father, so also it is proper that the priest should resemble His Divine Model when representing and renewing the Sacrifice of the Cross. "The altar becomes not merely the Cross, but also the crib; for at the moment of Consecration the marvels of Bethlehem as well as those of Golgotha are renewed. While deep silence pervaded all things and the night was in the midst of its course, the Almighty Word of God descended from His royal throne in heaven to the crib of Bethlehem; in like manner, does the King of Glory at the consecration come down upon the altar, amid the most profound silence" (Fr. Gihr).

Is not this sacred stillness a worthy preparation for the approach of God?

> Words are necessary, but as means, not as ends; they are not mere addresses to the throne of grace, they are instruments of what is far higher, of consecration, of sacrifice. They hurry on as if impatient to fulfill their mission. Quickly they go, the whole is quick, for they are all parts of one integral action. Quickly they go, for they are awful words of sacrifice, they are a work too great to delay upon; as when it was said in the beginning, "What thou doest, do quickly." Quickly they pass, for the Lord Jesus goes with them, as he passed along the lake in the days of his flesh, calling first one and then another. Quickly they pass; because as the lightning which shineth from one part of the heaven unto the other, so is the coming of the Son of Man. (Venerable John Henry Newman)

As soon as the priest has invoked the Holy Name, he makes three Signs of the Cross over the gifts. The insight of St. Thomas Aquinas on this and on all the times the Sign is used during the Canon shows how full of symbolism this hidden action of the Canon really is:

> The priest, in celebrating the Mass, makes use of the sign of the cross to signify Christ's Passion which was ended upon the cross. Now, Christ's Passion was accomplished in certain stages. First of all there was Christ's betrayal, which was the work of God, of Judas, and of the Jews; and this is signified by the triple sign of the cross at the words, *these gifts, these presents, these holy unspotted sacrifices.*
>
> Secondly, there was the selling of Christ. Now he was sold to the Priests, to the Scribes, and the Pharisees: and to signify this the threefold sign of the cross is repeated, at the words, *blessed,*

enrolled, ratified. Or again, to signify the price for which He was sold, viz. thirty pence. And a double cross is added at the words *that it may become to us the Body and the Blood*, etc., to signify the person of Judas the seller, and of Christ Who was sold.

Thirdly, there was the foreshadowing of the Passion at the Last Supper. To denote this, in the third place, two crosses are made, one in the consecrating the body, the other in consecrating the blood; each time while saying *He blessed.*

Fourthly, there was Christ's Passion itself. And so in order to represent His five wounds, in the fourth place, there is a fivefold signing of the cross at the words, *a pure Victim, a holy Victim, a spotless Victim, the holy bread of eternal life, and the cup of everlasting salvation.*

Fifthly, the outstretching of Christ's body, and the shedding of the blood, and the fruits of the Passion are signified by the triple signing of the cross at the words, *as many as shall receive the body and blood, may be filled with every blessing*, etc.

Sixthly, Christ's threefold prayer upon the cross is represented; one for His persecutors when He said, *Father, forgive them*; the second for deliverance from death, when He cried, *My God, My God, why hast Thou forsaken Me?*; the third referring to His entrance into glory, when He said, *Father, into Thy hands I commend My spirit*; and in order to denote these there is a triple signing with the cross made at the words, *Thou dost sanctify, quicken, bless.*

Seventhly, the three hours during which He hung upon the cross, that is, from the sixth to the ninth hour, are represented; in signification of which we make once more a triple sign of the cross at the words, *Through Him, and with Him, and in Him.*

Eighthly, the separation of His soul from the body is signified by the two subsequent crosses made over the chalice.

Ninthly, the resurrection on the third day is represented by the three crosses made at the words, *May the peace of the Lord be with you.*

In short, we may say that the consecration of this sacrament, and the acceptance of this sacrifice, and its fruits, proceed from the virtue of the cross of Christ, and therefore wherever mention is made of these, the priest makes use of the Sign of the Cross. (*S.T.* III, q. 83, a. 5.3)

Each time the priest pronounces the name of the Body or Blood of the Savior, he makes the Sign of the Cross over the host and the chalice, to confess that he has before him the same body that was crucified.

The kiss he gives the altar is symbolic of the reconciliation of heaven and earth (*justice and peace have kissed*, as David prophesied [Ps. 84:11]).

From the elevation to the Pater Noster there are five prayers in the Canon, and we can unite ourselves with each of the Five Holy Wounds at each prayer. In the first one we can unite ourselves with Mary, the Mother of Sorrows; the second with the beloved disciples; the third with the penitent tears of St. Magdalen; the fourth with the holy women; in the fifth we beg for mercy like the Good Thief.

In these silent signs are a complete theology of the Holy Mass and what takes place at the Consecration: the one Christ in two forms, the Son of God, lies with His wounds upon the altar of sacrifice; the altar's long, narrow linen cloths are the grave cloths of the sepulcher at the Resurrection.

THE MEMENTO OF THE LIVING

The remembrance or Memento of the Living follows the first blessings of the Canon. After the words "thy servants and handmaids" the letters *N.N.* are in the text of the missal. In the early Church certain persons were named; the deacon came down to the ambo and read the names on a writing tablet called a diptych (meaning two tablets—one for the living and the other for the dead). A relic of the practice may be found in the parish bulletin, where a list of the names of the living who need prayers (the sick and the suffering especially) and a list of the dead recently deceased are published. In missionary countries that are too poor to have bulletins, the names are often read from the pulpit.

If a diocese has an auxiliary bishop, his name is not read in the Canon. Since only the Roman Pontiff can change the Canon, and since the Canon mentions only the ordinary of the diocese (*antistite nostro*), the auxiliary is not named, but his is the first name to be mentioned in the private prayer of the priest in the Memento.

Next, if the intention of the Mass is for the living, that intention is named. After that, the priest is free to pray for whomever he chooses, such as his family, friends, the poor, his enemies, the president, parishioners who are vexed with him, et cetera. He also prays for those present; only those who come to Mass receive its special fruits and choicest blessings. In the case of the sick, or of someone who is in the habit of daily Mass and all of a sudden cannot come, they receive special graces by these prayers. But the Sacrifice is intended to procure for them and those dear to them the redemption of their souls; that they might have hope of salvation and receive final perseverance.

Two adjectives are used to describe the Church in the first words of the Canon—*holy* and *Catholic*—to express the prayer that the grace of God might be given to all people throughout the world (*toto orbe terrarum*). For the Church we petition peace (*pacificare*), or putting it negatively, for defense from every threat of danger (*custodire*) so that the leaven of divine power within her might penetrate every level of society.

We also pray that the Church might be held together by love, like a family bond (*adunare*), and that the Spirit of God might Himself lead and govern her (*regnare*). The Church needs to be held together as a visible society (*una cum famulo tuo*).

Orthodoxi refers to those Catholics who profess the Faith, and the *fidei cultoribus* ("guardians of the Faith") refers to the pope and the bishops. *Circumstantes* refers to those present at the Mass, literally standing around the altar—which indicates the common position of prayer in the early Church at the Mass.

THE COMMUNICANTES

The *Communicantes* is a prayer of comradeship with the saints, even though we recall the great distance between us with the phrase "venerating the memory."

There are two well-balanced groups of twelve names; twelve apostles and twelve martyrs (who were very dear to the Romans when the Canon was being composed); led by the Queen of all saints and all martyrs. She is called the Queen of Martyrs for having stood by the Cross, and while her maternal tears were mingled with the His blood and the sword of sorrow pierced her soul, she offered her Crucified Son for the redemption and salvation of the world. She was nailed to the Cross in spirit with her Son and felt the pain of His wounds in her heart.

In the second list there are six male and six female martyrs, led by St. John the Baptist, since the Lord called him "the greatest born among women" (cf. Mt. 11:11). The twelve martyrs are aligned in hierarchical order; six bishops, five of whom were popes. Then a non-Roman, St. Cyprian, is named; he was a contemporary of St. Cornelius, and St. Cornelius is taken out of chronological order, so he can be side by side with St. Cyprian. Of the next six martyrs, two are priests (SS. Lawrence and Chrysogonus); then follow four laymen.

The *Communicantes* brings to a close the first section of intercessory prayer and is marked by the phrase *per Christum Dominum nostrum*, which appears for the first time. It may seem odd that these are the only intercessory prayers, since there were many more of them in the Sacramentary of St. Gelasius I (on which the Roman Canon is based). But the intentions of the faithful became too earthy—ailing pets and menacing school exams stuck into the Canon—so the practice was stopped by St. Gregory the Great; the intentions became just the intentions of the clergy and the people present at each Mass.

This is the Memento of the Church Triumphant. The priest extends the appeal of clemency to the whole of heaven and commemorates the saints. The sacrifice is offered to God alone; to commemorate the saints is to unite them to our prayer so that their prayers and sacrifices (which derive their value from Christ's) may reinforce our own. An *amen* is said at the end, showing that the three preceding prayers make up the Memento in three stages.

These saints are invoked like Moses calling on the Lord to "remember Abraham, Isaac, and Jacob, thy servants" (Ex. 32:13), and like Azarias in the fiery furnace crying out to the Lord, "Take not away thy mercy from us for the sake of Abraham, thy beloved, and Isaac, thy servant, and Israel, thy holy one" (Dan. 3:35).

So, just as in the Old Law, the names of the twelve tribes of Israel were engraved on onyx stones, and on the rational were twelve stones, and on each stone the name of each of the twelve fathers of Israel, so we see how that prefigured the names of the twelve apostles and twelve martyrs in the Canon of the Mass (cf. Ex. 28:21).

HANC IGITUR

The *Hanc igitur* comes next. The priest extends his two hands horizontally over the chalice and Host, with his right thumb placed over his left thumb in the form of a cross. This action not only harmonizes with the tenor of the text (the oblation, indicating the sacrificial elements in a reverential manner) but has a mystical meaning too. The ritual of laying hands over the oblation is found in both testaments of the Bible, and it is always a symbol of transferring something to others—the guilt of sin or a blessing.

The Levite priest of the Old Covenant spread his hands over the scapegoat. Originally this was done by Aaron (cf. Lev. 16:11-14), and there were actually two goats then: the High Priest would cast lots between the two to decide which would be the scapegoat (reminding us of Christ and Barabbas); that is, one goat would be sacrificed, and the other would escape by being released into the wilderness. The goat to be sacrificed was laden with the sins of the people and sacrificed, its blood taking away the sins; it represents Christ laden with our sins at each Mass, in order to take them away. We are the beneficiaries of this; we are the scapegoats set free.

We should note one more thing about the goat: when a victim was presented in the Temple to be offered in sacrifice, it was set apart forever from all profane use and devoted to the service of God alone. In the same way, the bread and wine were set apart from profane use at the Offertory. And the laying on of hands is done in the name of the Father, "Who hath laid on Him the iniquity of us all" (Is. 53:6).

It is a difficult part of the Mass for the priest sometimes, since he regrets the necessity of having to lay any sin, especially his own, on the Sinless. But at the same time it must be done; there was a price that had to be paid.

This is similar to the terrible holiness of Mary, who was present when Pilate offered the crowd the choice between Barabbas and her Son, and the crowd chose Barabbas and, concerning Our Lord, shouted, "Crucify Him!" The Fathers of the Church have Our Blessed Mother saying the same thing, but in a radically different way from the way the crowd said it.

We are now at the threshold of the Consecration, with the prayer *Quam oblationem* ("which oblation"). For the first time in the Mass there is an explicit mention of the Body and Blood that the offerings are about to become.

It is as if the priest is saying in this prayer, "The general meaning of our offerings are nothing in themselves; give them their value, O

God, by transforming them into Your Son. We have done what we can by bringing our offerings with our poor efforts, but now render them worthwhile. It was accomplished when Your Son took on our humanity; apply this great benefit to us today . . . that it may become for us the Body and Blood . . ."

There are five terms in this prayer that are borrowed from Roman law that should be understood in this sense:

+ *Benedictam*: blessed, set aside for God, a holy victim free from every stain of sin; original or actual, mortal or venial.

+ *Adscriptam*: registered, in the sense that we are begging God to write it down in the Book of Life, but also approved—that is, figured in the victims of the Old Testament, in the Paschal lamb, in Isaac on the mountain, in the lambs of the flocks of Abel.

+ *Ratam*: ratified, as in approved and confirmed by God, such that this is not a sacrifice to pass away like the sacrifices of the Old Covenant, but a sacrifice of bread and wine according to the order of Melchisedech.

+ *Rationabilem*: reasonable, in the sense that even the animal sacrifices of the Old Covenant make sense insofar as they were connected to the Sacrifice of the Cross; and for us St. Paul urges, "Present your bodies in a living sacrifice, holy, pleasing to God, your reasonable service" (Rom. 12:1). Reasonable, in the sense that this is not a sacrifice of beasts that are without reason, as in the Old Law, but of a reasonable Being; the Body, Blood, Soul, and Divinity of Jesus Christ, a sacrifice that will cleanse our conscience from dead works (cf. Heb. 9:14).

+ *Acceptabilemque*: acceptable like the sacrifice of Abel; not like the sacrifice of the Temple, for "sacrifice and oblation thou didst not desire" (Ps. 39:7).

This prayer is a plea for the final hallowing of the earthly gift that it may become "the Body and Blood of Thy most Beloved Son, Our Lord Jesus Christ." *Beloved* here (*dilectissimi*, which signifies a love of choice between two) is a word filled with emotion, in contrast to the legal language that preceded it.

This part of the Canon is also called the Epiclesis (invocation). It is a plea for God to send the Holy Ghost, that He might "make" the gifts into the Body and Blood of the Lord. This is similar to the sacrament of Penance, where the Holy Ghost takes our incomplete contrition and joins it or makes it into the contrition of Christ.

To tell us of the price at which our divine Victim was sold by Judas Iscariot, the priest makes three crosses over the bread and wine for thirty; then, to remember both the buying and selling, the celebrant makes two crosses, one over the bread and one over the wine. It is as though the celebrant is saying that the selling of Christ for thirty pieces of silver was accursed, forbidden, invalid, wicked, and detestable, but dear Lord, bless, approve, ratify, make reasonable and acceptable the Holy Victim we are about to sacrifice. For Judas "loved cursing and it shall come unto him"; "he would not have blessing and it shall be far from him"; Judas's posterity is cut off: "in one generation may his name be blotted out," but Thou, O Lord, approve this sacrifice, by which we may be numbered with the elect; "Judas hanged himself with a halter" and "his bishopric let another take," but Thou, O Lord, ratify this offering of Thy holy Son, the price of our redemption. Judas is damned; "may he go out condemned and may his prayer be turned to sin" (Ps. 108:7), but Thou, O Lord, make this mystic death reasonable and acceptable in Thy sight, that it may become the Body and Blood of Our Lord Jesus Christ.

Again the three crosses are made over the offering, because at the Last Supper Jesus did three things with regard to the bread: He received it, blessed it, and gave it; and the two crosses over the bread and wine remind us of the words in giving the bread: "Take ye and eat; this is my Body"; and His words in giving the wine: "Drink, this is my Blood."

These crosses also recall the three kinds of persons to whom Judas sold his Master: the Scribes, the Pharisees, and the priests.

These five crosses, three over the whole offering, one over the bread, and one over the wine, according to some writers, signify the sufferings of Our Lord in His five senses during His Passion: in seeing, when the Jews veiled His eyes at Herod's palace; in hearing, when they mocked Him; in tasting, when they gave Him vinegar and gall; in smelling, when they brought him to Calvary—a place offensive and stinking from the bodies of victims crucified by the Romans; in His sense of touch, when they nailed His hands and feet to the Cross.

The liturgy begs us at this point to adore our Blessed Lord. The five wounds cry out to us. We do well at this point to recall the hands that were overflowing with healings, benedictions, and mercies; those feet that had become weary from walking in search of the lost sheep on the thorny field of the earth; that Heart which glowed with the love of God and mankind.

THE CONSECRATION

In the Consecration of the Mass, God will answer our prayer. It is His turn to speak, and He does so in the terms used by His Son at the Last Supper to change the bread and wine into His Body and Blood. So far in the Mass, the priest's tone has been one of supplication. Now it changes and becomes one of narration.

The words of Institution are not taken word for word from one evangelist or any particular text of Scripture. They are instead a compilation of the Synoptic Gospels and the Epistles of St. Paul. Some words have been added by tradition (e.g., "his holy and venerable hands").

The form for the consecration of the wine does not complete that for the bread in such a way that the bread would not be consecrated without it. The moment the bread is consecrated, Christ is whole and entire under the species of bread: Body, Blood, Soul, and Divinity. But for the perfection of the sacrifice; for the full sacramental representation of Calvary, both forms (consecration of bread and wine) must be said. If a priest forgets to consecrate the wine, for example, the bread would be truly the Holy Eucharist, but there would be no Sacrifice of the Mass; the Mass would be invalid, in other words. In the laws governing the Sacrifice, we see that if a priest dies before completing the Consecration (this has happened), another priest must finish it. Such is the overwhelming importance of the Mass.

The miracle that takes place at this point of the Mass can be understood in a number of ways. However, the best that has been thought of is the doctrine of Transubstantiation. This means that the whole substance of the bread and the whole substance of the wine are changed into the Body and Blood of Christ. From that moment, Christ is there, whole and entire, not dead, but living; He who is seated at the right hand of the Father, ever making intercession for us. But the accidents, or everything we associate with the bread and wine, remain.

The words of Consecration are *Hoc est enim corpus meum* for the bread, and *Hic est enim calix sanguinis mei*. It is these words that effect the Transubstantiation. Mention of the chalice in the second form is an allusion to the Passion: "Father, let this chalice pass from me" (Mt. 26:39). In the chalice is the blood of the New and eternal Testament (or Covenant). The New Testament is new in time, but eternal in its value and lastingness. This Testament makes our inheritance possible. It is the mystery of faith. The blood of Christ justifies and saves believers, those who cleave to the mystery of faith.

The phrase *shed unto the remission of sins* refers to the blood of Jesus being shed for the remission of our sins, which stood in the way of this justification. *Vobis* ("you") refers to the priest and faithful who participate in the sacrifice. *Multis* ("many") refers to the countless others for whom the blood of Christ was shed.

Christ does not "come down" on the altar. It is our oblation that goes up and is joined to the eternal sacrifice in His offering. There is no new immolation, no new sacrifice again, only the one on Calvary that is made present to us, and at the same time the one eternal liturgy celebrated in heaven by the One Eternal High Priest.

The Mass must not be looked upon as a vehicle for communion. The Mass is especially the gift of all gifts, the offering of the Son to the Father in the Holy Ghost, the essential adoration and glorification of the Holy Trinity. The action on the Cross, that love of the Son for the Father and for sinners is present on the altar. Our action is not only adoration and devotion, but the effort to become Him, to be one with Him in giving the Trinity everything.

Once the Consecration has occurred, notice that the fingers of the priest that touched the Holy Eucharist are kept together. I love this rubric. It started in the eleventh century, when the monks of Cluny would keep them together from the Lavabo so that the fingers would not have any profane contact from the washing to the time they touched the Host. Now the canonical digits are held together from the moment of the consecration of the bread to the ablutions at the end of Mass.

In the Transfiguration of Our Lord, "A bright cloud covered them with its shadow" (Mt. 17:5). In the three poor disciples who were present we see men of no exceptional merit of their own, who enter into the cloud, the loftiest image of divine power. They have no direct access to the Father, for they are close to Jesus and are His friends. Their dullness, their incomprehension, does not matter; their hearts are given totally to Jesus, and that is enough. They were told by the Father to listen to Jesus, but He has nothing to say to them for the moment other than to keep quiet. Solitude in the company of Jesus has introduced them into a great silence. From that day on, they carry in their hearts this vision that will stay with them to the end of their days: *Vidimus gloriam eius,* "and we saw His glory" (Jn. 1:14). But already the cloud has passed, "Arise, do not be afraid" (cf. Mt. 17:7). They are astonished: Jesus is alone; there is silence; life continues.

Jesus prays apart and seems not to communicate with those around Him. It is at the heart of this deeper solitude that a more intimate communion is revealed: a communion coming from God, manifested in different ways, but always the sign and reality in us of the communion among the Divine Persons.

Such is our ideal: to enter into the great Paschal Mystery with our good Lord, especially at the time of the Consecration, and to receive from the Father the revelation that His Son has been given to us and is ours to welcome. We have *no other call here below as great as this one*; to bear this mystery, in silence, in our hearts.

What is the one thing that God will not spurn? We read in the Fiftieth Psalm, "A sacrifice to God is an afflicted spirit: a contrite and humbled heart, O God, thou wilt not despise." There is above all one Heart of which this is true, the Sacred Heart of Jesus. His Heart is infinitely contrite (broken, literally, from the Latin *contritus*) because He is God, infinitely humble in perfect obedience to the Father, and infinitely afflicted since He was bearing the sins of the world. So we may say that this sacrifice is so powerful that God is forced, if you will, to look upon it, accept it, and grant all that His Son asks as a result of it.

The Father cannot refuse this sacrifice. He will not refuse a contrite heart. Because of this, the words "the new and eternal testament" are used in the consecration of the wine. The acceptance of the Father of the sacrifice of His Son is eternal. All this takes place in silence, since silence is best suited to what is eternal.

When the priest lifts his eyes to the crucifix and then bows his head, he is imitating Christ at the Last Supper, who looked to His Father for blessing, then bowed His head in thanksgiving.

THE MAJOR ELEVATION

Once the bread is consecrated, it is lifted in a precise manner. The Elevation, as it is called (sometimes it is called the Major Elevation), was not used until the thirteenth century, when it was instituted as a reaction against the heresy of denying that the bread when consecrated was Christ. Berengarius was a French priest who taught that Transubstantiation was effected only when both forms had been pronounced—the bread supposedly not consecrated until the wine was. The Elevation is a superb development of the liturgy. Originally only the Host was elevated, but by the fourteenth century, the practice of elevating the chalice was introduced. These practices were received with joy by the faithful.

To adore Christ at the Elevation of the Host, we can imagine Him bowing His head to extend the kiss of peace, His arms open to embrace, His hands pierced to give us the bounty of His gifts, His feet nailed in order to stay with us. We are kneeling to make reparation for the crowd at His Crucifixion that made mock genuflections to him, and we bow our heads slowly in respect of His.

An ancient custom was to sound a trumpet at the execution of the condemned criminal, in order to drown out the cries of the next of kin or the exaltation of his enemies. Many cultures did this, and the practice was known in Judea. The Romans did not use it, since they relied more on terror as an instrument of the state, wanting the wailing of relatives to be heard. While there is no mention of a trumpet in Sacred Scripture, tradition has it that it was sounded at the death of Christ. We ring bells at the Consecration in memory of that moment.

The Elevation may be said as well to be a fulfillment of the ancient prophecy, "For in the hand of the Lord there is a cup of strong wine full of mixture" (Ps. 75:8). Indeed the One truly holding the chalice in the heavenly liturgy is Christ. The priest is only standing in for Him as an *alter Christus* ("another Christ").

Mystically, the chalice is elevated in order to catch the balm of the sacrifice of Our Lord's life: the blood from Gethsemane, the thorns, the scourging, the Cross, and the lance. It also holds in a sense the tears Christ shed in the crib, at the tomb of Lazarus, when He beheld Jerusalem, and over each one of us. His whole life may be worshipped in the Mass. These sentiments may be found in the private revelation of different saints.

At least one sentiment or act of faith should be made at every Elevation, and it is to say with St. Thomas the Apostle, "My Lord and my God."

Once the Consecration is completed, the priest keeps the canonical digits (thumb and forefinger) held tightly together until the ablutions. This is obviously a mark of great respect; that once something has touched God, it cannot touch anything else that is not God, until it goes through a rite of purification. But there is also a symbolic reason for keeping the fingers together: that our hearts should be joined to Him Who is now on the altar in a more profound way than before and that we should struggle mightily to give our hearts to Him at this level until the end of Mass, when the ablutions are complete and we prepare to leave.

Unde Et Memores

The prayer that immediately follows the Elevation is called the *Unde et memores* and is the answer to Christ's command "Do this in memory of me." Technicians of liturgy call this the *anamnesis*, a Greek word meaning "remembrance."

"We Thy servants" refers first to the priesthood as a whole and then to all the people who are mindful of the mystery of redemption. It's interesting that in other forms of the *Vetus Ordo* (this is how Pope Benedict XVI refers to the Rite of St. Gregory, as the "Old Order," which includes such as the Lyonnaise, Dominican, Carthusian,

Carmelite, and Sarum rites), we see the priest stretching his arms
out in the form of a cross at this point.

The phrase also refers to the fact that in the early Church, the
Mass was concelebrated in some way that is lost to us. The Church
in her wisdom did away with the practice of concelebration, and
the modern practice in the Ordinary Form of the Roman Rite was
largely assembled by a committee from various practices such as
may be found in the Eastern rites. There is no way of knowing how
the ancient Roman practice was done.

The phrase "we Thy servants" should also strike us in that the
Lord, by an unmerited favor, elevates His priests and faithful to the
rank of good friends or messmates and honors us with a very intimate,
confidential discourse; but we must always remember at the same
time that we are servants. So it is that the priests are exalted above
the laity in dignity of office but obliged to serve the flocks that have
been entrusted to them, trying to imitate the Master, "Who came
not to be ministered unto but to minister, and to give His life as a
redemption for many" (Mt. 20:28).

And mindful of His Passion, we do what He did: we offer to God
gifts and presents, which are Christ Himself with His merits and
His glory; a pure Host, a Host that sanctifies, a spotless, food-giving,
saving Host. This prayer expresses the very essence of the Mass:
Memorial (*unde et memores*), sacrifice (*hostiam*) and Eucharistic
banquet (*panem sanctam*).

Five crosses are made over the consecrated Host after the
Consecration. The first three are made over the Host and Chalice
together, for now the Body and Blood are united in Christ, Who
can die no more; the last two are made over the Host and Chalice
separately, signifying the separation of His Body and Blood at His
death on Calvary.

Supra Quae Propitio

"For although the consecrated offering is always pleasing to God both in itself and because of Christ who principally offers it, yet in respect of the minister or the people present who offer with him, it may not be pleasing. Therefore we pray that God may look kindly upon this offering, inasmuch as it is offered by us" (St. Robert Bellarmine).

The Consecration done, we now ask that it may be accepted in the prayer *supra quae propitio*. The meaning of the prayer may be seen in the last words of it: "Vouchsafe to accept . . . this holy sacrifice, this spotless host as you accepted the sacrifices of the Old Testament, figures of the true sacrifice which was to be offered in the New."

For a man—even a whole congregation—to offer God gifts, no matter how holy, is the utmost daring. For this reason the oblation is expressed in another manner, to show that it is nothing less than grace to expect the acceptance of these gifts. All we can do is offer (*offerimus*); it is up to God to cast a favorable glance upon the offering (*respicere*) and consider it with approval (*accepta habere*).

The plea that God accepts this sacrifice does not refer to that of His Son, which has just been made, but to our sacrifices, that they would not be offered by unworthy hands (cf. Amos 5:21-23). We can never be sufficiently worthy of God, so we unite ourselves to those sacrifices that were offered worthily:

✙ Innocent Abel offered to God an acceptable sacrifice; the best of his flock (Gen. 4:4), but the blood of Christ "speaketh better than Abel" (Heb. 12:24).

✙ The sacrifice of Abraham, a hero of obedience to God, who was willing to immolate his son by an act of obedience, recalls the heavenly Father immolating His only Son, who, like Isaac, let Himself be bound and stretched out on the wood, "obedient unto death, the death of the Cross" (Phil. 2:8).

✣ Melchisedech, the King of Salem, offered bread and wine (Gen. 14:18), foreshadowing Christ the King, who applied to Himself (cf. Mt. 22:44) the verse of Psalm 109: "Thou art a priest forever after the order of Melchisedech" (cf. also Heb. 7:17). Melchisedech had no father or mother or children as he appears in Genesis, also making him truly a figure Our Lord.

✣ The sacrifice of Christ was accepted from the moment of its offering; we ask that it may be accepted in our favor and for our benefit—for that reason it must be offered with "clean hands"— that is, with wills ready to obey God.

A gift is fully accepted not just when it has drawn a favorable glance, but when it is in the recipient's possession. This final phase of human gift-giving is transferred to our sacrificial gift and to God.

SUPPLICES TE ROGAMUS

Supplices te rogamus is the next prayer to be offered. At the beginning of this prayer the priest joins his hands before his breast and laying the points of his fingers on the altar bows down profoundly. At the words "the partaking of this altar," he kisses the altar, near the Host. Then joining his hands at the word "Body," he makes the Sign of the Cross over the Host, at "Blood," over the chalice, and while saying, "enriched with every heavenly blessing and grace," he makes the Sign of the Cross on himself, then joins his hands again at "through Christ Our Lord. Amen."

To understand this prayer and the gestures that go with it, we should look at what happened after the Last Supper.

A hymn being said they went out unto Mt. Olivet . . . into a country place, which is called Gethsemane . . . and taking with him Peter and the two sons of Zebedee, he began to be sorrowful and to be sad. And going a little further he fell upon his face praying. Again the second time he went and prayed, and leaving them the third time he prayed, saying the self-same words. . . . Then he came to his disciples and said . . . rise, let us go: behold he is at hand who will betray me. And as he spoke behold Judas, one of the twelve, came . . . and forthwith coming to Jesus he said, Hail, Rabbi, and he kissed him. (cf. Mt. 26)

To recall the prostration of Our Lord in the garden, the priest bows. To tell of the hands of Our Lord spread out on the ground, the celebrant spreads his hands on the altar. To bring into our minds the three times Our Lord prostrated himself, the celebrant makes three crosses, one over the Host, one over the chalice, and the third over himself. He places his hands on the altar as though he would embrace it, telling of the embrace of Judas, who betrayed the Savior; the celebrant kisses the altar, for the altar signifies Christ, and the kiss recalls the betraying of Our Lord with a kiss.

By the Consecration, the Church on earth is joined to Christ offering Himself in heaven. There is no break in continuity; it is the same offering. The connection is established at this moment. The presence of Christ on our altar is effected not by His coming down, but by the mystery of the carrying up of our offerings, assumed in Him.

This is the altar that St. John saw in the Apocalypse, upon which the Lamb appeared as immolated (Apoc. 5:6), and the angel of sacrifice whom we see in the Old Testament as carrying the prayers and good actions of men, bears our sacrifice, whence it will be returned to us in graces and blessings.

As to who the angel is that takes the sacrifice, there are differing opinions. Several saints think it is the unnamed angel in the Apocalypse: "And another angel came and stood before the altar, having a golden censer, and there was given him much incense that he should offer the prayers of all the saints upon the golden altar, which is before the throne of God" (Apoc. 8:3). But Dom Gueranger thinks that this work is wholly beyond the power of any created being, even an angel, and that Christ is the Angel of Great Counsel.

THE MEMENTO OF THE DEAD

The Memento of the Dead is the next prayer in the Canon, and originally this memento followed the Memento of the Living: the word *etiam* ("also") connected these two prayers.

The letters *N.N.* which appear in the missal are a reference to the diptychs (cf. the section on the Memento of the Living). If the intention of the Mass is being offered for the repose of someone's soul, or for the Poor Souls, then they are first to be mentioned.

"Nor can it be denied that the souls of the dead are helped by the piety of the living, when for them the sacrifice of the Mediator is offered, or when offerings are made in the church" (St. Augustine, *On the Sacrifice of the Mass*).

"Those who have gone before us with the sign of faith" refers to the baptized, and the "sleep of peace" to those who died in the communion of the Church. Should the soul or souls for whom prayers are offered be in heaven or hell—where these prayers would avail them nothing—then the merits of those prayers fall into the general treasury of the Church and are dispensed to the Church Militant and Suffering by way of indulgences. We remember the just who died in His grace. "And the graves were opened: and many of the bodies of the saints that had slept arose" (Mt. 27:52).

It is interesting that the word *death* was not used in the early Church, but rather a particular kind of sleep. We would do well to think of these souls as resting; waiting for the sound of the archangel's trumpet to call them from the grave. So it is that our burial grounds became known as cemeteries. The root of that word is from the Greek and is similar to dormitories or sleeping places. The departed were deposed in a cemetery, like a precious treasure locked away for later. The ancient Teutonic word for graveyard is *Gottes-acker*—that is, "God's field," for the dead are like the seed sown, from which will spring the great harvest on the Day of Judgment, and the gravestone is like a label placed by the gardener to tell of the seed planted there. This notion of likening death to sleep runs all through the Scriptures.

As the celebrant begins to recite this prayer, he moves his hands slowly before this face, so that they will join at the words "the sleep of peace." This movement is to tell of the slow, weak acts of the soul about to leave the body, and the resting hands joined together tell of the motionless body after death. The priest keeps his eyes on the Blessed Sacrament while he prays for the departed, in order that he might recommend them in a special manner to the favor and mercy of God.

As our Sacrifice is carried by the hands of angels from the earthly to the heavenly altar and united with the homage of the blessed and thus presented before the throne of God, it becomes in a most sublime sense a fountain of living waters that descends in a strong stream (Cant. 4:15) upon the earth and into the flaming abyss of purgatory, to refresh and revive the suffering children of the Church.

It may seem odd in the prayer to implore a "place of refreshment, of light and of peace" for the souls in purgatory, but keep in mind that there is a peace and rest even in purgatory, inasmuch as the poor souls have been removed from the discord and turmoil of this sinful world, but we wish them in this prayer the fullness of peace that will be found only in heaven. Fr. Gihr puts it this way: "When the just soul has reached purgatory, she sees before her but two objects—the excess of suffering and the excess of her joy. The greatest bitterness there is mixed with the most serene peace. These souls are full of pure and strong love of God, full of patient contentment, full of touching resignation to God's holy decrees. In a manner inexplicable to us, they are at one and the same time filled with a holy suffering and a holy joy. Suffering is not unhappiness" (cf. also *The Treatise on Purgatory*, by St. Catherine of Genoa).

NOBIS QUOQUE PECCATORIBUS

After we have prayed for the dead, we pray the *Nobis quoque peccatoribus*; for those whose sins still keep them back from their abode of blessedness; the sinners of this world who are gathered before the altar.

Similar to the Memento of the Living, where the saints in heaven are associated with the offering of the sacrifice with the faithful on earth, so the names mentioned here form a complement to the former list. As in the Memento of the Living the name of Mary was followed by a diptych—twelve apostles and twelve martyrs—here the name of St. John the Baptist is followed by a further diptych—seven men and seven women—ending with St. Matthias (last to be added to the College of Apostles), and St. Barnabas, companion to St. Paul, the first local bishop. These saints were held in particular veneration at the time of Pope Symmachus, when the prayer was written. Notice that there are no virgins or confessors in this list; they were not yet recognized as saints in the early Church; only martyrs received that recognition.

"In the commemoration of the saints before the body of Christ is consecrated, their prayers were requested; now that the body of Christ has been consecrated, the company of the saints is sought. For before the body of Christ, which is the Church universal, has been consecrated, that is, before the Kingdom comes, we who are on pilgrimage require prayers. But when the body of Christ is once consecrated, that is, when the Kingdom has come, we shall enjoy the company of the saints in our homeland" (Durandus).

At the *Nobis quoque*, the priest raises his voice—the only time he does so in the Canon. In the early Church, with very small congregations, this was unnecessary. By the time of Charlemagne it was a signal to warn the assistant ministers that it was time to go and prepare the vessels for Holy Communion.

"He says, *And to us sinners*, who intercede for others, when we ourselves have greater need of others' prayers. Therefore the priest at this moment raises his voice a little and strikes his breast. The striking denotes the work of satisfying for sin, since a blow brings pain. The audible speech denotes the act of confession" (St. Albert). The celebrant strikes his breast once, that our humility might be as becoming as the prayer of the publican who struck his breast, and also to signify that Christ died once for us sinners.

This is the prayer of the Good Thief, who openly acknowledged his sins: "We receive the due reward of our deeds" (Lk. 23:41). It also recalls those who returned from the Crucifixion, "lamenting and striking their breasts" (Lk. 23:48).

At the end of the list of these glorious saints named in the prayer, the priest closes his hands and says, "Through Christ Our Lord. Amen." For not on Apostles, or on the Virgin, or on the saints, or on any creature do we depend for our salvation, but on Christ alone, Who is our God. Through Him alone salvation comes, "nor is there any other name under heaven given to men whereby we must be saved" (Acts 4:12).

So with the conclusion of this last prayer, the priest bows his head, as the dying Redeemer bowed His, when all was finished.

Per Quem Haec Omnia

"Through Whom all of these" was originally a blessing of the unconsecrated offerings that were destined for the distribution to the poor and other uses, and also the fruits of the earth, the firstfruits. These were also used for a particular meal that followed the Mass known as the Agape or brotherly meal (dropped rather early in the worship of the Church, because of misuse). This is a literal reason why we see the crosses of blessing in this little prayer. We see here a remembrance of the benefits of creation side by side with the greatest benefit of all, which is Christ, who has just been made present for us sacramentally. But in the Middle Ages the Church began to see a deeper theology in the prayer, which shows why she was reluctant to dismiss the prayer even though the Agape Feast had long since ceased.

So instead of a meal following, it was here that at certain times and on special feasts there were blessings of various objects such as water, milk, honey, bread, fruit, and grapes. These blessings were in time transferred to the Roman Ritual as their number began to grow. But one of the original blessings has been kept in the Mass, and that is done on Holy Thursday when the holy oils to be used throughout the year are blessed at the Chrism Mass by the bishop. How appropriate that after the prayer "for us sinners" (*nobis quoque peccatoribus*), which implores for sinful man from the Divine Mercy a share in the beatitude of the saints, that oil should be blessed, whose sacramental power and grace fortifies the soul for the combat of death and tends to remove all the remains of sin—that is, the last obstacle to admittance into eternal glory. This places before us the truth that every blessing, grace, and consecration done by any bishop or priest proceeds from the Sacrifice of the Mass.

"Through whom, O Lord, thou dost always create"—that is, the Father created and always creates through the Son, making creatures from nothing but His Word; "thou dost sanctify"— that is, dedicating and consecrating all things at their creation to God's honor and glory; "thou dost vivify"—that is, infusing life into beings having life, as vegetables, animals, men, and angels, so that they reflect in an imperfect manner the life infinite in God; "thou dost bless"—that is, showering graces on men, so that they are capable of knowing, loving, and serving Him.

On a different level we see that *creating* refers to the bread and wine created by God; *sanctifying* refers to their being brought to the altar to be made holy; *vivifying* refers to their being the means by which the Body and Blood bring us everlasting life.

"These words bring the Canon to a most fitting end, since they briefly enumerate all God's blessings in this sacrament, beginning with the first production of the matter with which it is confected. It is first of all *created*, when the bread is created. It is *sanctified* when it is dedicated at the Offertory as that from which the sacrament will come. It is *quickened* when the mystery of life is wrought, and by the Consecration it is changed into the true Body of the Lord, who is our life. It is *blessed* when it obtains the effect for which all blessings are given—that is, when it unites the members with the Head by its sacramental power. It is *given* when we receive it so that we may draw life therefrom" (St. Robert Bellarmine).

Per Ipsum

Next comes the prayer called the *Per ipsum*. This clause refers to the whole of the Canon and forms a conclusion.

"The pall is removed from the chalice to denote that when Christ gave up the ghost, the veil of the temple was torn from top to bottom, and those things which had before been concealed were made known to us" (Durandus).

The priest makes several Signs of the Cross over the chalice, only this time he does not use just his hand but holds the Host above the chalice for the first three Signs and says, "Through Him, with Him, and in Him," and then mention is made of the Father and the Holy Ghost, making two more Signs, but between the chalice and the priest. Then he raises slightly the Host and chalice together in what is sometimes called the Minor Elevation. The Minor Elevation is the more ancient elevation, predating the Major Elevation by almost a millennium.

The first three Signs are made over the chalice because the Flesh and Blood of the Savior are contained therein, and the last two are made outside of the chalice when mention is made of the Father and the Holy Ghost, signifying that the highest honor given to God is through and with Christ.

The doxology that ends the Canon is a perfect summary of the doctrine of Christ. First, it is through Christ that we go to the Father; Christ is the only Mediator. Second, we go with Christ, for He does not go alone to the Father; He does not pray alone; the whole Mystical Body goes with him in fulfillment of His Ascension. And third, we are in Christ, for He is the vine and we are the branches—that is, by grace there is one and the same life in Him and in us. It is by this complete offering of humanity redeemed in Christ that all honor and glory is given to the Father, in the unity of the Holy Ghost.

The priest then raises his voice by singing *per omnia secula seculorum*, so that the faithful may respond with an *amen* to show their agreement. In the early church (around A.D. 150), this was shouted by the faithful. With this doxology, the silence of the Canon is ended.

To understand why the silence of the Canon ends here, we should see the *Nobis quoque* and the *Per ipsum* as symbolic of the death of the Savior, which is a rich medieval interpretation of the prayer.

According to this interpretation, the three crosses signify the sufferings of body and mind and the compassion of the soul of Christ. Of the first the prophet says, "O all ye that pass by the way attend and see if there be any sorrow like to my sorrow" (Lam. 1:12); of the second the Lord said, "My soul is sorrowful even unto death" (Mk. 14:34); of the third He said, "Father, forgive them, for they know not what they do" (Lk. 23:34). Because only the human nature of Christ suffered (God's nature cannot suffer), two crosses in reference to the Father and the Holy Ghost are made apart from the chalice (the chalice of suffering).

Two Signs are made outside of the chalice, and this recalls the separation of Christ's soul from His body, which occurred at His death; His body is seen as the Host, His soul by the blood, and both of these are encased in the chalice, if you will, as in the tomb.

The server rings the bells as a symbol of the convulsion of nature at the supreme hour of the death of the Son of God, at which occurred an earthquake and a darkening of the sun. It was as if the sun was ashamed to shine at the death of its Creator, and the earth shuddered when the last drop of the Precious Blood fell upon it.

The priest raises his voice after this (at *praeceptis*), recalling that terrible moment recorded in the Gospels when Our Lord cried out with a loud voice, "It is consummated" (Jn. 1:30) and then, "Father into thy hands I commend my spirit, and saying this He gave up the ghost" (Lk. 23:46).

"And because a great stone was rolled at the door of the tomb, the deacon covers the chalice once more with the pall" (St. Peter Damien).

THE PRAYER OF THE INSOLVENT DEBTOR

The Pater Noster

THE CANON HAS JUST FINISHED; the Minor Elevation is the last breath of the Savior. What was the little band of His faithful doing at that time? The Bible does not say. But surely they were praying for forgiveness, as that was His last dying wish—Father, forgive them.

Once the Crucifixion is ended with the *Consummatum est*, and the Canon is ended with the "forever and ever" in a clear tone meant to be heard by the faithful, the deacon and the subdeacon come up to the altar. The end of the Canon said aloud signifies the voice of the Centurion, who saw that Christ was truly the Son of God and announced it. The deacon and the subdeacon tell us of Joseph of

Arimathea and Nicodemus the Pharisee, who went up Mount Calvary to take down the body of Christ from the Cross.

Here we remember that the Body and Blood of the Lord were raised twice off the altar during the Mass and then placed back upon it. This is because He was taken twice: the first time he was taken by the soldiers and thrown upon the Cross to be crucified, signified by the Major Elevation; the second is here at the Minor Elevation, when Joseph and Nicodemus take Him down and place Him in the sepulcher; thus, the deacon covers the chalice with the pall. Then the two sacred ministers walk away from the altar, as did Joseph and Nicodemus (and all the apostles) walk away from the sepulcher.

The Mass is not a prayer to Christ or to the Holy Ghost; it is an offering of Christ through and with the Holy Ghost to the Father, and when we worship God in the Mass, we try to make this offering our own.

In the *Per ipsum*, we experienced a glorious praise of God through Christ, a turn of thought that was lost in most of the Oriental liturgies in consequence of the Arian turmoil. At this moment the word of St. Malachy is fulfilled: "The Name of the Lord is great among the peoples" (Mal. 1:11). Christ here is not a lone petitioner as in His earthly pilgrimage when He spent quiet nights praying alone on the mountaintop; now His redeemed are with Him.

The five Signs of the Cross made at this point in the Mass may be understood as follows: the first signifies the eternity of the Son with the Father; the second, the equality of the Son with the Father; the third, the essential unity of the Son with the Father; the fourth, the Son having the same mode of existence as the Father; and the fifth, the unity of the Holy Ghost with the Father and the Son.

One last thing is done before we are ready for the Pater Noster, and it is to pray a small preface. This preface is the priest calling the faithful to mind that the Pater is prayed by Christ's command. We dare to say it because Christ taught it. No one knows who wrote that little prayer; its origins are lost in the silence of apostolic times. In pagan worship, the gods were dreaded masters, so daring to pray to them was like approaching a Mafia Don for some favor. And in the Old Testament the faithful did not even mention the name of God or approach Him; they did not go to make a visit to Him as we do the Blessed Sacrament. When the God of Abraham, Isaac, and Jacob was around, there were earthquakes, plagues, and storms. We had to be commanded to approach God by God Himself.

The prayer *Praeceptis salutaribus* together with the next paragraph *Pater noster*, and followed by *Et ne nos* are three paragraphs that recall the three days and nights when Our Lord's body was in the grave.

Up to St. Gregory's time, the Pater Noster came after the Fraction—the breaking of the Host—just before Communion. St. Gregory adopted the Eastern practice of placing it just before Communion, thus connecting the sacrificial prayer and Communion, and giving a chance for the fulfillment of our daily bread.

The Pater is a prayer of an insolvent debtor. All of us are that debtor.

We know that "if thou bring thy gift to the altar, and there shalt remember that thy brother hath anything against thee; leave there thy gift before the altar and go first to be reconciled to thy brother" (Mt. 5:23-24). We are rarely if ever fully reconciled and can be scrupulous about this. When will we be sufficiently reconciled? When we can pray, "Forgive us our trespasses as we forgive those who trespass against us" honestly, or from our hearts and not just saying the words, then we have the indication we need for sufficient reconciliation for Communion.

There are seven requests in the Pater, and they correspond to the Seven Last Words that were prayed on the Cross. The requests are: "Hallowed be thy name," "Thy kingdom come," "Thy will be done," "Give us this day our daily bread," "Forgive us our trespasses," "Lead us not into temptation," and "Deliver us from evil." There are seven beatitudes in heaven represented by these petitions but seven deadly sins in us; these are to be destroyed by the seven graces given in the Lord's Prayer.

The Pater ends with the phrase "but deliver us from evil" and is followed by a short doxology. The doxology "For thine is the kingdom and the power and the glory forever" comes from the *Didache,* a manuscript used by second-century bishops and priests for the instruction of catechumens. It was so good that many copies of the New Testament included it as part of the Bible (the canon of books that should be included in the New Testament had not yet been resolved at that time). But the version of the Pater used in the Mass comes from the Gospel according to St. Matthew and not the *Didache,* and so we do not use the doxology of St. Irenaeus (though it is a beautiful prayer).

During the *Praeceptis*, the priest is required to look at the small cross on the bottom of the chalice. During the Pater, the priest is required to look at the Host. This may seem odd, to look at the Son while addressing the Father, but it is to be understood in the context of John 14:8-9, when St. Philip asked of Christ, "Lord, shew us the Father, and it is enough for us." Christ responded by saying, "Have I been so long a time with you and have you not known me? Philip, he that seeth me seeth the Father also."

Going back for a moment to the words "And forgive us our trespasses": the deacon and the subdeacon make a genuflection and go to the altar, where the subdeacon gives the paten to the deacon during the High Mass. The paten is always hidden at a Low Mass under the corporal and purificator and at a High Mass by the humeral veil on the shoulders of the subdeacon. That hiding of the paten signifies the Divinity of Christ being hidden during His Passion. When the paten is held in front of the eyes of the subdeacon, it first signifies the blindness of the Jews, who would not see Christ as the Messiah. It also signifies the blindness of the pagans who would not see Him as God, and lastly it signifies the Catholics who would not see Him as King.

For those of us attending the Mass in faith, we see in this action our blindness to the mysteries of the Crucifixion hidden in the sacrifices of the Old Law and, for some (including some priests), their blindness to the continuation of the Crucifixion in the Sacrifice of the Mass.

But the subdeacon comes up at the words "And forgive us our trespasses," signifying that the forgiveness obtained for us by the sacrifice of Christ is what takes away our blindness and puts into our souls the gift of faith instead, sight coming with the faith.

The Pater is placed in the Mass before the act of Holy Communion. St. Augustine explains this by saying, "If perchance, in consequence of human frailty, our thought seized on something indecent, if our tongue spoke something unjust, if our eye was turned to something unseemly, if our ear listened complacently to something unnecessary, it is blotted out by the Lord's Prayer in the passage: Forgive us our trespasses, so that we may approach in peace and so we many not eat or drink what we receive unto judgment."

The Pater is said by the priest, since it is still in that portion of the Mass that represents the Passion, during which the Son prayed primarily in a hidden way to His Father. The termination of the Passion is the Resurrection, which is symbolized by the commingling of the Body and the Blood.

At a Low Mass the celebrant takes the paten, hidden under the corporal, and the purificator, lying on the altar covering the paten, and after quickly wiping it to make sure there is nothing but the gold to contact the Host, he holds it upright in his right hand, resting it on its edge at the right of the corporal. This is done by the deacon in the Solemn High Mass.

At the words "benignly grant peace in our days," he crosses himself with the paten; since only the Cross will bring peace. Then carefully sliding it under the Host he says, "helped with the aid of thy mercy." That Christ would deign to be so humbled as to be handled even in such a reverent way is mercy itself.

Libera Nos

The silence that follows the Pater is an echo of the silence of the tomb, when Our Lord's soul went down to the souls of the just who were awaiting His coming, to announce the nearness of their hour of deliverance (when He would be resurrected). The *Libera nos* is the lively expression of their sighs. At this part of the Sacrifice, Our Lord goes to console those who sigh in the hope of heaven.

"And yet Christ was not silent, for he who according to the flesh rested in the tomb, in spirit descended into hell, that he might come upon the strong armed man, and in his greater strength overcome him. For this reason, the Roman Church recites this prayer aloud on Good Friday" (Durandus).

When the priest takes the paten after wiping it, he says the *Libera nos* (called technically the Embolism, from the Greek meaning "insertion"), which requests the same things as in the Lord's Prayer. It is said in silence, which reflects the silence of the Lord in the tomb during those three days in Jerusalem after His death, when no preaching was heard.

We ask in this prayer to be delivered from all evils, "past, present, and future." Three apostles (Peter, Paul, and Andrew) are mentioned because of the three days and nights the Savior was in the tomb, but also because they represent the three states of the faithful: St. Peter was married when he was called, St. Andrew was a widower, and St. Paul was a virgin.

St. Mary is mentioned first, of course, being the Mother of God, and in the High Mass the deacon and the subdeacon coming up to the altar tell us of the holy women who, buying spices and sweet-smelling incense, came to the grave that they might anoint the body of Our Lord.

While the prayer is being said, the paten is brought forth by the deacon and the subdeacon in the High Mass.

The deacon and the subdeacon represent the holy women who with their hearts broadened by charity brought spices for ministering at the tomb. The priest accepts the paten, that is, Christ receives the heart made wide by charity. And since it was the Crucified whom they sought with such keen desire, the priest makes the sign of the cross with the paten upon himself; then he kisses it, to show that Christ forthwith fulfilled the women's desire, coming to meet them and saying: All hail. (St. Peter Damien)

The Fraction

The Fraction (as we now call it) takes place right after the prayer *Libera nos.*

Before the Host is broken, the pall is removed, and the mouth of the chalice is like the door to the rent tomb; the pall is like the stone rolled to the door; the deacon moving the pall to the side is like the angel rolling the stone from the door of the tomb at the Resurrection. The Host laid on the paten recalls the body of Christ laid on the stone slab in the grave after the custom of the Jews.

The Host is taken from the altar and broken, for in the original tabernacle of Moses the Loaves of Proposition were taken from the altar and broken before being eaten. At the words, "Through the same Christ our Lord thy Son," the priest breaks the Host from top to bottom (there is already a thin line creased in the altar bread before Mass to facilitate the Fraction) over the mouth of the chalice, so that if some of the particles fall, they will be received into the chalice. Laying the half in his right hand on the paten, he takes the part in his left hand, breaks a small piece off the bottom, and lays the rest on the paten with the other portion. At the words "in the unity of the Holy Ghost" he holds the little piece in his right hand over the chalice.

The Host is thus broken into three pieces. Similar to the Holy Trinity, it is separated into three, but remains one Lord, Who is divided only in appearance. Another way to see the Host in three parts may be in the three states of the sacred Body of Christ, first living among men, and then laid dead in the tomb, now reigning in glory in heaven. It is also an image of the Church Triumphant, Militant, and Suffering—three yet one Church.

We see in the Fraction the fulfillment of what St. Paul spoke of to the Corinthians: "For we, being many, are one bread, one body: all that partake of one bread" (1 Cor. 10:17). So (somewhat ironically) the Fraction is a sign of unity. The Host is broken in order to distribute or share—Christ giving Himself to put us back together.

The Fraction represents that time when Our Lord died and a soldier opened His right side, from which flowed water and blood. Our Lord is the new Adam. As the first Adam had a rib taken from his side, from which Eve was made, so the Church is the new Spouse whom Our Lord has chosen. We see clearly the symbolism in the particle taken from the Host and placed in the chalice.

After breaking the Host the priest makes three Signs of the Cross over the chalice, in memory of the Lord's three days in the tomb.

In each of these crosses, made in the form of a Greek cross (the horizontal and vertical being of equal length), the Host is moved over the chalice as if in four corners. This represents the peace of Christ reaching out to the four corners of the earth, even to men who are the most distant from Him; physically from the Real Presence and spiritually by sin.

St. Thomas Aquinas sees the Fraction in the following light: "The breaking of the host denotes three things: first, the rending of Christ's body, which took place in the Passion; secondly, the distinction of His Mystical Body according to its various states; and thirdly, the distribution of the graces which flow from Christ's Passion. The chalice represents to us the sepulcher, and the pall the stone which sealed its mouth, the corporal is the figure of the winding-sheet, and the host, which we see, is no longer bread, but the flesh fastened to the cross."

THE COMMINGLING

The mingling of the particle of the Host with the Blood reminds us of the Resurrection, when Our Lord's blood was reunited with His body, so to speak; His blood flowing once again through His veins.

Scholars refer to the commingling as the *Fermentum*; the Eucharist permeating and uniting the Church as leaven ferments the dough. "Another parable he spoke to them: The kingdom of heaven is like to leaven which a woman took and hid in three measures of meal, until the whole was leavened" (Mt. 13:33). We see in this part of the Mass the fulfillment of that passage of Scripture.

When the priest says, "The peace of the Lord be always with you," we hear the echo of when Our Lord appeared to His disciples after His Resurrection from the dead and saluted them with the words "Peace be with you" (Lk. 24:36). Peace is the result of the obedience and submission of the lower to the higher in all ranks of creatures. There is peace in us when the lower powers (such as our appetite for food) are subject to our higher power of reason. There is peace in the Church when her members are subject to the Lord.

The fact that this salutation of peace is made precisely between the symbolical fraction and commingling signifies that Christ, by His redeeming death and glorious Resurrection, has become the author and source of true peace; likewise does the Sign of the Cross.

Next, for the Commingling, the priest drops the little particle into the chalice, to show that the Soul and Body of Christ are united at the Resurrection; to show that although the Body and Blood are separated, still there are not two sacraments or two sacrifices, but one.

In the prayer for the Commingling, the priest says as he drops the particle, "May this mingling and consecration of the Body and Blood of our Lord Jesus Christ be to us who receive it effectual to life everlasting. Amen." The sense of the word *consecration* here presents a difficulty, since the Consecration has already occurred. But since the object of the liturgical act of mingling the Body and the Blood is intended to symbolize the Resurrection, and since the previous separation of the species is intended to symbolize Our Lord's death, we see that the word *consecration* in this place denotes an action by which an object is raised to and made a symbol of a holy mystery. A church or a sacred vessel is consecrated in this same sense.

> In the Mass the passion and death of Jesus Christ are represented by the separation of His body and His blood. Although this separation can only be in a mystical manner, because the body could not be apart from the blood, nor the blood from the body, however, by the entirely mystical separation of the body from the blood, and the blood from the body, the passion and death of our Lord are perfectly represented. It remains then, but to express in the sacrifice His glorious resurrection; it could not be done more perfectly than by putting into the chalice a fragment of the host, and thus showing the reunion of the body and blood of Jesus Christ. (Benedict XIV, *De Sac. Missae*, 1.2.c.20)

The Agnus Dei

After this prayer comes the Agnus Dei, a most beautiful prayer that comes from the first person in history to call Christ the Lamb of God—St. John the Baptist. It was always sung during the Fraction—which could take a fair amount of time, since a deacon would be taking the particle to another bishop.

The wording is surprising. Those who know some Latin will wonder why the celebrant does not say *Agne Dei* in the vocative case, which would be proper grammar. But ancient languages would sometimes have as a grammatical rule that from a feeling of reverence, some religious terms were considered indeclinable, since they express a mystery, and a mystery cannot be declined or broken down for understanding. So the nominative case is kept in this instance.

Despite this great gift of the Son of God, we still remember with compunction why it is that the Lamb had to be sacrificed; it because of our sins. So we strike the breast ceremonially to acknowledge our being the cause of His suffering.

The word for *lamb* in the ancient Greek signifies "pure," aptly telling us of the most pure Victim offered on the Cross for us sinners and for our salvation.

The Agnus Dei is said three times, since Christ came to us for three reasons. First, that He might deliver us from the guilt of sin; secondly, that He might teach us how to live; thirdly, that He might open to us the gates of heaven. For this the prophets cried out for the coming of the desired of the nations: "Send forth, O Lord, the Lamb" (Is. 16:11); and of Him it was said in heaven, "This is the Lamb that was slain" from the beginning of the world (Joel 2:17); and of Him the Baptist cried out, "Behold the Lamb of God" (Jn. 1:29); and to signify these three revelations of the Lamb slain on the Cross, the celebrant says twice, "Lamb of God, who taketh away the sins of the world, have mercy on us." "Have mercy on us" does not differ from the prayers of the Jewish Temple in the times of the prophets, when the priests and the Lord's ministers stood weeping between the porch and the altar crying out, "Spare, O Lord, spare thy people, and give not thy inheritance to reproach," such as may be found in Joel 2:17.

To tell of the times when Our Lord after His death gave peace to the world and appeared to His disciples saying, "Peace be with you," the celebrant says the third time, "Lamb of God, who taketh away the sins of the world, grant us peace." The Kiss of Peace has been placed at this point.

During this prayer the chalice remains covered. This is for a practical reason, since great care must be taken by the priest that nothing fall into the chalice that does not belong there. But in the Commingling, the Resurrection is symbolized, so here the conferral of peace with the covered chalice represents Christ passing through the walls of the house and appearing to His apostles to give them the greeting of peace.

The Prayers before Communion and the Pax

Once the Agnus Dei is completed, the priest and faithful begin their immediate preparation for Holy Communion. The remote preparation is done the day and night before, the proximate preparation while entering the church and during holy assistance at Mass, but the immediate preparation is three prayers that the celebrant prays bowed down, with the points of his fingers on the edge of the altar and with his eyes riveted on the Host.

Note that it is only just before Communion that prayers are addressed directly to Christ (from the Agnus Dei to the Communion Antiphon exclusively). Most all the other prayers in the Mass are directed to the Father. These Communion prayers are fairly recent in the history of the liturgy. They were the priest's private prayers as a preparation for his Communion, then the faithful started making them, and lastly they were inserted into the missal.

The first relates to the peace left to the Apostles by Our Lord, the second to the death of Christ vivifying all men, and the third to the Communion of the priest. Notice that in Masses for the Dead, the first prayer is omitted, since it relates to this world and the peace we have here, while the dead are beyond the peace of this world.

As to the first of these prayers, St. Augustine once said, "So great is the gift of peace, that even in worldly and mortal things nothing more pleasant can be heard, nothing more desirable can be longed for and nothing better can be found." This is the peace that Christ left to His Bride and which the world can neither give nor take away (Jn. 14:27). It comes from heaven and leads to heaven.

It contains an entire theology of the peace of Christ:

1. We see a picture of Him Who will soon be our nourishment. Our gaze is fixed on Christ, of Whom we say, as St. Peter did, "Thou art the Christ, the Son of the living God" (Mt. 16:16).

2. Next, we see His gigantic work of renewing and reviving the world (*vivificasti*)—a work that will be continued in our Communion.

3. Third, our view takes in the grace-laden decree of the heavenly Father and the obedience unto the death of the Son of God and takes in the completion of that work in the operation of the Holy Ghost.

4. Lastly, we plead to the Lord with great confidence in Christ's Sacrifice of His Body and Blood, which He now wants to give us as a repast. The things we ask for are great: deliverance from all sin, the strength to be true to His commandments, and the grace of final perseverance, so that we may never be separated from Him.

The Kiss of Peace (or giving the *Pax*) is made immediately (and fittingly) after this prayer in a Solemn High Mass. The priest embraces the altar and kisses it, which is symbolic of the celebrant receiving the *Pax* from Christ; it proceeds from the altar like a message or gift that comes from the Lord.

In general, the kiss signifies union, charity, peace, repentance, and reverence. The Apostle, writing to the Christians of Corinth, says: "Salute one another in a holy kiss" (1 Cor. 16:20).

The rubrics of the 1962 Missal stipulate that the acolytes should reverently kiss every object they hand to the priest, afterward kissing the back of the priest's hand. This brings to mind Jesus' "holy and venerable hands," as the Canon puts it. The kissing takes place at the very moments when the priest acts out in gestures what he says in words, thus expressing that fact that he is now acting *in persona Christi*.

The Kiss of Peace is omitted on Maundy Thursday, as a kind of protest against the kiss of Judas, which betrayed our Savior, thus delivering Him into the hands of His enemies. It is also omitted on Holy Saturday, since it was not until the evening of Easter Day that our Risen Lord addressed the disciples with the words *Pax vobis.* For the same reason, by the way, the Agnus Dei is omitted on Holy Saturday, since that prayer uses the words *dona nobis pacem.*

The *Pax* is never given at a funeral, to signify that the souls of the dead are no longer subject to the conditions and changes and miseries of life, and so do not need the peace we do.

The second prayer before the priest's Communion recalls St. Paul's words about unworthy reception of Communion (cf. 1 Cor. 11:29) and emphasizes the one negative point in the first prayer: the curbing of sin. Whoever dares (*praesumo*) to receive must not be conscious of any grave sin, lest he eat judgment unto himself.

The third prayer emphasizes the divine condescension, goodness, mildness, and mercy to man (*sed pro tua pietate prosit mihi*). This mercy appeared in the manger, on the Cross, in the Ascension, on the altar—everywhere—and results in the protection and health of body and soul.

The Communion of the Celebrant

The priest then takes the Host in his left hand and says the verse: "I will take the bread of heaven and call upon the name of the Lord." He strikes his breast three times declaring his unworthiness to receive the Father, the Son, and the Holy Ghost, then crosses himself with the Host and receives with the right hand. He remains for a short time meditating on the Most Blessed Sacrament (as prescribed in the rubrics) and then carefully scrapes the corporal with the paten, and then with his finger brushes the particles on it (if there are any) into the chalice and says, "What return shall I make to the Lord, for all he has given to me? I will take the chalice of salvation and call upon the name of the Lord. Praising, I will call upon the Lord, and I shall be safe from my enemies."

The only thing the priest has to offer of himself that is 100 percent his and not the Lord's is his sins. This is not a worthy return for the overwhelmingly merciful gifts of the Mass, to say the least, so he must offer to the Father the only-begotten Son.

The Communion reminds us of the meals of Christ with His apostles after His Resurrection. As He hid His glory from the apostles under the guise of a pilgrim on the way to Emmaus, so He hides His glory within the person of the priest.

In the second prayer before Communion, the priest begins with the profession of faith that St. Peter once proclaimed ("the Son of the living God"), then confesses Christ's restoring to life a world dead in sin by His death. The Sacrament before the priest is then the powerful means for keeping the commandments and for being unified with Christ, and the means above all for final perseverance in good. Frequent, devout Communion was considered by the Fathers and Doctors as a mark of predestination. To feel the great need of Jesus is the wisdom and joy of life; there is something delightful in this feeling of utter dependence on Jesus. No loss can be comparable to the loss of Him; no sorrow to the sorrow of being separated from Him by grievous sin. Worthy Communion delivers us from this misfortune.

In the third prayer before Communion, the priest remembers the admonition of St. Paul: "but let a man prove himself, and so let him eat of that bread and drink of the chalice" (1 Cor. 11:28). The priest's unworthiness is the want of perfect worthiness and the absence of perfect purity, perfect reverence, love, and devotion, which Christ deserves. The frailty of the human nature of the priest and the weakness of his human will are so great that the disposition he should have for Holy Communion are almost invariably defective—far less perfect than they should be.

Sure, if he has done all in his power to prepare himself as carefully as possible, then yes, he may justly say that he is worthy to receive. But even then he is unworthy of so great a grace. It is precisely this avowal of his unworthiness that is required to make him in some degree worthy of Holy Communion. So even if holy fear and reverence keep him from the table of the Lord, it is better that he celebrates and receives through love and with confidence in the mercy of God.

Holy Communion preserves and protects the life of grace in the children of God that they may not die in the death of sin; for one of its effects is preservation from mortal sin. Christ declared that whosoever would eat of the Eucharistic Bread would not die (Jn. 6:50). That is, he would not die the death of the soul by sin. The world drinks in sin like water, the enemy lies in ambush, and everywhere dangers threaten, so we must work out our salvation in fear and in trembling (cf. Phil. 2:12). The Eucharist protects the life of grace principally in this: that, as a supernatural food, it imparts the life of grace, perfect health of soul, and refreshment of heart. It increases sanctifying grace, strengthens the spiritual life, awakens and fortifies the supernatural virtues, purity, and devotion, humility and meekness, patience and perseverance. It impels us to do good works and bestows earnestness and fervor to consecrate and devote ourselves with generosity to the service of God.

All through these three prayers, the priest is alone briefly with God. All of the sacred ministers remain at the bottom of the steps while he says the prayers. The priest is face-to-face with Him Who at once is the Immolated Victim and the Great High Priest; alone with Him in Whose place he stands as an *alter Christus*. He bends low, mere inches from the Host, and whispers these three beautiful prayers to His Lord. It reminds us of St. John the beloved apostle, who alone leaned close to the Savior and placed his head upon His breast. "My heart hath said to Thee: I have sought Thy Face. Thy Face, O Lord, will I still seek: turn not away Thy Face from me" (Ps. 26:8-9).

The priest does not take a long time for his Communion, but partakes of the Eucharist as the Hebrews took the manna during the Exodus. He receives Communion first, as Christ partook of food before His disciples at Emmaus.

He makes the Sign of the Cross over himself before he receives the Host, since the Host is the Victim Who was immolated on the Cross. Immediately after the Sign, he leans his forearms on the edge of the altar, which was done at the Last Supper, since one ate while reclining before a low table, with the forearms on the table.

This is a significant gesture. The "arm of the Lord" is a phrase used in Scripture to denote support, upholding, and the strength of the Lord. So when the priest places his arms on the altar, it is a gesture and a prayer at the same time, imploring the Lord to be his strength, as if he cannot even stand on his own power to receive such a grace.

Just as soon as he has placed the Host in his mouth, he rises and briefly calls to mind the enormous privilege of receiving God in such a way; so intimate, with such immense humility on the part of God, and this gives rise to a feeling of gratitude. Then the deacon takes off the pall over the chalice at a High Mass, or the priest does so at a Low Mass, wondering how he might adequately express his gratitude. He says to God at this time, "What will I return to the Lord for all that He has given to me? I will take the chalice of salvation and I will call upon the name of the Lord. Praising I will call upon the Lord, and I shall be saved from my enemies." While he says this prayer, he carefully takes the paten and scrapes the corporal to gather any tiny fragments that might be left on it and brushes these with his finger into the uncovered chalice.

In his heart, the priest recalls to himself that although God is almighty, He could not give the priest more; although He is omniscient, He does not know how to give more; although He is infinitely wealthy, He has no more to give. God has no need of our gifts (cf. Ps. 15:2), so the most acceptable thanksgiving to His loving Heart is for us to esteem His gifts, to receive them with fervor, and to use them with fidelity and zeal.

The celebrant now drinks the Precious Blood to a holy inebriation: "My chalice, which inebriateth, how goodly is it!" (Ps. 22:5). This holy inebriation is from the unity that God effects in the priest, so that he is one body, one heart, and one soul with the Divine Victim. Only after this unity happens is the priest ready to distribute Holy Communion to others.

The Communion of the Faithful

While the priest is preparing for his Communion, the faithful prepare for theirs. Given that there are no limits to the treasures of salvation and grace that are concealed in the Holy Eucharist, why is it that so many who receive Communion do not become richer in the goods of heaven? One place to look is our preparation and thanksgiving for Communion. These can be so short, so stingy, so careless, so defective, and, God forbid, so lukewarm, as to be not worthy of the words. The Lord longs to pour out the fullness of His grace into us, but we put a check on His liberality because we do not carefully prepare and guard the soil of our hearts. Catholics can be slothful, distracted, and unmortified during those moments when they should be preparing for the King of heaven and earth to come into their dwelling and abide with them.

But contrary to this sorry state of preparation, the greater our fervor before, during, and after Communion, the more bounteous will be the measure of the gifts that the Savior will put in place of our poverty. This is a great work, terrible in its significance, because in the preparation a dwelling is being prepared not for man, but for God. It is the fulfillment of the Old Covenant: "And king David said to all the assembly: Solomon, my son, who alone God hath chosen, is as yet young and tender; and the work is great, for a house is prepared, not for man, but for God" (1 Par. 29:1).

Once the priest and sacred ministers have received Holy Communion, the faithful receive theirs. The order of Communion is reflective of the hierarchy of the heavenly court.

Communion under both kinds is certainly acceptable; it was done in the *Vetus Ordo* perhaps as late as the twelfth century and is still done in the Byzantine Rite. Likely it was abolished in the Gregorian Rite because of the danger of spilling the Precious Blood or because of other concerns for the protection of it.

Originally the faithful communicated standing up, since this was the way in which the greatest respect was shown. For that matter, the faithful attended the whole Mass standing up, pews being an invention of the sixteenth century. The priest said, "*Sancta sanctis*" ("holy things for holy people"). They received in the right hand, which was covered with a veil, and communicated themselves. Then they received from the chalice; originally they drank directly from it, and later a tube was used. As the liturgy developed, the Church had the wisdom to discontinue these practices for various reasons.

The Lord has prepared the Eucharistic table against all that afflicts us (cf. Ps. 22:5), and in this festive and joyful banquet lies the mystery of all strength and fortitude for the spiritual life and for spiritual combat.

The Confiteor before Communion is not found in the 1962 Missal, but there is nothing contrary to preparing for Communion with a Confiteor and absolution, especially if it is used to ask God for forgiveness for willfully engaging in distraction during the Mass. It has been retained as a custom in many churches.

When the priest distributes Communion, He makes a Sign of the Cross in blessing, so as to lighten the cross of the communicant and to bless the communicant in his effort to leave sin and follow the Lord. But most of all he gives the blessing in the hope that the communicant will receive worthily as an act that will take him to heaven. He says while doing this, "May the body of our Lord Jesus Christ keep thy soul unto everlasting life" (cf. Jn. 6:55).

When a bishop distributes, it is customary to kiss the ring of the bishop before Communion, and this is still in the rite; it is an extension of the Kiss of Peace.

Since 1929 a silver or gilded plate called a paten has been required; the altar boy will hold this Communion paten underneath the chin of the communicant to protect the Host from falling. There was also in former times the requirement for a houseling cloth, a long linen cloth placed along the Communion rail. When the communicants knelt, their hands went underneath the cloth as an additional safeguard for the Blessed Sacrament. It is still used in some places out of great reverence for the Sacrament.

Only the priest (or at a Pontifical High Mass, a bishop) distributes Communion. If one of the priests serves as a deacon, he helps with Communion, but he is still a priest even if he serves as a deacon or a subdeacon. This policy comes from a belief in the reverence that is proper to the Mass. St. Thomas explains it this way: "The dispensing of Christ's body belongs to the priest for three reasons: (1) because he consecrates in the person of Christ; (2) because, as the appointed intermediary between God and the people, it belongs to him to offer the people's gifts to God and so it belongs to him to deliver the consecrated gifts to the people; (3) out of reverence, nothing touches the host but what is consecrated, like the corporal and the chalice, so, likewise, the priest's hands. Hence, it is not lawful for anyone else to touch it, except from necessity" (*S.T.*, IIa, Q. 82, a. 3).

St. Thomas is referring to the law of his own time; in ours it is lawful for unconsecrated hands to touch the Holy Eucharist, but only after training and formation, and only by way of exception, and only by appointment from the local ordinary. Still, it is less fitting for unconsecrated hands to touch the consecrated Host, and the Angelic Doctor's reasoning still holds.

The same reasons may be applied to the Consecration; not only do the altar boys refrain from touching the Host; they do not touch the sacred vessels either. Their hands have not been consecrated, so they can transport the vessels by using white gloves or holding the vessel by linen or the surplice. But if they do touch the vessels by accident, there is no cause for concern.

Communion is not given in the hand—not because the hand is dirty or unworthy, but because it is impossible to do the purifications necessary on the hands (i.e., return the hands to ordinary use). Our liturgy requires these purifications, in order to return the sacred vessels to ordinary use. I'll speak about this in regard to the ablutions.

The Ablutions

In the smallest particle of the sacramental species the whole Christ is present. On this belief are grounded the liturgical ordinances that are designed to prevent and avoid the slightest profanation of the smallest portion of the Host or a single drop of the Precious Blood. So, after the Consecration, the priest's thumb and forefinger must be continually held together; as often as they touch the Host they must be purified either over the chalice or in the ablution bowl, which is always placed next to the tabernacle for a priest who assists at Mass or in the case of Communion outside of Mass. St. Cyril of Jerusalem said, "Have the utmost care that no part of the Eucharistic species be lost. For, tell me, if anyone gave you grains of gold, would you not guard them with the greatest circumspection and be most solicitous that none of them be lost and that you thereby suffered no loss? How much more cautious must you be not to lose a crumb of that which is incomparably more valuable than gold and precious stones."

Once the faithful have received their Communion, the celebrant uses a little wine to wash away any remnant of the Precious Blood, and then goes to the corner of the altar on the Epistle side to have wine and water poured over those parts of his fingers that have touched the Host. All this was prefigured in the Old Law, when, after sacrificing the red cow, the priest washed his vestments and was unclean until the evening. (cf. Num 19:1-9). He was unclean in the sense of not being able to return to ordinary life after such a holy act of sacrifice.

So there are three washings the priest performs with each Mass; in the sacristy, before he proceeds out to celebrate; before the Consecration; and before his fingers are returned to the ordinary, during the ablutions; these recall the washing of the soul from the sins of thought, word, and deed. They also recall the wiping out of original, mortal, and venial sin, by the waters of Baptism, which Christ commanded to be given "in the name of the Father and of the Son and of the Holy Ghost."

Notice that the rites of "washing" the chalice and ciboria are called ablutions or purification. The word *purification* is used not in the sense that the sacred vessels are dirty in any way. It is used instead in the same sense as the rite of purification (churching) of women after childbirth. That is, the woman is not dirty after childbirth; the birth is holy—an imitation of God's creating. So, in order for her to return to daily life, she and her child come into the church to give thanks and be blessed. In the same way, once the vessels have been used for the holy act of the Consecration, they must be blessed before they can be returned to the ordinary.

In the same way, the mouth of the priest is purified since he has received Holy Communion under the species of wine. A little wine is poured into the chalice, and he drinks it to return his mouth to ordinary use. His fingers must be washed for the same reason.

There are two prayers that the celebrant prays that show joy and consolation for having been nourished with the Body and Blood of the Lord. Communion is the fulfillment of the prophecy of the time when "the poor shall eat and shall be filled, and they shall praise the Lord" (Ps. 21:27).

During these ceremonies, the subdeacon purifies and covers the chalice and carries it to the credence table during the Solemn High Mass, and during the Low Mass the priest puts the chalice back to where it was at the beginning of the Mass; veiled with the burse on top. "He covers the chalice, as a sign that a day will come when the truth will be hidden, above all at the time of antichrist. And this was prefigured also in Isaiah, in the vision of the six-winged seraphim, who with two wings cover the Lord's face, and with two cover his feet, and with two fly. The head is the beginning of the Church, before the coming of Christ, what would be revealed concerning him was veiled; and at the end, in the days of antichrist, the things to be believed and to be done will also be hidden, for deceitful error and wicked lust will hold sway" (Gabriel Biel).

The Communion Antiphon

During Communion a Communion Antiphon is sung. This is a relic of the psalm that was sung during the Communion of the faithful and is mentioned by St. Augustine. Originally it was Psalm 33; as the liturgy developed, various other psalms were used to connect the antiphon to the feast day. Sometimes it is necessary to look up the whole psalm before understanding why that particular verse is used for a particular feast day. But this effort will be rewarded, as the wisdom in the choices is deep.

The missal is moved back to the Epistle side of the altar, and the priest walks over to it. This movement of the missal and the priest signifies the fulfillment of the prophecy (Apoc. 7) that toward the end of the world the Jews in great numbers will be converted to the Faith, so the movement of the priest, who represents Christ, symbolizes Christ's return to His people.

While on this side, he reads the Communion Antiphon. Here we see an emphasis on the Resurrection of the Lord. We are reminded in the antiphon of how Christ, after His Resurrection, preached to the disciples and opened to them the mysteries of the Scriptures. The celebrant then goes back to the center of the altar, kisses it, and turns to the faithful, saying, "The Lord be with you." These words signify the words that the Risen Savior greeted his disciples with when He appeared to them after His Resurrection. I say *signify*, since what He said was "Peace be to you." That phrase is reserved for a bishop when he celebrates Mass, since the bishop more perfectly represents Our Lord. The peace referred to here has been won by Christ on the Cross and is the result of the Holy Ghost's being sent as our Paraclete, Who sanctifies the Church.

"The priest went first to the right side of the altar, to show the gladness of our Lord's birth as man. When about to read the gospel, he went to the left hand, to suggest the sadness of the passion. But now again he returns to the right, that he may announce the joy of the resurrection. And to whatever part of the altar the priest goes, the ministers follow behind him, showing the truth of our Lord's words, If any man minister to me, let him follow me, and where I am, there also shall my minster be" (Durandus).

The Postcommunion

The Postcommunion is a final prayer, corresponding to the Collect and the Secret. It alludes to the mystery that has been celebrated, and the Eucharist that has been received, so it is called a Postcommunion, because it always makes mention of the Communion just received. It is not an effusive pouring out of affections and protestations; it is instead a plea that the carrying out of the holy Mysteries, the gifts that have been given, may produce in us their effects as food, remedies, and resources for our journey through life. The Postcommunions are always recited by the priest in the plural—that is, for all and in the name of all who have taken part in the Mass, either by actual or by spiritual Communion. It is always a prayer of thanksgiving.

The Collect *Super Populum*, which follows immediately after the Postcommunion occurs only in the ferial days of Lent; it is related to a former practice in Lent in which the faithful would fast from Holy Communion. During this time a special prayer was said for their benefit, beginning with *"Humiliate capita vestra Deo"*—"Bow down your heads to God." It is a form of blessing pronounced over the faithful who have attended the Mass, so it is custom to do just that, even while kneeling. Most likely this was the old conclusion of Mass before the present blessing had been introduced. This Collect is prayed with a consciousness that the priest and the faithful are tied strongly together at Mass, but when they separate, they are still bound together in Christ.

THE DISMISSAL

The priest returns to the center of the altar to say to the faithful, *"Ite Missa Est,"* or "Go, the dismissal is at hand." The turning corresponds with Christ's showing His wounds to St. Thomas—an invitation for any who are hard-hearted to believe.

This phrase is shrouded in mystery.

Just as the ceremony of the paschal lamb, no simple matter, was called the *Phase*, which means "the crossing", so the ceremony of consecrating the Eucharist is called *Missa*, "the sending". Some have supposed that the word means "sending out" since the catechumens used to be sent out when the priest began the consecration of the sacred mysteries. Others claim that the word means a "sending down", since the living victim is sent down to us from heaven by the Father. Others again have supposed *Missa* to mean "sending across", since the prayers and oblations are sent across from the people to God through the priest, who plays the part of a mediator between them. Still others think that it comes from "sending back",

since when it is done, the people are sent back to their own homes.
(St. John Fisher)

But the deacon announcing this (as Durandus sees it) is representative of what was said to the apostles, *This Jesus who was taken up from you into heaven.*

At Masses for the Dead the ending is *Requiescant in pace,* or "May they rest in peace."

Then the priest bows low with his fingers on the edge of the altar, as has been explained earlier, and says a beautiful prayer: "May the ministry of my serving please thee, O Holy Trinity, and grant that the sacrifice which I unworthily have offered before the eyes of the divine majesty be acceptable to thee, and to me, and to all those for whom, through thy mercy, I have offered it may it be propitiatory."

Then he kisses the altar for the last time in the Mass, invokes the angels, and blesses the people with a large Sign of the Cross, though a bishop uses three crosses. "This last blessing over the people represents the sending of the Holy Spirit, whom our Lord sent upon the apostles after he had ascended into heaven, according to his promise, *You shall receive the power of the Holy Ghost coming upon you.* It also recalls the last blessing that will be given when Christ says, *Come, ye blessed of my Father, possess you the kingdom prepared for you from the foundation of the world*" (Durandus).

This marks the end of the Mass, and as Christ went to heaven to engage in the eternal thanksgiving to His Father, to which we are not privy, so in the High Mass the priest turns to the Gospel side of the altar to say the Last Gospel quietly as a formal thanksgiving for the Mass. It is said out loud in the Low Mass, as an expression that while we do not know the extent of the prayer of the Son to the Father and with the Holy Ghost, some of that conversation is known to us by revelation.

The priest leaves the sanctuary with downcast eyes, concentrating on thanking God for what just happened. "And going out of the people's sight he enters the place where he vested: for when Christ ascended into heaven, the clouds took him from the sight of those who gazed thereon" (Durandus).

All the united homage of creation and the world of the elect do not give the eternal Father such glory as He receives from the offering of His Son. It needs faith to understand the value of the Mass—that faith which is like a participation of the knowledge God has of Himself and of divine things. In the light of faith, we can regard the altar as the Heavenly Father does. What does He see upon the altar? He sees "the Son of His Love," *Filius dilectionis suae,* the Son in Whom He is well pleased, present in all truth and reality, *Vere et realiter,* and renewing the sacrifice of the Cross. God measures all things by the glory He received from them; and in this sacrifice, as on Calvary, infinite glory is rendered to Him by His Well-Beloved Son. God cannot find more perfect homage than that. It contains and surpasses all. (Blessed Columba Marmion, *Christ, The Life of the Soul*)

GLOSSARY

Ablutions

Liturgical actions that consist in washing one's body or part of it. They occur at Baptism, the Mandatum (washing of the feet of the faithful on Holy Thursday), and at Mass after Communion. The water and wine drunk by the priest after Communion is called the ablution. The word is from the Latin *abluere*, "to wash away."

Ablution Cup

A small glass jar with a semiprecious metal lid, kept near the tabernacle on the gradine of the altar. It is used by a priest who has helped distribute Holy Communion to purify his fingers that have come in contact with the Blessed Sacrament. A small finger towel (called a purificator in the Roman Ritual) is placed next to this cup to dry the fingers.

Acolyte

One of the Minor Orders, this is the conferral of the privilege of serving the Mass, in any function, whether as a thurifer or a master of ceremonies. The word is from the Greek *akolouthos*, "a follower."

Adoration

Reverences, postures, prayers, and sacrifices performed by mind, body, and will, recognizing God alone as the Supreme Being, from whom all blessings come. The word is from the Latin *ad + orare*, "to speak to."

Altar

From the Latin word *alta*, "high." A high altar has several parts. The mensa or table part for the sacrifice, the gradine (step) for the candles and reliquaries, a tabernacle for the Holy Eucharist, and a reredos for decoration, containing statues and other art. A side altar refers to a smaller altar, not used for the main or Sunday celebration of the Mass.

Altar cards

These are used by the priest to help him say the parts of the Mass he needs to when he is away from the missal. The priest normally memorizes the prayers, but the cards became the norm in the sixteenth century to help him remember.

Altar cloth

Three swaths of linen are used to cover the mensa of the altar.

Alb

From the Latin meaning "white," the alb was originally the dress of a clown, in which Herod clothed our Lord in contempt. It was also used by neophytes in the Faith after their Baptism and is now used by a priest to cover his cassock and worn underneath the chasuble. It is used only for Mass.

Ambo

Also called a lectern, this is the place from which the Scriptures are read in the vernacular at Mass, and from which a sermon is preached by the parish priest. A bishop normally sits in order to preach. The word is from the Greek *ambon*, "raised edge."

Ambry

This is a niche in the sanctuary in which the holy oils are stored.

Amice

From the Latin word meaning "to cover," this refers to a rectangular white cloth with two long strings that covers up the roman collar or religious habit beneath the alb. It serves a practical purpose of protecting expensive vestments from sweat and also serves as a reminder to the priest, before he says Mass, to put on the helmet of salvation.

Antependium

From the Latin meaning "hanging in front of," an antependium is a decorative cloth that acts as a veil for the entire length of the mensa of the altar. Its color varies according to the feast or liturgical season. The term is also used for a cloth that hangs from the pulpit or ambo.

Antiphon

From the Greek meaning "one sound against another," this is a short text sung or recited after a psalm or a canticle. It refers to the short prayer that usually consists of a few lines of a psalm that functions as its own prayer, but relates the prayer at the time with the feast day. For example, the Communion Antiphon of the Mass expresses both the action (Holy Communion) and the feast of the day. When the Divine Office is sung, one side of the choir sings two verses of a psalm, and the other side responds with the next two verses. This is called antiphonal singing.

Apse

A term in architecture that refers to the part of the church building that covers the sanctuary. The word is from the Latin *apsis*, "arch."

Archeologism

An error in liturgical theology that seeks to return to some liturgical practice in the past and bring it forward into the future, without regard to liturgical development. For example, a scholar finds some practice that he thinks is wonderful, which stopped in the fourth century. It is then reintroduced into the twenty-first century without regard to why it was discontinued. This error was condemned by Pius XII in his encyclical *Mediator Dei et Hominem*.

Archpriest

An ordained, experienced priest who helps the newly ordained with his first Mass. The archpriest is vested in a cope. The word is from the Greek *archos* ("leader") and *presbyter* ("old man" or "elder").

Ashes, Blessed

A sign of penance, blessed ashes are made from the burning of palms from the previous year's Palm Sunday. On Ash Wednesday, these ashes are blessed to become a sacramental that imparts grace to enable the recipient to make a good Lent.

Asperges

A prayer and rite that refers to the sprinkling of holy water just before the principle Mass of the parish on Sundays, outside of Paschaltide (cf. the *Vidi Aquam*). The words recall Moses' cutting a bull in half to establish the original covenant. Moses then dipped a branch of hyssop (a bush that grows there) into the blood of the sacrificed bull and sprinkled the blood over the heads of the Hebrews. It reminds us of the New Covenant, to which we were admitted by Baptism.

Aspergillum and Bucket

The aspergillum (from the Latin *aspergere*, "to sprinkle") is a metal stick of various length and thickness that can hold holy water to sprinkle over the heads of the faithful, or to bless objects. The bucket is used to hold the holy water. Both are usually made of some good metal.

Baldachin

From the Italian *baldacco* (Bagdad), this is a canopy of rich fabric, carried by four poles, to cover the Blessed Sacrament or relics in an outdoor procession. The word is also used (improperly) to describe a permanent canopy over an altar.

Balsam

A resinous fluid acquired by cutting certain trees or plants. Together with olive oil, it is an ingredient of the Chrism, blessed on Holy Tuesday and used for the administration of Baptism and Confirmation.

Banns

Banns are official announcements from a parish about an upcoming wedding, which would enable other members of the parish to inform the clergy if there is an impediment to the marriage. They are no longer required but continue as a custom in some parishes.

Baptistry

A small chapel within the church used only for Baptisms.

Basilica

The word is from the Greek meaning "ruler." Romans called a room for meeting and conversation a basilica. In each town there was a public basilica in which business was transacted and lawsuits heard. It was usually a rectangular room opening onto a porch (narthex); it had an apse at the farther end and was often divided by pillars. The early churches were built in this style, though expressly for worship. Today the word refers to a church that has received special privileges for the Mass of a Pope.

Bells

Bells are used to elicit joy and attention from the faithful and to indicate great events of joy or sorrow. They are also used to ward off evil, as devils hate the sound of bells. Bells predate the sixth century for use at Mass, though not much before, due to the Roman persecutions. Beginning in the Middle Ages, the distance that the sound of a bell traveled would determine the parish boundaries. The origin of the word is fascinating—from the Old English *bellan*, "to roar."

Benediction

This refers to a solemn blessing of the faithful with the Holy Eucharist enthroned in a monstrance. The word is from the Latin, meaning "to speak well of."

Betrothal

A solemn promise to marry made between a man and a woman. It is made before and blessed by a priest, in the presence of the Blessed Sacrament. It is the liturgical expression of engagement and obliges the couple by natural law to keep the engagement in conscience and in justice. But it does not impose the obligation to marry.

Bination

This refers to a priest celebrating the Mass more than once a day. The ancient rule is *nec bis in die*, "not twice in a day." The priest is not permitted to celebrate the Eucharist more than once a day except in cases where the law permits him to celebrate or concelebrate more than once on the same day (cf. Can. 905 #1).

Blessing

This has several meanings:

1. An action of God in which He grants favors or gifts to people.

2. Acts of praising God by prayer or song, i.e. "Let us bless the Lord."

3. A sacred rite by which the Church draws divine favors down on people and objects to sanctify them. The power to do this was granted to the Apostles and is passed down to priests by ordination.

4. Liturgical blessings, of which there are two kinds:
   a. Constitutive, which permanently bring about the dedication of a person or an object in the service of God, such as an altar or the consecration of a woman as a nun.

b. Invocative, which asks God to help those who are in need or who use blessed objects, such as a rosary. The object that is blessed should also be understood as being protected and a sacramental.

Boat, Incense

A small, oblong receptacle usually in the shape of a small ship, used to hold incense. The incense is transferred to the thurible by means of a small spoon.

Bow

Originally the gesture of presenting the neck to an oriental potentate, as a sign of supreme submission (thus offering the head to be cut off should the potentate wish it), but used in the liturgy as a great and humble mark of human respect to the Lord or to a superior.

Bread, Eucharistic

In order for a Mass to be valid, or real, the bread used must be baked from pure wheat meal. To be licit it must be unleavened. It is hard to know what kind of bread Our Lord used at the Last Supper; though it was celebrated on the Day of Unleavened Bread (*azymes*), it could have been leavened if the Pasch was anticipated. Once the bread is offered, it is called the Host, from the Latin *hostia*, "victim."

Breviary

Before the eleventh century, there were a number of books that priests and religious were required to pray: the Psalter, the Lectionary, the Martyrology, the Homiliary (a collection of sermons from the Fathers), the Antiphonary, and the Hymnary, which all together was called the Divine Office. All these books were combined into one, two, three, or four volumes and called the breviary.

Bugia

A low candlestick consisting of a small plate and socket in which a candle is placed. It has a handle so that it can be easily held out to provide extra light for a bishop when he says Mass. The name comes from Bougie (Algeria), which was at one time a major source of wax in Europe. The symbolism is stronger here than the mere practical use; it is clear that the Holy Scriptures can be read and understood only in the light of faith.

Burse

A cloth case used to hold the folded corporal for use at Mass and Eucharistic Adoration.

Calendar, Liturgical

This is a kind of table that divides the lunar or solar year into days, weeks, and months, in which the names of the feasts to be celebrated and the saints to be honored are inscribed. The civil calendar of the Romans, called the Julian calendar, was established in 45 B.C. and remained in use until 1582, when it was replaced by the Gregorian calendar. The Julian year was 365 days and six hours, so by the time of the Middle Ages the calendar was not synchronous with the seasonal dates, particularly Easter, which is always scheduled for the Sunday following the first full moon after the vernal equinox. So in 1582, Pope Gregory XIII reformed the calendar, cancelling ten days from that year (October 5 became October 15) to adjust for all the days that had been added because of the extra six hours per year in the Julian calendar. Pope Gregory also instituted the present system of leap year and restored New Year's Day to January 1. The Gregorian calendar remains normative for the Roman Rite.

Candles

To be used at the altar, candles must be made of at least 65 percent beeswax. Worker bees that make the wax are virgins. Bleached wax is used normally; it stands for the living who are not as they appear (we mask and hide what we truly are). Unbleached wax is used near the casket or catafalque in Masses for the Dead to symbolize that life has changed, not ended. The flame that comes from the two kinds of candles is slightly different. Six candles are used at a High Mass, two for a Low Mass, and four for a bishop's Low Mass. The Low Mass candles are removed for every High Mass. Candles are also used for procession and for devotions. All these candles are blessed and are sacramentals.

Canon

This is a Greek word that means "standard" or "rule." So when we say that some books are canonical, we mean that they are accepted as the standard. When we call the great prayer of the Mass the Roman Canon, we refer to the prayer from the Preface to the Doxology, or Minor Elevation. When a man is canonized, his life is proffered by the Church as a standard for holiness.

Capitulum

From the Latin for "little chapter," this refers to a short reading from Scripture read at the end of the psalms of a particular hour of the Divine Office. "Chapter" is also used for an official assembly of religious, since they open their meetings with a short reading from their Rule.

Capsula

From the Latin meaning "little round," this is a round metal receptacle in which is reserved the large Host for Benediction. It is reserved in the tabernacle.

Cassock

This close-fitting ankle-length garment for priests is also used liturgically by the ministers of the altar. Priests wear black, bishops purple, cardinals red, and popes white. The traditional Roman-style cassock has thirty-three buttons in the front, each buttoned in thanksgiving for one year of Our Lord's life here on earth.

Catafalque
A coffin-shaped wood structure used at Requiem Masses to represent the faithful departed when the body or bodies are not present. It is covered with a black pall, as for a funeral. The word is from the Latin meaning "scaffold."

Cathedral
From the Latin meaning "chair," this is the principal church of a diocese. Each cathedral has a throne or chair in which the bishop alone may sit. The anniversary of the dedication of the cathedral is celebrated by the whole diocese. It is the premier location of the authority of the apostles in a diocese.

Celebrant
This word is from the Latin *celeber*, "numerous" or in "great number," so a celebrated feast is one to which many people come. The celebrant is the one who performs the Mass and confects the Holy Eucharist.

Cerecloth
A linen cloth waxed on the side that is placed on top of the altar, before the altar cloth is spread over it. It is kept there until all traces of the holy oils used in the consecration of an altar are gone. Afterward, it is kept in order to prevent any drops of the Precious Blood from seeping into the altar stone. It is also called a chrismale. The Latin word *cereus* means "wax."

Chalice
From the Latin *calyx*, meaning a kind of cup for drinking wine, this is a consecrated vessel used for the Precious Blood at the Mass. A chalice veil is used to transport the chalice to and from the altar. Chalices

have three parts: the cup, the base, and the node separating the two. They should be made of precious metal, the cup lined with gold.

Chancel

From the Latin meaning "crossbar" or "screen," this is that area of the church assigned to officiating clergy. In the Middle Ages it was raised to a tall height and was expanded to cover not just the sanctuary but also the choir.

Chasuble

From the Latin word *casula*, "little tent," this is a garment worn by priests and bishops for the celebration of the Mass. Originally it was a winter traveling cloak that took the place of the toga. Two basic styles are used, a full tent-like garment called Gothic or semi-Gothic and a sleeveless garment called Roman. The Roman style is very practical when the tabernacle is on the altar.

Chrism

A blend of olive oil and balsam, blessed during the morning Mass of Sacred Chrism on Holy Tuesday by the bishop and used to anoint persons in Baptism, Confirmation, and Holy Orders. It is also used to anoint altars, bells, churches, sacred vessels, and baptismal water. It implies and is symbolic of grace and dedicated service to God.

Christening

Another word for Baptism, this refers to the putting on of Christ and to the naming of a child.

Church

From a word that means "assembly," this signifies the society of the faithful who are united to Christ. Later the word began to be applied to the place in which the faithful met to worship. The first church in that sense was the cenacle, or the Upper Room, where the Last Supper was celebrated. Afterward it was the best room in the house of one of the faithful. Before churches in this sense, our ancestors used underground cemeteries in Rome called catacombs. Catholics would meet there as legally constituted "funeral associations."

Church, Dedication of

This is also called a consecration of a church. As the construction of a new church starts, a blessing and the laying down of a cornerstone or foundation stone is done, to give God's blessing to the work and remind the faithful that the physical structure is a visible sign of the Church, built with living stones.

Churching of Women

This is the blessing of women after childbirth, which is an official or liturgical thanksgiving for the children as well as a blessing. It is also called the Purification of women—not because of any defilement during childbirth (the sacred vessels used for the Mass are purified after Holy Communion) but because the act of giving birth is so holy that as a chalice is purified to return it to ordinary use, so a woman is purified to return to the ordinary or daily routine.

Ciborium

From the Latin *cibus*, meaning "food," this is a consecrated vessel used to keep the Hosts given to the faithful for their Communion. The ciborium is veiled when consecrated Hosts are in it, which reminds us of the manger, and the veil reminds us of Our Lord's swaddling clothes.

Cincture

A lengthy cord tied at the waist to gather in the flowing robe of the alb, the cincture also stands for purity. It is usually white to symbolize purity but may also be the liturgical color of the day. The word is from the Latin, meaning "to gird."

Clapper

A wooden device used in place of the bell at the Mass, from after the Gloria on Holy Thursday until the Gloria of the Easter Vigil. It calls to mind the sound of the nails going into the hands and feet of our Savior.

Common of the Mass

The parts that remain the same in every celebration of the Mass.

Communion antiphon

A verse from the Bible that was a refrain for a psalm to be sung during the Communion of the faithful. Originally the singing during Communion was quite long, and now only the antiphon is retained. It is still proper however, to sing some other hymn or sacred music during Communion.

Communion cloth

A long linen cloth attached to the altar rail to catch any particles from the ciborium during the distribution of Holy Communion. A paten held by an acolyte is now used in place of the cloth, though the cloth and paten are still used in some churches according to custom.

Communion, Holy

The act of receiving worthily the Holy Eucharist. In Communion, we receive the glorified (resurrected and ascended) Body and Blood, Soul and Divinity of Christ. After reaching the age of reason, all the faithful are obliged to receive Holy Communion at least once a year sometime between the First Sunday of Lent and Trinity Sunday. To receive Holy Communion worthily, we should be (1) free from all mortal sins; (2) sorry for all venial sins and striving to overcome them; (3) fasting from foods and liquids (except water) for at least one hour before receiving, preferably three hours; (4) striving to be recollected and participating in the Holy Mass in which the Communion is received.

Compline

The last hour of the Divine Office that completes the day and is sung at night.

Confessional

A place where the sacrament of Penance is received. Originally the confessor sat on a chair or bench between the altar and the Communion rail, with the penitent next to him. By the sixteenth century, the place for confession became a large box-like structure of wood, intended to guarantee anonymity to the penitent and separate penitent and confessor, to protect the confessor from any accusation. It was moved to the side of the church near the ambulatory, or at the back of the church for greater privacy.

Confirmation

Ordinarily conferred by a bishop, this sacrament is giving by the laying on of the hand, anointing with chrism, and saying, "Be sealed with the Gift of the Holy Ghost." It perfects Baptism and orients the confirmed toward the Holy Eucharist. It consecrates the person in two ways: (a) priestly, enabling the person to take part more intensely in the Paschal Mystery; (b) prophetically, fortifying the Christian to bear witness to the world of Christ, the only way to the Father.

Confiteor

From the Latin for "I confess," this is an integral part of the beginning of the Mass, in which contrition is expressed for our sins of omission and commission. (Individual prayers in the Roman Rite are often named for the first, or first and second words of the prayer in Latin, such as the Pater Noster and the Ave.)

Conopaeum

A veil that adorns the tabernacle where the Blessed Sacrament is reserved. Its color is that of the feast of the day, with the exception of black. It is also called the tabernacle veil.

Consecration candle

A single candle lit at the beginning of the Roman Canon that is placed on the altar to signifies the presence of Christ in the Eucharist. It is symbolic of Christ appearing to the Apostles on the road to Emmaus, as they recognized Him in the breaking of bread. It is taken off the altar at the repose of the Blessed Sacrament.

Consecration of the Mass

The time of the Mass when the priest says the words of institution over the bread and wine, so that these elements change into The Body, Blood, Soul and Divinity of Christ. The Consecration includes the Major Elevation.

Contemplation

From the Latin meaning "to be with the temple," this mystical state of awareness of the being of God is one of the highest states of prayer. The Gregorian Rite favors this prayer, which needs a great deal of silence to practice.

Contrition

Heartfelt sorrow and aversion for sins committed, including the intention of sinning no more. To be sorry for sins for human reasons—such as shame or financial loss—is called natural contrition and does not suffice for forgiveness from God. Supernatural contrition is based on motives of faith, that the goodness of God was offended. Supernatural contrition is perfect when the motive of sorrow is true love of God as our highest good. This is expressed well in the traditional act of contrition: "because they offend Thee my God, Who are all good and deserving of all my love." Supernatural contrition is imperfect when it is based on motives of faith, but not love of God for His own sake ("because I dread the loss of heaven and the pains of hell"). Imperfect contrition (also called attrition, in which the penitent at least wishes that he could be sorry for his sins) suffices for absolution in the confessional.

Cope

A long cloak opened at the front and fastened at the breast with a clasp. Originally used as a vestment for the outdoors, it protected other vestments from the weather and had a large hood. The hood (called a cowl) is gone, and in its place on the back is an ornamental shield. It is used for the Asperges at the High Mass and for Benediction or the solemn singing of the Divine Office. The word comes from the Medieval Latin *capa*, "cloak."

Cornerstone

The first stone placed in the foundation of a church during its construction. It is engraved with the name of the church and the date of the foundation on its surface, and inside the cavity other souvenirs of the time can be placed. It is blessed and set in place according to the ritual for the dedication of the church. It is symbolic of Christ; the "cornerstone rejected by the builders."

Corporal

From the Latin meaning "body." Originally the corporal was a white cloth on which was set aside some of the bread and wine brought to the Agape Feast, which in the early Church was eaten right before Mass. The bread and wine placed on that cloth were used for the Mass. Now the corporal is a square piece of white linen that is folded twice vertically, and twice horizontally, so that there are nine squares, symbolic of the nine choirs of angels. For each Mass, the priest intends to consecrate only the bread and wine that are on the corporal.

Credence table

A small table on the Epistle side of the altar on which are placed the cruets, the basin, and the finger towel for the Mass. In the case of a Solemn High Mass, the veiled chalice and burse are placed on it.

Credo

From the Latin for "I believe," this is the opening line of the Nicene Creed.

Crozier

A bishop's staff. When the Lord sent the messengers of the gospel out, He told them to take nothing for their journey except a staff as a badge of their vocation; to be pastors of souls, and to guide, sustain, correct, and lift up the flock. It is pointed at the bottom to signify that the bishop must fight against the enemies of the flock, and curved at the top for the sheep that have fallen into a pit or the brambles and need something to grab on to in order to get out.

Cruets

The small glass or metal containers used to bring the water and wine to the celebrant either to mix in the chalice or to begin the ablutions.

Custom

For a custom to have juridical value, it must last for at least forty years, be reasonable, and be accepted by the legislator. The Holy See has reserved to itself all rights in liturgical matters. Custom is also used for nonjuridical practices, such as when the faithful stand and sit during the Mass. There are no rubrics or laws about this; we simply say it is customary for the faithful to stand for the Gospel or to kneel for the Canon.

Custos

From the Latin *custodire*, "to guard," this is a small, round, golden and glass case in which the Luna—containing the large consecrated Host for Eucharistic Adoration—is placed and stored in the tabernacle. It is veiled when the Blessed Sacrament is in it.

Dalmatic

The preeminent liturgical garment for a deacon, the dalmatic looks very similar to a tunic. It symbolizes the ancient duty of the deacon to bring Communion to the shut-in and to work for the widow, the orphan, and the poor. It is also worn by a bishop for a Solemn High Pontifical Mass. The word comes from Dalmatia, a Roman province.

Deacon

The first step in Major Orders, a deacon is the ordinary minister of the Holy Eucharist. He can touch the Holy Eucharist, sing the Gospel and preach, perform baptisms and witness marriages, and bless certain things. A transitional deacon is preparing for the priesthood. A permanent deacon will remain a deacon and not go on to the priesthood.

Dispensation

This is the relaxation of a law in a particular case by the lawgiver or by an authorized person. The Pope can dispense from all ecclesiastical laws; bishops and superiors can dispense from some of these laws. No one can dispense from divine laws, except the Lawgiver.

Divine Office

This great prayer of the Church consists of eight liturgical hours, which extend the celebration of the Mass throughout the day and prepare for it. These hours—not sixty-minute hours, for the Minor Hours take only ten minutes to say—begin with Matins (morning) and continue with Lauds, Prime, Tierce, Sext, None, Vespers, and Compline and consist mostly of the psalms. All 150 psalms are prayed in a week.

Divine Praises

Written in 1797 by Fr. Luigi Felici, S.J., to make reparation for profane language and blasphemy, the Divine Praises are recited publicly at Benediction of the Blessed Sacrament.

D.O.M.

Abbreviation for the Latin words *Deo Optimo Maximo*, "To God, the best and the greatest." Often put on a cornerstone, they indicate the dedication of a church to God.

Doxology

From a Greek word meaning "praise," a doxology is a particular praise to the Holy Trinity. One of the best known is "Glory be to the Father, and to the Son, and to the Holy Ghost. As it was in the beginning, is now, and ever shall be, world without end. Amen."

Dyptych

From the Greek *diptukon*, "folder," this is a painting used on the altar that can be folded in such a way as to show two different scenes. A triptych can be folded to show three scenes or three panels. It is also a folder of wood or metal on which were written the names of the Christians who were to be remembered in the Canon of the Mass. This ancient diptych is now the prayer called the Communicantes of the Canon of the Mass.

Easter

The greatest and most solemn of all the feasts, Easter is the celebration of the Resurrection of the Lord. It is also called the Pasch, after the Jewish feast commemorating the emancipation of the Jews from their slavery in Egypt. It was in His last celebration of Passover, on the first Holy Thursday, that Christ instituted the priesthood and the Holy Eucharist of the New Law. Easter is the Christian Passover, by which man was delivered from the bondage of the devil. The word comes from the Old English *Eastre*, "to shine from the East."

Elevation, Major

The lifting of the Host and chalice high into the air at the Consecration. It is symbolic of the offering of Christ to the Father.

Ember days

The word does not come from embers as in coals, but is a corruption of the Latin *Quattuor Tempora*, "four times." Celebrated in the Roman Rite but not in the Eastern rites, Ember days are meant to thank God for the gifts of nature, to use those gifts in moderation, and to assist the needy. The ancient Romans gave thanks to or implored their deities for a rich harvest; and the Church sanctified this practice, as she has sanctified other pagan practices that were good in themselves but misdirected. So these are days of fast and abstinence to assist the effort of moderation in the use of the goods of the earth.

Eucharist

From the Greek meaning "thanksgiving," this is a technical term for the Mass, since during its institution at the Last Supper, Christ gave thanks to His Father, and in sacrificing His life for us, He offered the supreme act of Christian gratitude to God.

Ex opere operantis

This Latin phrase meaning "from the work of the worker" states that the dispositions or state of grace of the one who confers a sacrament do not affect the efficacy of a sacrament. In the case of a sacramental or an indulgenced prayer or good work, however, the disposition or state of grace of the person using the sacramental or seeking the indulgence does determine the amount of grace he receives or does not receive.

Ex opere operato

This Latin phrase meaning "from the work of the work" refers to the validity of a sacrament, which comes about not through the work of the worker (i.e., the personal disposition of the one doing the work), but from celebrating the sacrament correctly, with proper matter, form, and intention. So our Lord shepherds us well despite the constant failure of His priests.

Exultet

From the Latin for "exalt," this is a superb hymn sung only once a year at the Easter Vigil, in conjunction with the blessing of the Paschal Candle.

Evangelarium

A book containing only the Epistles and the Gospels to be sung at the Mass.

Extraordinary Form of the Roman Liturgy

This is the technical, or juridical, term for the traditional Latin Mass. Pope Benedict has referred to it as the *Vetus Ordo* (the Old Order) of the Mass; the Eastern churches and Cardinal Hoyos refer to it as the Gregorian Rite; commonly it is called the Tridentine Mass.

Faculties

Authorizations granted to bishops by the Holy See, or to priests and deacons by ordinaries, to allow them to employ their powers in favor of the faithful they serve. A priest receives the power to absolve from sins at his Ordination, but he may not use that power unless he receives this permission from the local bishop. All the sacraments demand faculties for their licit administration. Preaching also requires faculties.

Faldstool

A portable or folding stool (the old Teutonic word for fold was *fald*) for the bishop to sit on or, when he is kneeling, for support. It is used when the bishop is not seated on the throne.

Fast, Eucharistic

Refraining from food and drink at least one hour before the reception of Holy Communion out of reverence for the Holy Eucharist. Medicines and water are exempt from the fast, as are the faithful who are sick or pregnant or aged. A priest who binates or trinates may eat and drink between the celebrations.

Feasts

Days of the Church year that commemorate certain events or sacred mysteries. The celebration of feasts consists primarily of the Mass in honor of the saint or mystery, and the Divine Office in honor of the same. Some feasts are fixed; that is, they occur on the same date each year. Some are movable, and their dates depend on the day assigned to Easter.

Fermentum

A particle of the Eucharist was sent by the Pope after his Mass (fourth century) to parish priests who were unable to be at the Papal Mass. The fragment was placed in the priest's chalice at his parish at the moment when the Pax (Sign of Peace) was said, thus indicating the unity of the Pope and the faithful. The practice is today symbolic, as the particle from the Pope's Mass cannot be distributed.

Flowers

These are used as adornment for the sacred things in the church to express joy and affection. They are not used at the Requiem Mass or in penitential seasons. Like a votive candle, cut fresh flowers represent a sacrifice, since they must be replaced. Artificial flowers cannot denote the same sacrifice, and therefore generally are not used in the church. Flowers can be represented however, as on sacred vestments. Traditionally the tulip represents prayer; the myrtle and lily represent chastity; the hawthorn, hope; the violet, humility; the hyacinth, peace.

Flowers tell us of the graces and virtues that we must bring as we approach the Holy of Holies. They also tell us that virtue blossoms best in the atmosphere of the Eucharistic King, and that our hearts should be like beautiful gardens for the King to enter.

Font

This primarily refers to the Baptismal font, where all the baptisms of the parish take place. Originally it was quite large and below ground so that the one to be baptized went down to symbolize union with Christ dying and then came back up to symbolize union with Christ rising from the dead. Sometimes the small containers near the doors that contain holy water are called holy water fonts; they are also called holy water stoups.

"For the Kingdom and the Power and the Glory are Yours . . ."

This doxology is not a part of the Our Father and thus is not used when the Pater is prayed at the Mass. It was written by St. Irenaeus of Lyon. The Gregorian Rite uses the version of the Pater, which can be found in St. Matthew's Gospel.

Forty Hours' Devotion

The Blessed Sacrament is solemnly exposed for forty hours at the parish church to honor the time that the body of Our Savior rested in the tomb after His death.

Fraction

The breaking of the Host into three parts during the Mass, just before the Agnus Dei.

Fruits of the Mass

The Mass applies the merits of the Sacrifice of the Cross to souls. Both spiritual and temporal blessings are derived from the Sacrifice (we call these fruits), and the whole Church—both here and in Purgatory—benefits from the general fruits of the Mass. The special fruits of the Mass are shared first by the priest who celebrates the Mass, then by those for whom he offers it in a special way (by means of the reception of a Mass stipend), and lastly by all those who participate in the Sacrifice (*omnium circumstantium*, as it says in the Canon—those who are present at the Mass). The one who gives the stipend so that the Mass may be said for an intention also benefits from the special fruits of the Mass.

Genuflection

This is the touching of the right knee to the ground in adoration of the Lord, which is done before the Blessed Sacrament, or a relic of the True Cross, or at certain times to objects that represent Our Lord, such as the crucifix. Only Christ receives the honor of the right knee.

Gloria

This is an ancient hymn of praise to the Holy Trinity, sung by the angels at the Nativity. It is also called the Major Doxology, because of its length, and the Angelic Hymn. The word *glory* comes from the Latin and means "light." It has the connotation of honor, praise, splendor, and majesty.

Gloves

Worn by the bishop for a Solemn High Pontifical Mass, these were originally made only from the skin of the kid of a goat. As Jacob's hands were covered by the same, and with them he received the blessing of Issac with the wine and bread, so the bishop prays when he puts them on that he might be in a state of grace to receive the highest food of all, which is the Holy Eucharist.

Greater Litanies

A day of prayer and fasting observed on April 25 to ask for God's blessing and protection for crops. The Litany of the Saints is sung in procession through the fields to be blessed, followed by a Rogation Mass.

Gregorian Water

A mixture of blessed water, wine, ashes, and salt used in the Roman Ritual for the blessing of altars and churches.

Gremial

A ceremonial apron placed on the lap of the bishop to protect his vestments from oil, candle wax, ashes, et cetera, with which he comes in contact during various ceremonies such as Ordinations.

Hebdomedarian

From the Latin *hebdomeda*, "week." This refers to the priest who leads the prayers for one week, at the principal Mass and at the hours of the Divine Office that are prayed or sung in common.

High Mass

This refers to a Mass in which the celebrant sings the prayers. A sung Mass is one in which the priest sings the Epistle and the Gospel; a Solemn High Mass has a deacon and a subdeacon; a Solemn High Pontifical Mass has a bishop or an abbot as its celebrant; a Solemn High Mass of a Pope is celebrated by the Holy Father.

Holocaust

From the Greek meaning "wholly burned," this refers to animal sacrifice in ancient Jewish ritual. Only the blood and certain parts of the animal were offered to God; the rest was divided among the priest and faithful who had offered it. The whole large Host is consumed by the priest, as is all the Precious Blood during the Mass, which is the liturgical or sacramental fulfillment of the ancient holocaust.

Holy oils

Used at the celebration of sacraments, and for the consecration of persons or things, holy oils are consecrated by the bishop once a year at the Mass of Holy Chrism. There are three: the Oil of the Catechumens, Holy Chrism, and the Oil of the Sick. They are kept locked in the ambry in the sanctuary or, lacking an ambry, in the safe with the sacred vessels.

Holy Week

The holiest week of the year, commencing with Palm Sunday and concluding with Holy Saturday. It is the last week of Lent, immediately before Easter.

Homily

This is a kind of preaching that explicates a particular text of Sacred Scripture. A sermon is a preaching on some subject and not necessarily an explanation of Scripture. A ferverino is a short sermon that aims to stir up the fervor of the faithful.

Honorarium

This is another word for the Mass stipend, or some gift to the priest for services he has rendered. Great care must be taken by priest and laity to make sure that not even the appearance of charging money for a sacrament takes place.

Humeral veil

This is a veil that is put over the shoulders of the sacred minister to hold a sacred vessel during the liturgy, such as the subdeacon holding the paten in a Solemn High Mass or the priest holding the monstrance during Benediction.

Hymn

Hymns are used for the praise of God, usually in metric or strophic form. Vernacular hymns were introduced to the Gregorian Rite in the thirteenth century.

Kiss

Liturgical kisses are used especially with the bishop at the Mass. When an object is handed to him, it is kissed first, then the back of the hand of the bishop is kissed; when the bishop hands something back, the opposite protocol is used. This reminds us that the bishop can give blessings, but he can also take things away, such as privileges. The action reminds us of the words: "The Lord giveth and the Lord taketh away. Blessed be the name of the Lord" (Job 1:21). Liturgical kisses may also be used with the priest but are done in a lesser manner, since the power of the priest to discipline or dispense is far more limited than that of the bishop.

Liber Usualis

"The book of use" has almost all the prayers of the Roman Rite, plus all the official music, which is Gregorian and Ambrosian chant. This is like the missal used by the faithful to assist at Mass, but the so-called hand missal has only a portion of the chant of the Church.

Litugical colors

There are several colors used for the liturgy, and each symbolizes something different: black for mourning; green for hope; red for fire and for blood; rose for the flowering of the next liturgical season; violet for penance, affliction, and humiliation; and white for joy and purity.

Liturgy

Two Greek words, *laos* ("the people," from which comes the word *laity*) and *ergon*, "work." "The work of the people" is usually given as the meaning of liturgy. But if it is the work of the people, it is the whole people (*ecclesia*), stem and root, manifested by this person here. The work done is the work of Christ, and not a deed or set of practices undertaken by the assembly. Christ is the head of the Church, and it is His work that is the essence of the liturgy.

Low Mass
This refers to the celebration of Holy Mass without music and only with the spoken word of the priest. There can be music at a Low Mass, but the priest does not sing. The Low Mass is derived from, is oriented toward, and takes its meaning from the solemn forms of the celebration of the Mass.

Maniple
Originally an ornate Roman handkerchief, the maniple was later used to give or receive something precious (such the paten) in the Mass. When not in use it was folded over the arm. Now it is like a small stole that hangs over the left wrist, symbolic of good works and holy labor, and it is used only for the Mass and for no other sacrament.

Minor Elevation
A slight lifting of the Host and the chalice before the Pater Noster.

Missa Cantata
A Mass that is sung by the priest but without a deacon or a subdeacon.

Missal
From the Latin meaning "to be sent," this is the book that has all the written text and musical notes for the priest to be able to say or sing the Mass.

Miter
A kind of crown worn by the bishop in the Roman Rite for liturgical functions; the precious miter has jewels in it since the bishop represents the Lord who was crowned with many diadems (Apoc.

19:12). It does not resemble crowns of earthly kings. Instead it has two horns like the light that encircled the brow of Moses when he descended from Mount Sinai. As Moses was both a guide and a legislator for the Israelites, so the horns represent this and also the Old and New Testaments.

Monstrance

This refers to the cross-shaped golden vessel used to expose the Blessed Sacrament to the faithful that they may adore Him. It is from a Latin word meaning "to show."

Oblation

A Latin word meaning "gift." Our oblations at the Mass are the gifts of our attention, devotion, worship, et cetera.

Octave

A feast day celebrated for eight days in a row. It originated with Solomon's dedication of the Temple and was renewed at the re-dedication of the Temple of Jerusalem after it had been desecrated by the Roman vassal king Antiochus Epiphanes. The rededication took eight days; the record of this may be found in the book of Maccabees. The first Christian feast of dedication is the historical octave of Easter, the eight days between the Resurrection and the second appearance of Christ to the Apostles. The connection between the original Jewish octave of the rededication of the Temple and the ancient octave of the dedication of a Church is profound. Christ's body is the true Temple; desecrated by scourging, crucifixion, and death and rededicated by the Resurrection. Christ's death removes once and for all the Jewish prohibition from contact with or touching the dead.

Ostensorium

Another word for *monstrance, ostensorium* refers to the cross-shaped or round golden or silver vessel used to expose the Blessed Sacrament to the faithful that they might adore Our Lord.

Pall

A decorated or plain square card of varying weight that is used to cover the chalice during the Mass. The word is also used for the black cloth that is placed over a casket at the funeral Mass, called the funeral pall.

Pallium

Reserved for archbishops, this is a woolen, white band from the fleece of lambs and has black crosses on it. It reminds the archbishop that he must toil to carry the little sheep on his shoulders regardless of the cost. It is worn over the chasuble and has three pins that fasten it to the chasuble. This is a reminder of the three nails that fastened Christ to the Cross, when He willingly died for love of His sheep.

Paten

From the Latin *patena*, "open," this is a small golden plate used as the vessel to bring to the priest the consecrated Host before his Communion. It was originally very large to accommodate all the hosts needed for the faithful. Now a ciborium is used. A hand-paten is used by the acolyte to place under the chin of the communicant at the altar rail.

Pectoral cross

Worn over the chest (*pectora* in Latin), this is a cross of precious metal with or without jewels and representing not only the crucifixion but the Resurrection and the Ascension.

Prayer

From the old English, meaning "please." "Pray pass the salt," one used to say at table. We use the word liturgically to refer to any loving or respectful address to the God, the saints, or the angels. St. Francis de Sales once defined prayer as "a loving conversation with God."

Procession

This is the movement of the celebrant and the ministers from the vestibule to the sanctuary. In a Solemn High Pontifical Mass, the subdeacon represents the Old Testament, and the deacon represents the New Testament. The closed book carried by the subdeacon represents the mystery of the prophecies of the Old Testament. The assistant priest is a figure of the Law of Moses under the high priest Aaron. The two deacons at the side of the bishop represent Abraham and David, who received the majority of the promises of the Incarnate Word. The Gospel also puts them at the head of the ancestors of Christ: "The book of the generations of Jesus Christ, son of David, son of Abraham."

Processional

This is a book that provides the texts and all the manners of the processions used in the liturgy.

Processional cross

An ornate crucifix mounted on a pole and carried by a cross bearer before the ministers and the celebrant while in a liturgical procession. It can also be a plain cross as opposed to a crucifix, in order to emphasize the Resurrection, but it should be jeweled or highly decorated in that case.

Pyx

A small, round metal case in which the Blessed Sacrament is placed in order to bring Communion to the sick or to those who cannot come to Mass. The word is from the Latin *pyxsis*, "box."

Real Presence

This refers to the presence of Christ, the Second Person of the Holy Trinity—Body, Blood, Soul, and Divinity—in the Blessed Sacrament.

Reliquary

This refers to a simple or ornate vessel in which is placed a first-class relic of a saint. A first-class relic is some part of the saint's body, such as a chip of bone or a lock of hair; a second-class relic is something that belonged to the saint; and a third-class relic is some blessed object, such as a rosary, that has been touched to the tomb of the saint or to a first-class relic.

Reverence

From a Latin word meaning "fear," this is a deponent verb, meaning that it is a respectful fear that comes over one when confronted with the holy but is also desired. When a priest reverences the altar, he kisses it with a loving fear—that is, a fear of harming the One whom he worships.

Ring

A ring is worn by a prelate, such as a bishop or an abbot, to help represent his preeminent dignity among the clergy and to signify that he acts as the spouse of the Church, ready to lay down his life for her.

Roman Martyrology

Divided by days of the year to be read at the end of the Office of Prime, the Roman Martyrology provides a list of saints who are celebrated or commemorated that day and in many cases a short hagiography or life of each.

Roman Pontifical

One of the four liturgical books used for the Gregorian Rite (the Missal, the Breviary, and the Ritual are the other three), this has additional texts and forms to be used by a bishop for sacraments and sacramentals reserved to the bishop, such as Confirmations, Ordinations, et cetera.

Roman Rite

This is not a single, homogenous rite, but a historical family of rites that all developed from the ancient Diocese of Rome. Some dioceses had their own rite of Mass—such as the Sarum (Diocese of Salisbury) or Braga (Diocese of Budapest). All showed a high degree of congruence. All used the Roman Canon. Other rites, such as the Dominican, Carthusian, Cistercian, and Carmelite rites, are best spoken of as part of the Latin Rite of Mass. The 1962 missal is the last of a series of revisions to the missal issued after the Council of Trent by Pope St. Pius V in 1570, by the Papal decree called *Quo Primum*. It was revised by Clement VIII in 1604, Urban VIII in 1634, Leo XIII in 1884, St. Pius X in 1910 (though his revision was not promulgated until Benedict XV in 1920), Venerable Pius XII in 1955 and St. John XXIII in 1962. The great majority of the changes to the missal concerned the calendar of saints.

A popular error concerning *Quo Primum* is that it forbade anyone from ever changing the missal until the end of time. Since no pope can bind his successors in matters of discipline, a well-catechized Catholic should be able to see the error in this position. The problem St. Pius V was addressing had to do with printing presses at the time, which would regularly change texts to make them fit more easily on a page, or just to save some money. The pope was forbidding this kind of usurpation of the texts.

But a pope does have the legal right or authority to make a change in the Mass, such as adding St. Joseph's name to the Canon (this was done by St. John XXIII). Whether Pope Paul VI should have promulgated a new order of Mass is another question. That he had the right and authority to do so cannot be questioned.

Roman Ritual

This book has sacraments and blessings and liturgical functions that a priest performs outside of Mass, except for things such as the Divine Office.

Rubrics

From the Latin meaning "red," these are instructions on how to say the Mass or the Breviary, which are in the altar missal or in the Breviary and are written in red. The words to be prayed are written in black.

Sacrarium

A special sink whose drain goes not into the sewer system but straight into the soil. All blessed water, or water used to purify the sacred linens, is poured into the sacrarium. If there is no sacrarium, then blessed water left over from Mass is poured onto the ground where people don't walk.

Sacred linens

This is a collective term for the following furnishings used at Mass: the altar cloth, corporal, pall, and purificator. They are washed three times in the sacristy after use, with the water poured into the sacrarium, before they can be put into a regular washing machine.

Sacristy

Adjacent to the sanctuary, this is the place where the priest and servers store the sacred things needed to celebrate the liturgy, prepare for the liturgy, and return after the liturgy to put the sacred things away.

Sanctuary lamp

A burning candle is placed in a special lamp that is either suspended, affixed to the wall, or on a stand on the floor, to signify the reservation of the Blessed Sacrament. It should be in close proximity to the tabernacle. Custom has it that the glass case in which the candle is kept is red.

Signification

A theological term used to describe the value of signs and symbols used in the liturgy, as to whether they truly signify the mystery they symbolize.

Solemn High Mass

A sung Mass with a priest, deacon, and subdeacon. A Solemn High Pontifical Mass is similar, only a bishop or an abbot sings the Mass. When a bishop sings the Mass, the Blessed Sacrament is removed from the tabernacle in order to intensify the understanding that the bishop is in the place of Christ, and it is Christ who is really doing the work that makes the Mass possible. When a bishop vests for Mass, his vestments are all laid out on the altar at which he will celebrate for a Pontifical Low Mass. For a Pontifical Solemn High Mass, the vestments are laid on an altar in the sacristy or on the altar in the church if the bishop vests at the throne or the faldstool; in both cases the vestments come from the altar to signify that his entire identity comes from Christ.

Solemnity

This refers neither to an overtly happy or sad demeanor or expression for the Mass, but a serious expression, as befits being in the presence of God.

Stational churches

We can celebrate something here that occurred there. Thus, the stational churches are a representation by the Pope of our Lord's own pilgrim journeys around Jerusalem and the surrounding areas. They reproduce in Rome the priestly significance of Christ's own movements in the Holy Land during His life. They indicate the physical sanctification of the land and, by implication, the whole of Christendom and the world.

Stole

A preeminent sign of the office of the priesthood, the stole is a long cloth that is draped around the neck of the priest and used for all the sacraments. Originally a linen cloth, and later a scarf, it has been in its present form for centuries. It symbolizes many things, but among them is immortality, that a priest is ordained forever according to the order of Melchisedech.

Subdeacon

Subdeacon is the lowest of the major orders. The subdeacon's function is to sing the Epistle at a Solemn High Mass. A layman can also fill this role, however, and when he does, he is called a "straw" subdeacon. He does most of what a subdeacon does but does not wear the maniple.

Surplice

A shortened form of the alb, this white garment is worn over the cassock and used as choir dress for priests and acolytes.

Tabernacle

From the Latin word meaning "tent," in reference to the Old Testament prophecies that said that God would "pitch his tent amongst His people," the tabernacle is a strong, secure, ornate metal box in which is reserved the Blessed Sacrament. Originally it was in the form of a dove, hanging from a crook above the altar. It is veiled to reveal what it is.

Temporal and sanctoral cycles

The temporal cycle refers to the liturgical season, such as Lent. The sanctoral cycle refers to an individual holy day, such as the feast of St. Thomas of Becket. These two cycles make up the liturgical calendar of the Roman Rite.

The octave day of Christmas (temporal) is at the same time as the Circumcision (sanctoral). Various octaves overlapped, such as those of St. Stephen, the Holy Innocents, and St. Thomas of Canterbury. These would be celebrated especially in the Divine Office, so that not only the extra prayer at Mass, but an antiphon, versicle, and Collect were added at the Office of Lauds. The feasts do not crowd each other out; they overlap. So Lauds becomes Lauds in miniature here on St. Becket's Day, but in the Cathedral at Canterbury it is Lauds in full. The sanctoral cycle is not grounded in an abstract recollection of saints or holy events. It is founded at the ground where the saint's bones are kept or where the event occurred. That place is brought here, if you will, by a commemoration.

The simplification of the calendar with the Ordinary Form of the Roman Rite had many consequences for the sanctoral and temporal cycles. For example, the Feast of St. Agnes had two dates in the old calendar, eight days apart. At the age of ten she consecrated herself to Christ. Her martyrdom occurred because the Prefect of Rome asked for her hand in marriage, which she refused. Surviving an attempted rape, she was beheaded. The legend about her reports her saying to the executioner, "Strike without fear, for the bride does her spouse an injury if she makes him wait." Her antiphon at Vespers has her addressing Christ; "Behold I hurry toward you, whom I have loved, whom I have sought, whom I have held in the highest." One week after her martyrdom, she appeared to her parents, who had come to pray at her tomb. This is the basis for the second feast, which connects her to the appearance of the Risen Christ to His apostles (eight days). She represents all Christians who will be reunited with their spouse, their sacrificial lamb, their true high priest. To eliminate this feast in the name of simplicity is to drop a wonderful connection for the faithful to the Resurrection of the Lord. I can remember at my seminary being told by a good priest that "One feast day for her is enough." This misses the point entirely.

The pope had the authority to change the calendar. There are still many misperceptions about the new calendar, however. For example, St. Christopher was removed from the liturgical calendar under Paul VI. This was not a matter of the pope's forbidding someone to pray to St. Christopher. It was instead a disciplinary decision, based on the paucity of information we have about St. Christopher. The pope wanted devotion to go to saints about whom we knew a great deal. Whether this was a good or prudent decision is one question. But it is not questionable that a pope has the authority to change the calendar.

Tenebrae

The celebration of the Office of Matins and Lauds for the last three days of Holy Week. The word is from the Latin meaning "shadows." It is symbolic of the setting of the Sun of Justice, Our Lord, and the sadness of those who rejected the Messiah. A special candlestick with fifteen candles is lit, and they are extinguished one by one.

Throne

Used for a bishop in liturgical functions, as he is the image of Christ seated on His throne in heaven. The bishop is surrounded by many ministers, as in the court of heaven.

Thurible

From the Latin *thus*, "incense," it is a metal container in which burning coals are placed so that when incense is put on the coals, it smokes. Also called a censer, the thurible can have one or three chains by which it may be swung.

Thurifer

The minister who carries and is in charge of the thurible and who incenses the celebrant and the faithful.

Tract

The psalm or verses of a psalm sung or recited immediately after the Gradual in Masses from Septuagesima to Easter, and in Masses for the Dead. It replaces the Alleluia versicle at these times. The word comes from the Latin *trahere*, "to draw," and apparently derives from either the drawn-out style of singing or the continuous structure without a refrain.

Tradition

From the Latin *tradere*, "to hand down," this refers to the Word of God given to the apostles by Christ and the Holy Ghost and handed down to their successors through the Church by such things as prayer, Creeds, liturgical practices, and authoritative writings (such as papal encyclicals and councils). The Sacred Liturgy is an essential means to pass down Sacred Tradition.

Transubstantiation

The conversion or complete change of the substance of bread and wine into the substance of the Christ's Body and Blood, which occurs through the actions of a validly ordained priest at the Consecration, with the result that only the accidents (appearances) of bread and wine remain. These accidents (taste, smell, appearance, et cetera) do not inhere in any substance whatever, but are sustained in a miraculous way.

Tunic

A vestment worn by the subdeacon for a Solemn High Mass, which matches the dalmatic worn by the deacon and the chasuble worn by the priest. It calls to mind the seamless garment woven by the Blessed Virgin, for which the soldiers gambled under the Cross.

Umbrellino

This is a canopy used to cover the Blessed Sacrament in procession. If the Sacrament is being simply transferred from the tabernacle to a temporary location (such as for Good Friday), a humeral veil is used to cover the ciborium. If the monstrance or ostensorium is being held in procession, the umbrellino is held over the celebrant and the Host.

Vernacular

The language native to a region or country. A limited use of the vernacular in the Mass was permitted or called for in the Second Vatican Council. Latin was to remain the primary language of the New Order of Mass, and Gregorian chant was to have been the primary form of music. The vernacular is not used during the Mass in the Extraordinary Form of the Roman Rite. That is, from the beginning of the Mass to its conclusion, only Latin is used. This means processional and recessional hymns can be used (they are outside the Mass), and the vernacular is used for the sermon (which is an interruption of the Mass). However, permission was given by Pope Benedict in *Summorum Pontificum* for the readings to be done in the vernacular at a Low Mass.

Versicle

A phrase of a psalm, normally complete in itself, divided into two parts ordinarily equal in length and even symmetrical, followed by a responsory. An example is: *V.* Our help is in the name of the Lord. *R.* Who made heaven and earth.

Vestment

This refers to any garment used for the liturgy, from the Latin *vestire*, "to clothe." The solemn rites display and make visible what the life of the angels is like in heaven and what we will be if we are blessed with heaven. The rites and gestures are not spontaneous but laid down and required—like the virtues we must put on and accept in order to be what we are to become at the end of time. These actions and gestures accompanying the clothing of the priest in vestments should be seen as coming from beyond and outside of us, not from within—that is, from our imagination, which is the effect of spontaneity. This is also why the ministers (e.g., altar boys) at the altar are vested. They should not glory in what they wear, but they are made glorious in Christ, resurrected and glorified. So the putting on of vestments (which is done very carefully and with special prayers for most of the vestments) represents the putting on of the virtues of Christ.

Our baptismal robe of white is further made to shimmer with vestments. St. Thomas Aquinas speaks of how the angels shimmer with light; not as shining by emitting light, but shimmering, which means retaining to themselves the light by which they are illuminated. The vestments are not mere coverings, but they are replaced or folded (as at an Ordination) or exchanged (as on Palm Sunday) and lifted up by ministers (as at the Consecration) in a sophisticated language to reveal the meaning of the liturgy. The liturgy is so deep and mysterious that only such complexity will suffice to make it clear.

Vidi Aquam

Similar to the Asperges, this is used before the principal Mass on Sundays during Paschaltide to bless the faithful with holy water.

Vigil

The eve or day before a specific feast or holy day, characterized by special offices and prayers, frequently having a specific Mass distinct from the one celebrated on the feast. The vigils of Christmas, Easter, and Pentecost are the most important of all the vigils.

Wine

Only wine that is made exclusively from grapes and has no additives can be used for the Mass. It is symbolic of our union with Christ, Who is the true vine (Jn. 15). It is changed into the Blood of Christ at the Consecration.

Worship

From the Old English *weorth* ("value") and *scipe* ("condition or character"); that which we give worth to—by giving it our time or energy—is what we worship. When it is given to God to acknowledge His dignity and supreme dominion, we speak of worship as adoration, which can be given to God alone. In the Greek this is called *latria*. When we use the term in relation to the saints, we use it because of their special relationship or closeness to God. In this case it is more properly called veneration (*dulia* in the Greek). Our Lady is singled out for a special veneration above the other saints (called *hyperdulia* in the Greek). The forms of worship are varied: praise, petition, repentance, thanksgiving, adoration, and sacrifice. The highest form of worship that man can give God is the Sacrifice of the Mass, since in it we unite ourselves to the worship that Christ gave the Father on the Cross.

LATIN IN THE LITURGY

T HREE LANGUAGES ARE USED IN THE MASS: Latin, Greek, and Hebrew. Above the crucifix you will often see an abbreviation of the decree of Pontius Pilate about the death of the Lord; the original declaration read *Iesus Nazarenus Rex Iudeorum* ("Jesus of Nazareth, King of the Jews," abbreviated INRI). It was written in Latin, Greek, and Hebrew so that anyone living in that part of the world who could read would have been able to read it. These languages are retained in the Mass, since the Mass is the proclamation of the death of the Lord, as St. Paul put it. For besides the Latin, there is *Kyrie* in Greek, and certain Hebrew words are left untranslated, such as *Amen* and *Alleluia*. But the greatest portion of the Mass is in Latin.

In medieval commentaries, there is little about why Latin is used for the Mass, likely because its use was not questioned. However, as its use has been regularly attacked not just by Protestants, but even by some Catholics, we need to spend some time understanding the importance of Latin in the Liturgy. We may begin with St. Robert Bellarmine.

> The language in which the sacraments are administered is not a matter of divine law. Yet for many serious reasons it has seemed to the Church, and to the Holy Ghost who rules her, that they should not be administered in the vernacular, unless perhaps by necessity. For the majesty of divine worship surely requires a language that

is more weighty and venerable than those which are in common use, if this is possible. Just as in administering the sacraments we use another building, other vestments and other vessels than those in common, daily use, so in just the same way, it seems, we should use another tongue. We do not say that Latin is holier or weightier than other languages, if we consider the bare words, but rather that the very fact of its being not in common use makes it weightier and more venerable.

And much later, St. John XXIII said the following: "The Catholic Church has a dignity far surpassing that of every merely human society, since it was founded by Christ the Lord. It is altogether fitting, therefore, that the language she uses should be noble, majestic and non-vernacular. In addition, the Latin language is a most effective bond, joining together the present age of the Church with ages past and yet to come."

If someone tells you, "In the Middle Ages, the people did not understand what they were doing, because they couldn't understand Latin," you can respond by just pointing a finger to the cathedrals they built. Those cathedrals, monasteries, and simple parish churches were built in perfect harmony with the liturgy, as was the music written, the stained glass produced, and the miracle plays performed. If you want to read a thorough study of just how well informed Catholics were in the fourteenth and fifteenth centuries, read *The Stripping of the Altars* by Eoman Duffy. The knowledge of our ancestors in the Faith was in many ways deeper than our own.

And as St. Thomas Aquinas noted, "Three kinds of attention are possible when we offer vocal prayers. First, we may attend to the words, lest we make a mistake in what we say. Next, we may attend to the meaning of the words. Finally, we may attend to the goal of our prayer, namely, to God and to the thing for which we pray. This last is the most important kind of attention, and can be enjoyed even by the uneducated. And sometimes the mind is borne so powerfully to God by this form of attention that it is no longer aware of anything else."

Martin Luther thought the Mass should be in the vernacular. He thought the essence of the Mass to be vernacular words. *Vernacular* is a Latin word that means "that which is familiar to us," whether visual, auditory, or olfactory. The old Protestant idea was that as long as we hear sacred words in our own tongue, we will have liturgy. Contrast that idea with the example of Mary, who stood by the Cross silently. Christ said only seven things when He was on the Cross, but what He did was far greater than what He said. Of course, what Luther was up to was far more than just wanting people to understand the Mass. His motivation was deeply nationalistic, and above all he was more concerned with people understanding *him*, since in his liturgy the preacher effectively becomes the center and not the Eucharist.

The Latin language was first consecrated for use at the Mass when it was inscribed above the Cross by order of Pontius Pilate. Divine Providence selected Rome as the center of the Catholic Church; from Rome the messengers of the Faith were sent in all directions to spread the light of the gospel. It was natural that Latin became the language of worship. But why keep it after it had been superseded by other tongues in civil life?

Why Latin Is Fitting in the Liturgy

First, in Latin was developed the incomparably valuable music of Gregorian chant, and from chant came sacred polyphony. Try as they might, composers of vernacular hymns will never be able to equal the beauty and appropriateness of chant for the Mass. Trying to come up with a new or modern equivalent of Gregorian chant is like wishing for an American Shakespeare to be born.

Second, the genius of the Latin language possesses great perfection.

It is distinguished for its dignity and gravity, for its clearness and precision, for its richness and euphony. It is very difficult to render the complete sense and still more difficult, if not impossible, to bring out in a translation the beauty, strength, dignity, unction, depth, and wealth of thought of the original Latin.

Third, Latin can serve as a strongly unifying factor for the universal Church. I can remember being in a small group of pilgrims (before I became a seminarian) on a special tour of the tomb of St. Peter beneath St. Peter's Basilica. There were a couple of Hungarians, three Mongols, and an Ecuadorian, a couple from the Ivory Coast, a Scot, some Latvians, and about four Americans. We wanted to pray together, but we couldn't settle on which language to do it in. One of the Hungarians started to pray the Pater Noster, and we all joined in. Everyone knew it. Then we said a Hail Mary and the Apostles' Creed in Latin together. It was a joyful experience; unlikely to be sure, but everyone was just beaming at that liturgical unity.

Fourth, vernacular languages are constantly changing, as they must. For this reason, I can remember a bishop once saying that there ought to be a minor change in the liturgy every two or three years, and a major one every five. He reminded me of Thomas Jefferson, who, when asked about whether the generation that came after the Revolution should obey the government and the laws and institutions that the Revolutionaries set up, responded that they should not (at least he was consistent). He thought there should be another revolution and a continuing revolution every twenty years or so. So I see the point. If a man holds the position that the Mass ought to be in the vernacular so that the people could "understand" what is going on without explanation, then the ceremonies, gestures, and objects used in the Mass would also have to be changed in order to be consistent with the vicissitudes of the language. But the Mass would lose continuity—a serious loss.

Fifth, the practical difficulties of the use of the vernacular have proven far more difficult than we can imagine. I know of a priest who serves in a diocese in India where there are as many as twenty-seven languages used. Which one should be chosen as the liturgical language? If the diocese chooses one, then the others will be slighted. If it chooses all of them, then the task is monumental. Furthermore the Church has an obligation to see to it that these translations are faithful to the Latin text. Translations are easily spoiled and disfigured by interpolations, omissions, incorrectness, errors, and misinterpretations, not to mention a complete loss of poetry.

Sixth, Latin possesses in the eyes of the faithful a certain sacredness, due in no small part to its withdrawal from daily life and from the ordinary conversation of the man on the street. No one would dispute that ecclesiastical Latin is a sacred language. As to what makes it sacred, well, that is another question beyond the scope of this little work. Trying to pin down the qualities of a sacred language is not easily accomplished. For example, most have a notion that Elizabethan English has taken on the quality of a sacred language, probably from the influence of the King James Bible. But there is much more to a sacred language than the use of archaisms such as *thee* and *thine*.

Seventh, Latin possesses a mystical character that derives from its withdrawal from common use. This is admirably suited to the Holy Sacrifice, which in itself comprises many mysteries. This mystical Sacrifice calls for vestments, architecture, demeanor, music, and a language that is elevated, majestic, dignified, and consecrated. Latin meets all these requirements.

Fr. Nicholas Gihr has a good passage about Latin: "The majesty of the divine worship depends, indeed, chiefly on the devout, dignified, and reverential demeanor of the celebrant; but the liturgical language contributes also its share thereunto, and a foreign language is suitable, in a measure, to veil the defects and repulsive routine of many a priest, and to prevent them from appearing so glaring." Latin thus prevents the linguistic peculiarities of the priest from dominating the liturgy, provided, of course, that he makes a bona fide attempt to pronounce the Latin correctly.

The Sacrifice of the Mass contains "much that is instructive." This phrase (*magnam eruditionem*) is from the Council of Trent. Erudition is a simple, introductory kind of learning, such as a child's learning to hold a fork correctly or a medical student a scalpel (see appendix II). But erudition or instruction is by no means the principal object of the Mass. The altar is not a pulpit, and the Mass is not a lecture or instruction of the people. The Sacrifice is essentially a liturgical action for glorifying God, as well as for the salvation of the faithful. The faithful should join in spiritual union with the celebrating priest *plus medullis cordis quam labiis vocis*—more with the heart than with the lips, as the great council put it. And granted, this is not possible without some understanding, but there are many means to acquire this understanding, such as reading this book.

However, even if the faithful could understand the words that are sung or recited at the altar, little would be attained for the real understanding of the Mass. For the formulas of the Mass, taken principally from Holy Scripture, are often very deep and difficult to comprehend; the mere rendering of them into the vernacular would rarely disclose the hidden meaning, and translations are often the occasion of misconceptions and misunderstandings and arouse disputation and dangerous hypercriticism.

Merely understanding these in one's own language does not enable one to share abundantly in the fruits of the Sacrifice. For that, we must become as little children; trusting in God and being pure of heart and mind. A child at his first Communion is far more advanced in union with God than is the brilliant professor who can tell you everything about the history of the liturgy but whose violations of the Third Commandment block even the smallest amount of merit. The most perfect disposition for Mass is a lively faith, fervent love, sincere compunction, profound reverence and devotion, humility of heart, and a longing for mercy and help. The Mass has its own, peculiar, significant, and eloquent language, produced from the symbolic character of the liturgy, and faith, hope, and charity access this language better than the vernacular.

The unity of the liturgy for all time and places can be maintained only insofar as it is always and everywhere celebrated in the same language. What consolation this would be to a Catholic in a foreign land; with his missal he could follow the Mass as if here were at home, with the exception of the sermon! Everything would be accessible to him. He would be spiritually at home. When national languages are adopted for the Mass, this uniformity and harmony are rendered almost impossible.

Notice how this unity of language would help the immigrant. I recall a conversation with a good priest with whom I often argued (in the best sense of that word) about the Mass in Latin. He said that the Mass was put into English "so that the people could understand what they were praying." It sounds logical. But I pointed out that when that happened, the immigrants from Mexico and other Spanish-speaking countries were automatically cut off from this understanding (it was hard to say how many there were; sixty thousand in legal residence, maybe another sixty thousand illegally, but who knows?). Of those who were Catholic, the Mass in English would necessarily cut them off. The same could be said for the local Korean or Vietnamese immigrants who were Catholic. The effort to find priests who could celebrate Mass and the other sacraments in their native tongues was daunting. But if the Mass had stayed in Latin, then what was in their native country would be here too, and I am convinced that we would not have seen so much apostasy as a result. The Mass in the vernacular alienates in a certain way every immigrant who does not speak the vernacular in which the Mass is said.

The unity of liturgical language is also a very efficient means for preserving the integrity of the Faith. As Fr. Gihr puts it: "The liturgy is the main channel through which dogmatic tradition is transmitted. Dogma is the root of all ecclesiastical life, of discipline and of worship. Worship is developed out of the doctrine of faith; in the liturgical prayers, in the rites and ceremonies of the Church the truths of the Catholic faith find their expression, and can be established and proved therefrom. But the more fixed, unchangeable and inviolable the liturgical formula of prayer is, the better it is adapted to preserve intact and to transmit unimpaired the original deposit of faith."

He goes on to say "The bond of a universal language of worship, which embraces the head and the members of the Church, supports and promotes everywhere the unity and the common life and operation of the Church. History confirms this; for it proves that a difference of liturgies, that is, the introduction of national languages into the liturgy, frequently gave or threatened to give rise to heresy and schism." The enormous dissent from the Magisterium that we saw after the Second Vatican Council cannot be separated from the loss of Latin. That dissent—which is subsiding but still quite active—could not have had such success if the dissenters were worshipping in Latin.

Fr. Gihr concludes, "In her bosom we behold how the Holy Ghost has 'gathered all the nations from out of the babel of tongues into the unity of faith.' Being formed of 'all nations and tribes and peoples and tongues,' she constitutes but one family of God, one kingdom of Christ, a kingdom not of this world, but exalted above every nation of the earth. Therefore, it is proper that the Church, when celebrating divine worship, when offering the divine Sacrifice, should make use not of the language of some one single country or nation, but of a language that is universal, consecrated and sanctified. Thus at the altar it is a figure of the heavenly Jerusalem, where all the angels and saints in unison (*una voce*) sign their 'Holy, holy, holy' and alleluia."

This gives us an insight as to why so many dissidents were so adamant in their opposition to Latin. And not just for the recited parts; they were strongly opposed to Gregorian chant and Latin polyphony. Chant, above all forms of music, constitutes a formidable obstacle to heresy. It cannot be manipulated to fit an agenda. The same goes for the polyphony that has been consecrated by long use and Church approval.

Dr. Peter Kwasniewski of Wyoming Catholic College has more to add on this subject from an article he wrote for the *Latin Mass Magazine* (Summer 2013):

> It is a rationalist fallacy to think that languages are all equal to one another, so that it is a matter of indifference whether readings are given in Latin or in a vernacular language. Every language is a bearer of cultural aesthetic, and even political values; every language flows from, evokes, and reinforces a certain world, greater or smaller, older or younger. It is therefore not the same experience to give or to hear readings in Latin and to give or hear them in English; for the one vehicle is universal, tied down to no particular people or nation or age, redolent of the ages of faith, suited to the ambiance of the church, while the other, whatever its merits, has not the same qualities.
>
> Another argument in favor of preserving Latin for the lections at Mass—and by no means a negligible one, given the sanctifying function of the liturgy—comes from the experience of worshippers accustomed to the unity and coherence, formality and dignity of the traditional Roman Rite. Akin to the seamless garment of the Lord, this rite is woven of ecclesiastical Latin from top to bottom. To shift from Latin dialogues and orations to vernacular readings is experienced as a jarring disruption, an awkward movement away from theocentric focus and ceremonial formality. One steps outside of the realm of the liturgical action which is oriented towards the adoration of God into a didactic mode directed to

the people. There is a time and place for such instruction, namely, the homily; and it is neither inappropriate nor surprising that in many places the readings are read in the vernacular from the pulpit prior to the homily. The inclusion of such vernacular readings is *not* considered to be part of the liturgical action, and for good reason; it is a moment of teaching the people, and is not directed to God *per se*. In the classical Roman rite, in contrast, the readings, whether spoken or chanted, are offered up to God as a kind of verbal incense, a spiritual offering of the word to the Word before Whom we come in adoration. The words here are a prayer of praise and petition. They teach us, indeed (how could they not?), but their function in the Eucharistic liturgy goes far beyond conveying a doctrinal message.

The integrity of the parts of the Mass—that fact that many disparate elements come together in one great offering of worship—is strongly brought home to the worshiper by the use of this noble, ancient, and worshipful language. The whole is a flowing river, a seamless garment, a landscape in which the various distinct objects are gathered together into a natural unity of environment. Think of mountains covered with pine trees—one can see many individual items, but the whole view is utterly *one*. There is no awkward transition or lack of transition from part to part; there is simply the flow of one great action of Christ the High Priest, teaching, ruling, sanctifying.

One may not, of course, deny that the word of God is the word of God regardless of what language it is in. The point is rather a symbolic one, at least as regards the lections at Mass, and it should be readily apparent that symbolism is not something incidental to the liturgy but is rather a constitutive dimension of the entire sacramental system. Put differently, *how* we do the readings, how we treat the book and the handling of it and the chanting of it, is just as important, and in some ways more important, than the specific message delivered in any given set of readings. The special way Scriptures are treated at the Extraordinary Form is already a powerful formation of the soul of the believer.

Among the most moving and beautiful signs of the latreutic or adorational function of the readings in the *usus antiquior* are those times in the course of the liturgical year when the priest, ministers, and faithful genuflect during the reading of the Gospel at a passage that narrates some reality that *cries out* for the total response of the believer, in body and soul.

One way in which the ancient Mass sets apart the word of God for special veneration and allows the faithful to perceive its unique character is by treating it in a way that mere profane texts are never treated, namely, by chanting it in its entirety. Right away, we are catapulted, as it were, into a different world, the world of God, in which His holy words, so beautiful and so beloved, must be lovingly lingered over, savored and reverenced, lifted up in a solemn sacrifice of song. One cannot overestimate the formative power of the chanted readings to communicate immediately to the faithful that we are plunged into the very midst of God's holiness when we encounter His word in Scripture. This liturgical action of reading puts us in contact with the source of sanctification, and does so in a way that deserves a treatment no less noble than any part of the Ordinary (*Kyrie, Gloria, Credo, Sanctus, Agnus Dei*) or Preface of the Mass receives. How strange it would be to chant so many other prayers, written by holy men but not equivalent to the revealed and infallible word of God, and yet to leave unchanted the very words of God Himself! If it is only the lover who sings, according to St Augustine, should not the lover of God sing most of all the words of God?

With this theological background in mind, it is fair to say that the chanting of the lections would suffer considerably if a sudden and rash change were to be made in favor of vernacular readings.

The chanting tones for the various classes of readings are ancient, solemn, noble, and perfectly fitted to the language. Although vernaculars can be sung by those capable of adapting the tones to the character of a particular language, the Church of the Roman Rite had never done this historically, and so an organic opportunity for developing vernacular chant never occurred.

In the Low Mass, by contrast, when the Epistle and Gospel are merely spoken, proper reverence for the Word of God is assured by the priest reading it *at the altar*, signifying two things: first, that this word of Scripture is *derived from* and *ordered to* the primal Word of God, Jesus Christ the High Priest, the Lawgiver, the very *life* of the word; second, that this word of Scripture is so sacred that it is not treated like any other word (e.g., announcements or homily), but is reserved to the spiritual domain symbolized by the altar of divine sacrifice. This is a guarantee that the uniquely *sacred* character of the text will be appreciated and respected. There is ample room in the homily to *apply* the word of God to the lives of the faithful, so that there is no need to fear too great a "separation" between the domain of the spiritual and the domain of life in the world. The word of Scripture should never be severed from its home—the Word, the font of life, the fire of love, the pleasing and acceptable sacrifice of holiness.

Appendix III

HOW THE LITURGY TEACHES

W HAT A MISTAKE to think of liturgy as being largely of a didactic nature, meant only to teach or evangelize for its primary purpose! As Cardinal Ratzinger put it in his excellent book *The Spirit of the Liturgy*, "That is why St. Augustine could say that the true 'sacrifice' is the *civitas Dei*, that is, love-transformed mankind, the divinization of creation and the surrender of all things to God: God all in all (cf. 1 Cor. 15:28). This is the purpose of the world. That is the essence of sacrifice and worship."

St. John Paul II warned us about those attempts that seek to fashion the liturgy into a didactic exercise, where every implicit thing is made explicit, with endless explanation. Conscious participation, as he points out, does call for increased learning about what the liturgy means. However, "it does not mean a constant attempt within the liturgy itself to make the implicit explicit, since this often leads to a verbosity and informality which are alien to the Roman rite and end by trivializing the act of worship. Nor does it mean the suppression of all subconscious experience, which is vital in a liturgy that thrives on symbols that speak to the subconscious just as they speak to the conscious" (October 9, 1993, address).

The ceremonies of the liturgy do many things, and "instruction for simple folk," as Pope Pius XII quotes Cardinal Bona as saying, is only one of them:

Exterior worship, finally, reveals and emphasizes the unity of the mystical Body, feeds new fuel to its holy zeal, fortifies its energy, intensifies its action day by day: for although the ceremonies themselves can claim no perfection or sanctity in their own right, they are, nevertheless, the outward acts of religion, designed to rouse the heart, like signals of a sort, to veneration of the outward acts of religion, designed to rouse the heart, like signals of a sort, to veneration of the sacred realities, and to raise the mind to meditation on the supernatural. They serve to foster piety, to kindle the flame of charity, to increase our faith and deepen our devotion. They provide instruction for simple folk, decoration for divine worship, and continuity of religious practice. They make it possible to tell genuine Christians from their false or heretical counterparts. (*Mediator Dei*)

All men require some sort of liturgy, because it has always been a primary way to express their thoughts about life and death. Liturgy is, among other things, putting into action, in gesture, movement, song, clothes, and speech, what we think. And from the earliest time of history, men have been engaged in some sort of liturgy. As a Benedictine monk from Le Barroux put it:

The ripe fruits of a whole civilization, hanging heavy in beauty, are often caught up in the civilization's fall. Sometimes they survive it like a refined and fragile flower (think perhaps, for example, of the outdated etiquette of the French court). We forget that these sacred rites were first of all the poetry of mankind in his infancy, barbarous and crude but the expression of men who danced out their theology before they ever thought to write it down. These religious rites in their earliest manifestation from the very first graspable expression, from across the long night of the ages, have come down to us from our remote ancestors. For well before we have any written inscription, any wall painting, any hieroglyph from primitive man, we discover in what survives of his funeral rites the first and moving witness to a belief in a reality beyond him. The dead man, his legs drawn up to his chest in a fetal position, is once more entrusted to mother earth like the seed of eternity.

It is clear as well that liturgy is required by every culture or civilization, in order that its religion be apprehended and that moral duties demanded by the culture be inculcated beginning with the youngest child. This is not exclusively a Western notion. It may be found in the East as well. From the same monk of Barroux:

> Every mode of religion, to make a deep and lasting impression on the human mind, must exercise our obedience, by enjoining practices of devotion; and must acquire our esteem, by inculcating moral duties analogous to the dictates of our own hearts. The religion of Zoroaster was abundantly provided with the former, and possessed a sufficient portion of the latter. At the age of puberty, the faithful Persian was invested with a mysterious girdle, the badge of the divine protection, and from that moment all the actions of his life, even the most indifferent, or the most necessary, were sanctified by their peculiar prayers, ejaculations, or genuflections; the omission of which, under any circumstances, was a grievous sin, not inferior in guilt to the violation of moral duties.

Not only in the religion of Zoroaster, but in every religion worthy of the name, one may find liturgy, in which the actions, gestures, clothing, and words are of paramount importance not only to the believer but also to the honor of the deity begin worshipped. These ceremonies and the things that went with them taught the believer how to be faithful to the deity.

The religion of the Chosen People was no exception to this principle. In order to teach the children of Abraham what was sacred and what was not, a plethora of sacred paraphernalia, holy days, and clothing was employed in the service of God.

But there was yet another idea to be expressed by the priest-hood. The object of reconciliation was holiness. Israel was to be "a holy nation"—reconciled through the "sprinkling of blood"; brought near to and kept in fellowship with God by that means. The priesthood, as the representative offerers of that blood and mediators of the people, were also to show forth the "holiness" of Israel. Everyone knows how this was symbolized by the gold-plate which the high-priest wore on his forehead, and which bore the words: "Holiness unto Jehovah." But though the high-priest in this, as in every other respect, was the fullest embodiment of the functions and the object of the priesthood, the same truth was also otherwise shown forth. The bodily qualifications required in the priesthood, the kind of defilements which would temporarily or wholly interrupt their functions, their mode of ordination, and even every portion, material and color of their distinctive dress were all intended to express in a symbolical manner this characteristic of holiness. In all these respects there was a difference between Israel and the tribe of Levi; between the tribe of Levi and the family of Aaron; and, finally, between an ordinary priest and the high-priest, who most fully typified our Great High-priest, in whom all these symbols have found their reality. (Alfred Edersheim, *The Temple: Its Ministry and Services*)

Not only were these sacred articles and vestments used to teach holiness; the very gestures of the priest were also packed with significance. The book of Leviticus is replete with these gestures, down to the slightest detail. "He is to dip his finger into the blood and sprinkle some of it seven times before the Lord, in front of the curtain of the sanctuary" (Lev. 4:6).

What was true for the Persians, and what was true for the Israelites, is also true for Catholics. In the *Catechism of the Catholic Church*, we read in the section on how the liturgy is to be celebrated: "In human life, signs and symbols occupy an important place. As a being at once body and spirit, man expresses and perceives spiritual realities through physical signs and symbols. As a social being, man needs signs and symbols to communicate with others, through language, gestures, and actions. The same holds true for his relationship with God" (no. 1146).

EIGHT MODES OF TEACHING

If it has been established that everyone needs signs and symbols in order to learn, then in what sense does the classic Roman liturgy teach, beyond the obvious case of the sermon? One way to answer this question is to look briefly at the art of teaching, of which there appear to be eight modes. The modes (from *modus*, "limit") are like the colors of the spectrum, or the notes on a musical scale, and are stages of a gradual act.

The idea of these modes comes from the thought of John Senior, who was a professor of Latin at Cornell University and later at the University of Kansas. His ideas on the different modes of teaching came from a variety of sources: from Plato to Sacred Scripture, St. John Cassian, and especially St. Thomas Aquinas, notably in the *Commentary on the Sentences of Peter Lombard*, from his reflection on the very words used for teaching, and from his long experience in the classroom. His ideas are certainly open to criticism and much disagreement (as one would find in any writing about art), but I hope you will find them useful. Then, after a brief explanation of each mode, I hope to apply the mode to the liturgy, to show how the liturgy teaches us in many ways and on many levels. This writing comes from an unpublished book of Dr. John Senior called the *Idea of a School*.

> Art, from *articulum* meaning "joint," is the joining together of things not joined in nature. It operates in four modes: two are transitive; that is, they result in something extrinsic to the artist—*ars faciens*,

the making art, like the carpenter's, and *ars auxilians*, the helping art, like the farmer's; and two are intransitive, intrinsic, remaining as habits in the artist—*ars perficiens*, the perfecting art, or skill, the habit of doing something well, like the violinist's, and *ars imitans*, the imitating art in which the artist imitates his masters and the operations and object of nature, becoming like them in love and knowledge. Each of these applies to teaching in a twofold way so there are eight in all: *Ars faciens* as erudition and formation; *ars auxilians* as information and education; *ars perficiens* as institution and instruction; *ars imitans* as imitation and exercise.

Although it is proper to think of these eight modes as stages of a gradual act, they can also be thought of like the scales of music, in which the musician sounds *do* here and *mi* there, and then ends on *fa*. A good teacher can go back and forth between the modes or stay in a single mode, depending on the need and capability of the student.

Erudition

The first of these modes is *erudire* (*ex* + *rudus*), and the word means to make what is rude smooth or polished. In other words, the task of the teacher in this mode is to bring the student out of rudeness—which is not necessarily ill will, but rather an inability to recognize the time and place of a thing. Erudition is then a kindly introduction, a pointing out of what and how things are done. Simply put, erudition inculcates good manners, and good manners are the right approach to things.

Of course, there are those who would deny that there are such things as good manners when speaking about the sacred. The idea of ignoring a proper way of doing something—which might mean some personal sacrifice—in favor of what is more expedient or comfortable, is a temptation to which many in the Church have succumbed, thinking that it is not important to make gestures such as the Sign of the Cross in a certain way, with accuracy and devotion. Perhaps some of the problem comes from philosophers such as Jean-Jacques Rousseau, who is famous for having elevated the petulance of the recalcitrant child to the level of ordinance. "Let the child do nothing on anybody's word. Nothing is good for him unless he feels it to be so."

In the mode of erudition, the smallest child can grasp the significance of the Holy Eucharist, by not only being taught the proper way to fold one's hands in order to receive Holy Communion devoutly, but by taking in, consciously or otherwise, the example of parents, other parishioners, and the priest.

An anecdote will illustrate this. I was speaking with a good and friendly bishop, who had asked me how he could restore reverence for the Holy Eucharist in his diocese. I should have answered like St. Joseph of Cupertino, who, when asked the same question, responded, "See to it that the priests in your diocese pray their breviaries and celebrate their Masses devoutly." But instead I asked him to repeat the question (to his surprise) simply because it was such a good and beautiful question, and I wanted to hear it once more and was unaccustomed to hearing bishops talk this way. I did not have a simple answer (though I recall stating that, above all, it was something he had to want, and if he really wanted it, he would find a way to accomplish such a noble goal), but I did bring up the aspect of erudition.

This mode of teaching is often neglected, especially if the priest who celebrates the Mass is negligent about paying attention to the details of reverence. In the Gregorian Rite, then, one finds many detailed instructions to ensure that the Eucharist is not treated as ordinary bread, but bread that is holy and set apart. This is evident from the necessity of keeping the canonical fingers together after the Consecration, from the many genuflections, from the use of the corporal, from kneeling for Communion, and from the use of the paten, to mention just a few of these safeguards—all of which teach the faithful what the Mass and the Eucharist are.

After we had conversed about this mode of teaching, the bishop told me a story about his childhood parish. The pastor of that very large parish was a highly respected and admired priest who took great care to ensure that the celebration of the Mass was dignified and orderly, according to the manifold specifications in the old rite. But while he was coming down from the altar, a mishap occurred and many of the consecrated Hosts dropped on the marble floor. Women gasped, men blushed, and the pastor was exceedingly nervous and upset at the incident; his normal composure was absent during the rest of the Mass.

But what most struck the boy who would one day become a bishop was that after Mass he observed the great man (for the tall monsignor was a great man in the boy's eyes) getting on his hands and knees and with a magnifying glass, holy water, and white linen carefully inspecting the entire area (guarded by an altar boy with a candle) and just as carefully (though unintentionally) purifying the whole area with tears in his eyes. The bishop then said something to this effect: "I think I learned more about what the Holy Eucharist was by that accident than by any sermon I ever heard. Is that what you mean by erudition?"

Well, in a word, yes. The boy saw with his own eyes the actions of a priest who paid attention to the details of reverence, so that whatever the Holy Eucharist was, it was *extremely* important not only to the pastor, but to everyone there who saw the mishap. It was, in a word, sacred.

Another example of erudition comes from St. Bernadette Soubirous. It is reported that some people who saw her make the Sign of the Cross learned more about prayer from that gesture than from anything they had heard in a sermon or read in a book. By making the simple Sign of the Cross, we too signify a profound theology. St. Francis de Sales said in his excellent little book *The Standard of the Cross*:

> We raise the hand first to the forehead, saying: "In the name of the Father," to signify that the Father is the first person of the Most Holy Trinity, of whom the Son is begotten and from whom the Holy Ghost proceeds. Then saying: "and the Son," the hand is lowered to the breast, to express that the Son proceeds from the Father, who sent Him down to the womb of the Virgin. Then the hand is moved from the left shoulder or side to the right, while saying: "and of the Holy Ghost," thereby signifying that the Holy Ghost, as the third person of the Holy Trinity, proceeds from the Father and the Son, that He is the love that unites both, and that we, through His grace, partake of the fruits of the Passion. Accordingly, the Sign of the Cross is a brief declaration of our faith in the three great mysteries: namely, of our faith in the Blessed Trinity, in the Passion of Christ and in the forgiveness of sin, by which we pass from the left side of curse to the right [side] of blessing.

No wonder St. Francis insisted on making the Sign well!

But as important as erudition is in the gradual act of learning what is sacred, it is much to the advantage of the learner to receive a higher mode of teaching, so that he can learn sacredness even more profoundly than he did in the acquisition of good manners. Erudition has its limits, and one would hope that the Catholic attending Holy Mass was able to do more than just fold his hands correctly and make a good Sign of the Cross. Thus, a higher mode of teaching is required of us, and it concerns beauty.

Formation

What is beauty? St. Thomas Aquinas defines it as "that which when seen pleases." This seems to go along with modern notions of beauty, such as Benjamin Franklin's famous line in *Poor Richard's Almanac*: "Beauty, like supreme dominion is but supported by opinion." Or as Margaret Wolfe Hungerford put it in one of her novels, "Beauty is in the eye of the beholder." Is it really? Or is there something objective to beauty that is independent of the eye of the beholder?

St. Thomas says it is objective. So even though Andy Warhol might think that a crumpled Schlitz can is beautiful, he does so because he lacks right reason. No, beauty has three elements according to the Universal Doctor: Wholeness (or integrity), proportion (or harmony), and radiance (or shine). This is what the Church uses to determine whether a thing or a collection of things is beautiful. A string of pearls is beautiful in itself, having all three qualities, but place it on the neck of a lumberjack, and it is not fitting, and there is a loss of integrity. An art deco altar might be beautiful in itself, but put it into a Baroque church, and the whole church suffers from the loss of integrity. A good rifle has pulchritude, but put it in a Christmas manger, and again, the whole thing loses its harmony.

True beauty not only pleases but teaches. This brings us to the second mode of the art of teaching: formation. The word comes from the Latin *formare*, and its root is from *forma*, one of the five types of beauty that philosophers distinguish. Each of these kinds of beauty is present in Holy Mass, and each has something to teach us.

SPLENDOR

The first of these formal kinds of beauty is *splendor*, a shining forth of form indirectly visible in the matter. So when the liturgy and the things that surround it are splendid, the one who participates in the liturgy is taught even more profoundly than when he learned the good manners of how to behave in the presence of the King of Kings.

Abbot Suger, a medieval Benedictine abbot to whom is credited the Gothic style of architecture, explained that what others were doing with literature and the decorative arts, he did in the field of architecture:

> I confess that I took great pleasure in devoting all the costliest and most precious things I could find to the service of the administration of the Most Holy Eucharist. If, to fulfill an order from God manifested through the mouth of the Prophets, golden chalices, vases and cups were used to receive the blood of goats, calves and the red cow of the expiation, how much greater is our obligation to use, in order to receive the blood of Jesus Christ, in perpetual service and with the utmost devotion, vases of gold, gems and everything that is considered most precious. Surely neither we nor our worldly goods can suffice to serve such great mysteries. Even if, in a new creation, our substance were changed into that of Seraphim and Cherubim, it would still be unworthy to serve the ineffable Host. We can however offer propitiation for our sins. Some, no doubt, would, in contradiction, tell us that all that is necessary is to bring to the cult a pure heart, a holy soul and true intentions; we also think that these conditions are a prime necessity and have a very special importance. But we likewise affirm that the ornamentation of the sacred vessels used for the Holy Sacrifice should possess an outer magnificence which, so far as is possible, equals our inner purity. We must serve in every way and with the utmost circumspection our Redeemer, Him from whom we receive everything without exception, and who has united His nature with ours in a Person who, placing us at His right hand, has promised us that we should truly possess His kingdom, Our Lord who lives and reigns world without end.

The good abbot understood well the importance of splendor in the celebration of the liturgy and insisted that splendid things be used in it.

Being formed with beauty is a great advantage to the learner, because beauty is one of the four transcendentals by which we can know God. These are existence, goodness, truth, and beauty. Each of them transcends this world and points us to the next. Where you find one transcendental, you find the others. These realities are filled with angels. Contrariwise, we find devils teeming in ugliness, falsehood, evil, and destruction.

SPECIFIC

The second kind of beauty is *specific* (from *spectare*, "to see"), which means "something beautiful to look at." When the church in which we celebrate the Mass is beautiful to look at inside and out, it can teach as eloquently as any sermon, though perhaps on a subconscious level. So if one takes the time to look at a church that grew from the Gregorian Rite and really reflects on what he sees, he will understand the teaching of the Church somewhat as he would in studying a text about a particular subject of theology, though not in the same way. Thus, when we attend Holy Mass in a beautiful church—and by that I mean one that accurately reflects the constant and traditional teaching of the Church—then we will be learning that teaching in a marvelous way, like a plant soaking up the sunlight.

DECOR

The third kind of beauty is *decor* (from *decere*, "to fit"). It is the beauty that results when accidentals are recognized as *fitting*. It is an often recognized fact that formal and specific beauty can be botched by bad taste in otherwise beautiful persons, because they are wearing clothes that are unfitting or unsuitable to them.

Here is another anecdote, related to me by my spiritual director when I was in seminary. My director was a convert from Judaism, and one day he brought a Jewish friend to Mass. The Church was beautiful, the music was good, but when the priest came out from the sacristy for Mass, he was holding a bunch of balloons in one hand and a hymnal in the other, and on his chasuble was a depiction of Snoopy (the cartoon character). The priest who celebrated the Mass was a very likeable man, as it turns out, but when the Jewish man saw him, he stood at once and said to his friend (my director), "I came here because you told me I would learn about God. You have insulted me. I am leaving."

It seems to me that the cartoon character on the chasuble was so unfitting, spoiling whatever formal and specific beauty there was to the beginning of the Mass, or to the likeableness of the priest, that one could even go so far as to say that the Jewish man who left the Mass knew more about God than the priest did. Of course, there will be some who might try to defend what the priest was wearing, according to the old saying, "*De gustibus non est disputandum*" ("There is no dispute over matters of taste"). Indeed, arguments about what is fitting are hard to present, since one's opponent will often insist on the subject at hand being simply a matter of one man's taste as opposed to another. But if the Mass is the proclamation of the death of the Lord, as St. Paul says, there are things that are fitting to such a proclamation, and things that are not.

An example of what is very fitting to such a proclamation is the work the medieval monks did, not only in their illuminated manuscripts, but in their commentaries. The Cistercians used to write long explanations in the prefaces of their antiphonaries. In these explanations, ideas on musical techniques were adapted to spiritual considerations.

> One of these concepts is explained by the theme of the "region of dissimilarity," so dear to St. Bernard: in this context, the *regio dissimilitudinis* is the confusion of poorly organized chant. The remedy is found in Scripture: the authority of the Psalter restores dignity to each note by suggesting the use of the ten-note scale. This biblical norm, unknown to pure musical science in combination

with the laws established by Guido Arezzo, was to make it possible
for the Cistercians as well as all the other monk-musicians to
achieve their ends: to add to the holy words of the Gospel the
color and beauty of song. (Dom Jean Leclerq, *The Love of Learning
and the Desire for God*)

Thank heaven we have a magisterial Church that can teach us
which songs are beautiful (fitting) and have just the right color for the
Mass. Heaven help the poor parish in which the songs used for the
Mass do not form the parishioners but actually deform them, with
sheer ugliness or more commonly, unfitting music for a proclamation
of the death of the Lord—music better fit for a picnic.

PULCHRITUDE

The fourth kind of beauty is *pulchritude* (whose root means "power"). It is the force of things and persons. Solomon pointed out that
the Blessed Virgin had this beauty when in the Song of Songs he
sang, "Thou art beautiful my friend . . . terrible as an army in array
of battle." Though a committed pacifist might object to the notion,
there really is a terrible beauty to seeing and hearing a regiment of
soldiers obeying the order "Fix bayonets" and seeing the sun glint
off the steel of the long row of blades. It is a powerful beauty and,
in the Church, is often deliberately ignored in the use of vestments,
architecture, sacred vessels, and music. It is certainly weak in the
imagination of modern man. There is a whole generation of clerics
who have imagined sacred things as cheap, in the guise of affection
for "noble simplicity."

The power of imagination of the medieval man, on the other
hand, was quite developed.

We are used to seeing, almost without looking at them unless with
a distracted eye, printed or moving pictures. We are fond of abstract
ideas. Our imagination having become lazy seldom allows us any

longer to do anything but dream. But in the men of the Middle Ages it was vigorous and active. It permitted them to picture, to "make present," to see beings with all the details provided by the texts: the colors and dimensions of things, the clothing, bearing and actions of the people, the complex environment in which they move. They liked to describe them and, so to speak, recreate them, giving very sharp relief to images and feelings. The words of the sacred text never failed to produce a strong impression on the mind. The biblical words did not become trite; people never got used to them. The Scripture which they liked to compare to a river or a well, remained a fountain that was always fresh. The spiritual men of those days counsel the renunciation of carnal images; but this is in order to substitute for them a holy imagination. The sanctification of the imagination results in their attachment to the slightest particulars of the text, and not merely the ideas it contains. (Dom Leclerq)

So the vestments the priest wears, the candlesticks, the altar cloths, the Stations of the Cross, the music—everything one sees and hears in the church ought to have a certain power in illustrating the majesty of God.

AMENITY

The fifth kind of beauty is *amenity* (from *amoenitas*, "without walls"). It is usually translated as "pleasantness," which comes from not needing walls, since there is no danger. Having formal, specific, and splendid beauty and pulchritude in the Mass is of great advantage to the parish, but, one hopes, we will not neglect the pleasantness of beauty. A perfect example of how the liturgy teaches us amenity, or pleasant beauty, is, of course, the singing of Gregorian chant.

At the monastery of St. Gall in Switzerland in the Middle Ages, there was a poet whose name was Notker. Around him grew a whole school of disciples to perfect the technique that had come to them from Jumieges, and the compositions that came from them and other monasteries were multiplied and amplified, resulting in tropes, sequences, versicles, and *prosulae*—to mention a few kinds of their works, with each form having its own laws and its own history. And the monks loved these texts.

> And all loved to sing
> The delightful kyrielles
> The sweet and lovely sequences
> With full voice and in rich tones. (Leclerq)

Listening to the sweetness and richness of Gregorian chant is like reading a copy of the Bible or the Psalms with excellent illustrations added. Chant is even more than that, since the very melodies of chant come from the text of Sacred Scripture itself, and the soul is being formed by the music of God and not mere human composers.

Information

Now, if the only thing a man knew about the Mass was how to perform all its gestures correctly and with devotion, and that the Mass was beautiful in all the meanings of that word, he would be well on his way to an understanding of God and of His court, which is heaven. But there is an even higher mode of teaching that the Church employs in the Mass, and it is to put forms into the student who has been polished and formed. This third mode is information, from *informare*, "to inform." Literally, it means to sow the imagistic and intelligible seeds of subjects in the bodies and minds of the students, like a farmer seeding his fields with corn. In fact, both formation and information are called "drilling," which means "piercing through" in Anglo-Saxon. To be technical, formation is a mode of beauty signifying a form apparent in matter, and information is an intelligible principle recognized by imagination and intellect through a process analogous to generation, the "conceiving" of images and concepts.

It is clear that the poems that the medieval monks composed—which are an important component of the body of Western chant—are ideal for putting the forms of doctrine into the listeners and singers of chant. In other words, if the ordinary man can sing a thought, he will remember it far longer and better than if he cannot sing it. That is one reason advertising agencies spend so much time trying to come up with those irritating little songs to sell their products.

Regarding the songs of the Mass, then, Leon Gauthier puts it this way: "Our monks are those theologians whose enthusiasm is not wanting in exactness." Furthermore, he was able (as any of us are able, should we so desire) to distill from their poems what he describes as "an exposition of Catholic doctrine." Not only the chant, but the very architecture that is consonant with the Gregorian Rite also informs the believer. "The few capitals from Cluny that have been preserved show, not the chimeras which St. Bernard deprecated, but the Christological symbols for the different tones of the chant. The third tone, for example, like compunction, moves the soul deeply and causes it, as it were, to experience Christ's Resurrection" (Leclerq).

So, by attending Holy Mass devoutly, especially High Mass, one may absorb a great deal of Catholic doctrine just by singing the Proper and the Common of the feast day, in Gregorian chant above all, but also in polyphony and hymnody, and if this singing is surrounded by a beautiful church, then together these sacred songs will penetrate, or inform, the soul with the melody and the sweet truth of God.

Another example of informing is the use of Sacred Scripture in the classic Roman Rite. To learn the meaning of Scripture, one must rely on far more than easy vernacular translations. Scripture is accessible to all, certainly, but it is always mysterious, always in need of further study and reflection. Mystery is in the very nature of Scripture, since it is the Word of God, and mysterious things must be heard over and over again. When we use the Rosary correctly, for example, we can almost hear the Blessed Mother telling us how important it is to look at the mystery once more. Like any mother who must tell her children over and over a particular lesson so that they can finally learn what is right and then *do* what is right, the Blessed Mother asks her children regarding the Mysteries of the Rosary (and hoping that they will respond in the affirmative), "Do you want me to tell you the story again about my Son?" Children love to hear the same story over and over. Would that the same would hold true for our attitude toward Sacred Scripture, for one must be like a little child to enter the kingdom of heaven. We need to ask to hear the story over and over again.

Here is a fine example by St. Gregory the Great of how mysterious Sacred Scripture really is: "For as the word of God, by the mysteries which it contains, exercises the understanding of the wise, so usually by what presents itself on the outside, it nurses the simple-minded. It presents in open day that wherewith the little ones may be fed; it keeps in secret that whereby men of a loftier range may be held in suspense of admiration. It is, as it were, a kind of river, if I may so liken it, which is both shallow and deep, wherein both the lamb may find a footing, and the elephant float at large" (preface to the *Commentary on the Book of Job*).

So even small children can be nursed with Sacred Scripture, and they do not have to hear it dumbed down in a slick, up-to-date translation to trick them into thinking it's cool. Rather, the key to unlock the secrets of Scripture, again, is to hear it over and over. The Church in her wisdom, then, proposes to us the Sacred Scriptures in the liturgy, over and over again. Thus, the repetition of the readings of Scripture at the Mass is the patient teaching of the Mother to the child so that he might learn to become a disciple of her Son.

I should add that while erudition, formation, and information are early modes in the art of teaching, that is not to say that one advanced in age cannot benefit from them. In fact, when a man enters the seminary he might be quite advanced in all good manners and even the virtues. But he will have to be well polished (*erudiebat*) before he first performs the liturgical role of thurifer. "This is how we hold the thurible up. This is how we incense the people."

Education

Once the believer has been polished, formed, and informed, he is ready to be educated, which is the fourth mode of teaching: *educare*, or education (*ex + ducere*, "to draw out"), and it is a kind of teaching that draws from students things already known but not yet recognized. In this mode, a good deal of the time spent in teaching is to let the student alone and, for the student of the Mass, perhaps to let him alone with the Missal and the Divine Office.

So we would do well to examine the Divine Office at this point, since it is such an integral part of the liturgy. Granted, few of the faithful (God forbid that this should apply to priests!) pray the breviary. It is true that many do not experience a higher level of learning than that of formation and information. But for those who do rise to the level of education, the breviary is a marvelous teaching tool of the Church. It draws out the meaning of the feast day, or of the liturgical season, in a way that the missal alone cannot.

The breviary is derived chiefly from the Bible, so that to meditate on the breviary is for the most part to meditate on the inspired word of the Sacred Scriptures. As the psalmist says, "I have been delighted in the way of thy testimonies. I will not forget thy words" (Ps. 118). The reproach of Protestants—that Catholics do not read the Bible—certainly does not apply to those who use the breviary. For that matter, it does not apply to those who read their missals either.

In the lessons and sermons of the breviary, we can follow the thoughts of the Fathers of the Church, who were and are still the great interpreters of Sacred Scripture. In meditating on these texts, we do not need to fear being led astray by false piety or unsound doctrine. There is no danger of illusions or spiritual aberrations such as one might find in some manuals of prayer, which seek to stir up the sensibilities by appeals to the imagination but neglect to furnish a sound doctrinal foundation for the learner, without which mere emotion is of no avail.

The missal is not enough for those who wish to be educated in the liturgy. The missal and the breviary go together; each complements the other. If those who love the Mass wish to carry their devotion to it to its logical conclusion, they must inevitably take up the breviary. The Divine Office (which is contained in the breviary) is at once a preparation for the Mass and a prolongation of it. If, therefore, the missal has taught us to understand the Mass as the Church does, then it makes perfect sense to make use of the Church's official preparation for Mass (First Vespers, Compline, Matins, and Lauds), and it makes just as much sense to continue throughout the day to dwell with the Church on the theme of the morning Mass, with the Minor Hours, Second Vespers, and Compline.

There is, moreover, a close correspondence in the content of the missal and the breviary. The theme for each day is the same in both of them, the same mystery of the same saint of the day. The Collect of the Mass for a given day appears also as the oration for Lauds, the Minor Hours, and Vespers. On days when the Mass is celebrated in honor of some saint, an account of that saint's life is read in the second nocturn of Matins. The lessons of the first nocturn often correspond to the Epistle of the Mass, which is again broken up into brief passages for the short lessons of the Minor Hours. The homily lessons of the third nocturn are a commentary on the Gospel of the Mass. Thus, in order to pray the Mass completely, one should pray the breviary.

Institution

Let us say then that the believer has been polished, formed, informed, and educated in his Faith by the Mass but yearns for more, desiring to cast his net into deeper waters. For him, there is the deeper water of institution which is, according to John Senior, the fifth mode of teaching, and its name is derived from the Latin word *instituere*. Institutes are sets of plans. The student who has been polished, formed, informed, and educated needs a *vademecum* ("come with me"), a summary or synopsis of what he has learned to prompt and correct him when knowledge is put to use, like the classical institutes of Latin by Donatus.

I would not dispute the point that a faithful Catholic could participate in the liturgy, bringing to it nothing but a crucifix, or a chaplet, or maybe nothing in his hands at all. But to participate in a deeper sense, going beyond even education, he will need a daily missal for his *vademecum*. The best missal of all is likely the *Liber Usualis*, because it has everything the daily missal has, plus the music that should go with it. Although it would be a mistake to use the *Liber Usualis* as the sole text for doctrine—thus ignoring such important developments as the catechism—this great book more than suffices for a *vademecum*.

> The liturgy is at once the mirror of a culture and its culmination. Just as the office of Corpus Christi, in the composition of which St. Thomas surely participated, crowns his doctrinal work, so the hymns, sequences and innumerable poems written by the monks are the culmination of their theology. The liturgy had been the motive for the renewal of monastic culture in the Carolingian period, and was also its fruit. During the following centuries, it is in the atmosphere of the liturgy and amid the poems composed for it, in *hymnis et canticis* that the synthesis of all the *artes* was effected, of the literary techniques, religious reflection and all

sources of information whether biblical, patristic or classical. In
the liturgy, all these resources fully attained their final potentiality;
they were restored to God in an homage which recognized that they
had come from Him. Thanksgiving, Eucharist, theology, *confessio
fidei*, all these expressions, in monastic tradition expressed only
slightly differing aspects of a single reality. In the liturgy, grammar
was elevated to the rank of an eschatological fact. It participated in
the eternal praise that the monks, in unison with the Angels began
offering God in the abbey choir and which will be perpetuated
in Heaven. In the liturgy, love of learning and desire of God find
perfect reconciliation. (Leclerq)

Although it would be a mistake to insist on using the liturgy as
the *only* text for learning, the texts contained in the *Liber Usualis*
nonetheless can and do serve as what Leon Gauthier describes as
"an exposition of Catholic doctrine."

Instruction

At this point, the believer is polished, formed, informed, educated,
and instituted in the sacred by his ever-deepening participation in
the Mass. But he can go deeper still by the sixth mode of teaching,
which Senior called instruction. *Instruere* means putting an army at
the ready for battle. "In the ancient times and in all the middle ages,
music was a part of the studies. Why? And why this pre-eminence
given to music rather than to any of the other arts? Music is the most
violent of all the arts, and the one which most powerfully affects the
senses. Music is very useful in forming sensitivity. . . . The slightest
beat of the drum, even if you are thinking about something else,
will produce a physical effect far more powerful than any painting"
(James Taylor, *Poetic Knowledge*).

The experience of the procession into Mass, with an organ thun-
dering, or with the silent power of chant, disposes us to "fight the
good fight" (1 Tim. 6:12) in the Mass, by rejecting anger toward

our neighbor as well as the common distractions of the world. Thus, music has the capability to put us at the ready for battle. But even before the procession starts, the priest's simple act of putting on the amice in the sanctuary *instructs* us in a marvelous union of Sacred Scripture, vestment, and gesture.

Fr. Gihr puts it this way: "The meaning of this rite is explained by the Church herself in the prayer which is to be recited by the celebrant when he puts on the amice: 'Place, O Lord, on my head the helmet of salvation, that I may overcome the assaults of Satan.' The question arises, what is to be understood by this helmet of salvation (*galea salutis*), with which the priest at the altar should be armed against the attacks of Satan. The expression is taken from Holy Scripture, which also contains its meaning. When the Apostle St. Paul exhorts Christians to put on the armor of God, to resist the attacks of Satan, he urges them 'to take unto them the helmet of salvation' (*galeam salutis assumite*—Eph. 6:17)."

In another place he says Christians should "be sober, having on the breast-plate of faith and charity, and for a helmet the hope of salvation (*induti loricam fidei et caritatis et galeam spem salutis*—1 Thess. 5:8)." The protecting helmet and, consequently, the amice, which covers the head in a similar manner, are accordingly symbolic of Christian hope; for hope in the goods of grace and glory acquired and promised to us by Christ is a powerful weapon of protection against "our adversary the devil who, as a roaring lion, goeth about seeking whom he may devour" (1 Pet. 5.8). Truly, the supernatural virtue of hope is our protection and shield in combat against all the enemies of salvation! "They that hope in the Lord shall renew their strength, they shall take wings as the eagles, they shall run and not be weary, they shall walk and not faint" (Is. 40:31).

The prayers that go with the donning of all the other vestments are also perfect examples of instruction. There are likewise many other gestures, prayers, and actions with which the Mass can instruct.

Discipline

Having been polished, formed, informed, educated, and instructed in the knowledge of the mysteries, there is an even higher or deeper mode of teaching in the Mass, and it is called discipline (from *disciplinare*, "two learning," or *discere*, "to learn"). It is a kind of tandem knowledge—teacher and student working together to learn—involving especially two acts: correction (the rod) and affection (the staff). As Psalm 22:4 puts it, "Thy rod and thy staff, they comfort me." The word *comfort* comes from the Latin and means "with strength." So St. David is saying that both correction and affection make us stronger. Monks call the flagellum (the whip with which they chastise themselves, as Pope St. John Paul II used to use before ordinations) the *discipline*, and spiritual sons are called *disciples*.

Many teachers think that students should never be corrected or who think the purpose of their subjects is to correct original sin. Both are incorrect. "Since there are infinite ways to miss a target and only one to hit it, error easily happens and uncorrected knowledge is worse than ignorance—the Devil had the highest knowledge next to God and misdirected it. But discipline can't be applied before there is a fault; you can't correct what doesn't exist. Unless the student has first been brought from a rude, unruly state, polished, formed to his natural but hitherto hidden beauty, informed, educated and instituted, he has nothing to rebel against and, if he has not rebelled, he can't be justly punished. It isn't novices but those in advanced stages of intellectual and spiritual development who need the sting, as St. Paul himself confessed: 'And lest the greatness of the revelations should exalt me, there was given me a sting of my flesh, an angel of Satan, to buffet me.' "

In what sense can the liturgy be said to discipline us, especially in the sense of a kind of tandem learning, receiving at once the rod of correction and the staff of comfort? I would suggest that this mode of discipline might be found above all in liturgical silence. It is probably not an accident that there are increasing numbers of spiritual books that teach the reader to empty the mind of the noise that clogs it up. A visit to any bookstore in the United States reveals a plethora of self-help books meant to lead the reader into silence or the more crass "quiet time." And many a denizen of a modern city goes into the countryside seeking the "quietness of nature" and silence. But they do not meet silence there; on the contrary, they carry the noise of the great towns and the noise of their own souls out into the country with them. The self-help books are not wrong, however, in pointing to the need for silence, nor are the spiritual books. "It is a blessing to have a common understanding not only about the meaning of things but also about the meaning of silence. Simply not to be talking is not the same as to be silent. Silence must be present within a man as a primary reality in its own right, not merely as the opposite of speech. This living in the primary silence adds another life to man, who is only man through the word: it adds the life in silence. It points him beyond the life that is in the word to a life beyond the word, and it points him beyond himself" (Max Picard, *The World of Silence*).

Now, just as ivy grows around a wall even for centuries, so it seems as if cathedrals have grown around silence. They seem to be built around silence. When I first visited the Romanesque basilica at Paray-le-Monial in France, I fell in love with that type of architecture, and it remains my favorite, if nothing else because of its silence. It was as if its silence existed as a substance there, and I thought it capable of producing men of silence, even cities of silence.

Likewise with the liturgy, it is clear that active participation in it does not preclude, as Pope John Paul II stated in his address to the American bishops in October of 1998, "*the active passivity of silence, stillness and listening: indeed it demands it.*" He explained further the nature of this active silence. "Worshippers are not passive, for instance, when listening to the readings or the homily, or following the prayers of the celebrant, and the chants and music of the liturgy. These are experiences of silence and stillness, but they are in their own way profoundly active. In a culture which neither favors nor fosters meditative quiet, the art of interior listening is learned only with difficulty."

Msgr. Romano Guardini puts his finger on the heart of silence in prayer very well.

> If we are to foster the awe, reverence, and adoration through which we may know the Word of Christ, then we must love, and not fear silence and stillness in the Mass and in our life. From silence comes the Word. From silence God spoke and created the world. From silence he spoke to Mary and came to dwell in her womb. From silence he sent his Holy Spirit at Pentecost to lead the Church. Meditative quiet, as the pope laments, is neither favored nor fostered in our culture. Yet there is no getting around the simple fact that only in stillness do we learn to listen with the interior ear. Only in stillness can we build the habit of listening, a habit that, when impeded by the jangle of noise, can never develop. Only in stillness do we calm down enough to sense the Lord's presence. Only in stillness do we find out that the Lord loves us and that we are made to love him. Silence, then, is not a den of terror; it is rather the place where we fall in love. (*The Spirit of the Liturgy*)

This is a very high level of teaching and learning we are discussing at this point.

> It is in this very aspect of the liturgy that its didactic aim is to be found, that of teaching the soul not to see purposes everywhere, not to be too conscious of the end it wishes to attain, not to be desirous of being over clever and grown-up, but to understand simplicity in life. The soul must learn to abandon, at least in prayer,

the restlessness of purposeful activity; it must learn to waste time for the sake of God and to be prepared for the sacred game with sayings and thought and gestures, without always immediately asking "why?" and "wherefore?" It must learn not be continually yearning to *do* something, to attack something, to accomplish something useful, but to play the divinely ordained game of the liturgy in liberty and beauty and holy joy before God. (Anne Husted Burleigh, *Common Wisdom*)

The silence of the Canon of the Mass in particular harmonizes perfectly with the accomplishment and the essence of the mystery of the Eucharistic Sacrifice. Indeed, the material elements are changed into the Body and Blood of Christ, without the senses perceiving it, or the created mind being able to comprehend it; the Real Presence and the sacrificial life of the Savior under the sacramental species is concealed beyond all discernment. The holy silence of the Canon is quite suited to indicate and recall the concealment and the depth, the incomprehensibility and ineffableness of the wonderful mysteries that are enacted on the altar. "The Lord is in His holy temple; let all the earth keep silence before Him!" (Hab. 2:20).

There is another reason for this silence at the Canon—a mystical one:

> The priest at the altar is the representative and image of the praying and sacrificing Savior. Now, as on the Mount of Olives and on the Cross, Jesus prayed not only in loud tones, but also in a low voice and in the silence of His heart to the Father, so also it is proper that the priest should herein resemble His Divine Model, when representing and renewing the Sacrifice of the Cross. The altar becomes not merely the Cross, but also the crib; for at the moment of Consecration the marvels of Bethlehem as well as those of Golgotha are renewed. Whilst deep silence pervaded all things and the night was in the midst of its course, the Almighty

Word of God descended from His royal throne in heaven to the crib of Bethlehem; in like manner, does the King of Glory at the consecration come down upon the altar, amid the most profound silence. (Gihr)

Although children may not appreciate silence as an adult would, they can sometimes appreciate it far more than the adult whose memory is crammed with images from video games.

For a Catholic, it is especially in silence that we receive the rod of correction and the staff of comfort.

Exercise

After having been polished, formed, informed, educated, instituted, instructed, and disciplined in the mysteries, the believer is now ready to put into action what he has been taught. This is the highest mode of teaching in John Senior's view, and it is called exercise (*exercere*), the putting into action of the things already learned.

Philosophers distinguish between potency (capable of being something else), act (the state of actually being it) and exercise (functioning). For example, a tree in the woods is potentially firewood; chopped and split, it is firewood in act and, in exercise, it burns. Since God is the only being purely in exercised act, when we achieve this state, we are His image (having minds) and His likeness (using them). The ultimate teacher is Christ, residing in the soul. Teachers act *in loco Christi* and students imitating them are indirectly imitating Christ, as St. Paul said, "Be ye followers (*imitatores*) of me, as I also am of Christ." (Senior)

It is a precept of the Church (Denz. 437, 1205) that Holy Communion must be received by all adults in virtue of the divine command: "You can have no life in yourselves, unless you eat the flesh of the Son of Man, and drink his blood" (Jn. 6:54).

As St. Thomas points out (*S.T.*, IIIa, Q. 80, a. 12, ad. 1), "On the part of the communicants, extreme reverence and caution are necessary to prevent anything happening which would not be fitting for so great a sacrament. This is most likely to occur in the drinking of the blood which might easily be spilt, if there were any carelessness in receiving it. And because the Christian community has increased . . . it is a prudent custom for the blood to be received by the priest alone, and not by the people."

Thus, it seems to me that the perfect example of how the liturgy teaches in this eighth and highest mode may be seen in the act of Holy Communion. What strikes me most at this point, about the priest acting *in loco Christi* at the time of the distribution of Holy Communion, is the supplication he makes for every one of his parishioners to whom he gives the King of Kings: "*Corpus Domini nostri Jesu Christi custodiat animam tuam ad vitam aeternam. Amen.*"

EVERYONE CAN LEARN FROM THE MASS

Everyone whom our blessed Lord met when He walked this earth needed some individual favor—a solution to some problem—from St. Peter to the most pathetic man suffering from leprosy. The people with whom He came into contact were not just faces in the crowd. They were individuals with particular needs. For example, the woman who suffered from an issue of blood came up to Him with the thought that if she could only touch the hem of His garment, she would be healed. He was in a hurry at the time, on His way to heal the daughter of Jairus, who was at the point of death. "And immediately Jesus knowing in himself the virtue that had proceeded from him, turning to the multitude, said: Who hath touched my garments? And his disciples said to him: Thou seest the multitude thronging thee, and sayest thou who hath touched me?" (Mk. 5:30-31).

The disciples pointed out that it was just a casual contact and that many had brushed up against Him, but Christ insisted on having an answer, because virtue had gone out of Him. This is partly because God is not interested in miracles that meet everyone's needs simultaneously, or mass-produced miracles, if you will. Every single person who met the Lord was brought into some personal relation with Him, and they were all able to say—with anger or delight—"He turned, and spoke to *me*." Everyone who met Him could carry away from the meeting some personal memory of His voice. "Go and sin no more." "Thy faith hath saved thee."

But He is fully able to distinguish between those who approach Him with pride and those who approach Him with humility. "And it came to pass, as they walked in the way that a certain man said to him: I will follow thee whithersoever thou goest. Jesus said to him: the foxes have holes, and the birds of the air nests; but the Son of man hath not where to lay his head" (Lk. 9:57-58). It seems like a curt response, but it was the right response to the man who would approach him with pride and self-assurance.

Should one approach Him honestly, however, and with humility, the result is quite different. "And the two disciples heard him speak and they followed Jesus. And Jesus turning, and seeing them following him, saith to them: What seek you? Who said to him, Rabbi (which is to say, being interpreted, Master), where dwellest thou? He saith to them: Come and see. They came, and saw where he abode, and they stayed with him that day: now it was about the tenth hour" (Jn. 1:37-39). The result of this enquiry is the Lord's entertaining them all day until sundown.

> How surely he recognizes, how gently he inspires, contrition, and at various levels! The woman of Samaria, with her pious platitudes, must be suddenly knocked off her perch with the command, "Go home, fetch thy husband." The woman taken in adultery is to be won by sympathy; "I will not condemn thee either. Go, and do not sin again henceforward." The Magdalen—she is pardoned already; "If great sins have been forgiven her, she has also greatly

loved." How nicely graded are the demands he makes on different souls! The young man who has kept all the commandments from his youth up must be sent home to sell all that he has. But when poor Zacchaeus, the publican, has been beckoned down from his eyrie in the sycamore-tree, and announces, "I give half of what I have to the poor," that is enough; "He too is a son of Abraham." How well he knows where faith is strong enough, where it is not yet strong enough, to do without reassurance! The Magdalen is to keep her distance; only Thomas may thrust his hand into the wounds. Everybody, to our Lord, from our Blessed Lady downwards, is a separate problem, needing a separate approach.

And so it is, if only we had faith to believe it, in Holy Communion. That long procession to the altar-rails, how interminable it seems! The priest, you would think, must get tired of muttering the same formula two or three hundred times over! But no, he is not allowed to say *"Corpus Domini Jesu Christi custodiat animas vestras"*, the sacred words must be said to each communicant individually. Jesus Christ is not simply coming among us, he is coming to each of us; and although the gift is always the same (for it is nothing less than the whole of himself), the purpose for which it is given, the influence which it is meant to bestow, on your soul or mine, is something special, in proportion to the needs of each, in accordance with the plan he has for each. He knows you, and makes allowances for you; knows you, and can gauge your capacity; knows you, and is not to be put off by excuses. He can tell whether you are really trying to find *him* when you go to the altar, or merely following the dictates of convention; whether you come in a spirit of humility, or expecting too much of him. He can tell whether the contrition you feel for your sins needs to be drawn out still more, or is ripening already into love; whether your faith is such that it still needs reassurance, or whether it can stand up to the test of a rebuff. (Msgr. Ronald Knox, *The Layman and His Conscience*)

So from the altar boy who is learning how to hold the paten correctly to the priest with many academic degrees, *everyone* can learn from the Mass, in any country, and at any time. The Mass runs up and down, touching each of the eight modes of teaching, like a schola singing chant; sometimes pausing at this note, or skipping to a higher note, or going back to the first note.

As Sacred Scripture has different senses to it, so that either the lamb or the elephant can be nourished from its waters, so the Mass can teach and nourish anyone, no matter what his level of knowledge might be, or what level of participation he might be capable of pursuing.

The Mass is like heaven, where the lowest angel and the lowest saint join their voices with the highest angels and saints, all of them singing, "Sanctus, sanctus, sanctus."

Appendix IV

THE FUNERAL MASS

W HY ALL THE CEREMONIES around the coffin and the grave? St. Augustine says in his great work *The City of God*:

All this, that is, the preparing of the bodies, the kind of burying, the pomp of funerals, is rather a consolation for the living than a help for the dead. The bodies of the dead must not be treated with disrespect or thrown away, especially those who have died in innocence and faith, because the Holy Ghost used these members like so many organs and vessels to do his work. If therefore our father's ring or clothes, or things of that kind, are dear and cherished, according to our love for him, for the same reason these bodies are to be honored, for they are nearer and united to us more closely than the clothes we wear. For our bodies are not for an ornament or as an aid to us, but these bodies belong to the nature of man; whence the funerals of the great and just men of old were considered as works of piety, and their burials celebrated; while they lived they chose the place of their tomb; they told their children how their bodies were to be carried; Tobias burying the dead merited heaven according to the words of the Angel; while the Gospel tells us with what care and honor they placed in the tomb the body of the Lord. Surely all this signifies not that there is any sense in the dead body, but that, by the providence of God, who is pleased by these works of mercy, these ceremonies tell of the faith in the resurrection from the dead.

And in his work on the *Care of the Dead*, he goes on to say:

> In the Books of the Maccabees we read that sacrifice was offered for the dead, and if it is mentioned in no other part of the Old Testament, that is of little account to the Universal Church, whose authority regarding this custom is so well known, for among the prayers of the priest offered at the altar to the Lord God, there is given a place for the remembrance of the dead. If for any reason the bodies of the dead cannot be buried, supplications for their souls must not be omitted, which must be given for all those who have died in the Christian and Catholic community; when they are not known, the Church prays for them in a general remembrance, so that if they have no parents, children or friends, their pious mother takes the place of all these.

The benefit to the living is not just for their consolation, of course; it is also to awaken in the minds of those present at the ceremonies the belief in the resurrection of the dead on the last day and above all to pray for the repose of the souls of the faithful departed and their speedy delivery from Purgatory.

Like many of our rites, our funeral ceremonies come down to us from the Jews. Their only way of disposing of the dead was by burial. It was a holy duty imposed upon their children and nearest kin; the latter coming sometimes from a great distance to give the last rites to the bodies of their departed relatives. The body was carried on a bier, often carved with ornaments and of great beauty, with the head of the deceased uncovered, and the family and friends following, singing songs of lamentation.

In Catholic countries the body is carried to the church with great ceremony, like that of our spiritual elders. The Fiftieth Psalm is sung, as is the Twenty-Ninth, as the body leaves the hearse and enters the church.

The coffin is placed such that if the deceased is a layman, his feet are facing the altar, and if he is a priest, his head is facing the altar; thus, in death the bodies are placed as they were in life. Another reason for this has to do with the ancient tradition of burying a priest facing west and the faithful facing east. This is indicative of the general resurrection of the dead, when the priest must rise to face his congregation and answer to them. If he lorded it over them in this life, then justice will be had when he must answer to them and to the Lord.

There are six candles placed in large candlesticks standing on the floor. These signify several things. First, they tell us of the light of faith burning in the soul of the deceased during his life, and of the faith in his soul in purgatory. Second, they remind us of the funeral of our Lord, when His body was laid in the tomb, and the holy women came to anoint it on the day of the Resurrection, and that body was surrounded with light. Third, these candles are made of unbleached wax, as opposed to the candles on the altar, which are of bleached wax. The ones on the altar represent the Church Militant—the living who do not appear to one another as they truly are—and the unbleached candles represent the Church Suffering, since they are now seen as they truly are. Fourth, the candles tell of the science and knowledge of all things coming from Christ and enlightening all men, both the living and the dead. Lastly, these candles burn with a slightly different light from the light of those on the altar, signifying a line from the Preface of the Dead in the Mass, *Vita mutatur, non tollitur*: "Life is changed, not ended."

Everything is in black, the color of mourning, the color of death; thus, the Church in mourning for one of her children clothes her priests and ministers in black. On the tabernacle, however, the veil is not black but purple (since our Lord lives) to symbolize the sorrow of the Savior at the death of one of His own, and the altar cloths remain white, which is a symbol of His Resurrection and Ascension.

The texts from the Proper of the Mass are all toward the praise of God, Who gives rest to the dead; toward the reality of sin, death, judgment, hell, purgatory, and heaven; toward hope and trust in a merciful Savior. All these may be found in the *Dies Irae*, the sequence for the Mass of the Dead.

The *Dies Irae* can hardly be translated with its splendor and sublimity, since poetry is always lost in translation. The author of it is not known for sure; it dates from the thirteenth century. Perhaps it was written in that century by a saint who was filled with heavenly perfection such that he did not want any recognition for his work. It could be argued that it is the finest piece of poetry ever composed by man. The secret of its power lies in the awful grandeur of its theme, the intense earnestness and pathos of the poet, the simple majesty and solemn muse of its language, the stately meter, the triple rhyme, producing an effect as if we heard the final crash of the universe, the commotion of the graves opened, the trumpet of the archangel summoning the quick and the dead, and saw the "King of tremendous majesty" seated on His throne of justice and mercy, ready to dispense everlasting life or everlasting woe.

The Mass is the same as usual, with some exceptions such as the Propers. Since the Forty-Second Psalm is for the living, it is omitted at the Requiem. The subdeacon does not receive the blessing after the Epistle, the celebrant does not bless the water before the commixture, since the Mass is for the dead and not to signify the union of the living with Christ.

Another exception is that instead of crossing himself at the Introit, the celebrant makes the Sign of the Cross over the missal, again because it signifies a blessing for the dead and not for the living.

At the end of the Requiem, the Last Gospel is said if it is a daily Mass of the Dead, but if it is a funeral, or a Mass with absolution at the catafalque, it is omitted, as is usual when another ceremony takes place immediately after Mass.

The subdeacon goes to the head of the casket, with the processional cross facing the deceased, and two acolytes with lit candles are on either side of the cross. This signifies that Christ is the Lord of the living and the dead; as He was Lord during the life of the deceased, so is He still the Lord over him in death, no matter where the deceased is. The two candles signify the knowledge of all things coming from the Holy Ghost, which enlightens all men, be they living or dead.

After several beautiful prayers that are fitting to the seriousness of what is going on, the *Pater Noster* is said silently, and the priest goes about the coffin, sprinkling it three times on each side, which symbolizes the three washings or pouring that were done at the baptism of the deceased. When he comes to the cross, he bows to it in gratitude for all the blessings poured forth by Christ in the rite, and passing in front of the tabernacle he genuflects to acknowledge that Christ is the Lord, and nothing happens outside the providence of God.

He then takes the thurible, into which incense was placed without the customary blessing, since that blessing is for the living. As incense is given only to God, or to the things relating to Him, we incense the body because it once contained the Body of Christ, Who sat as a king enthroned in that heart which is now cold, when he received Communion. The smoke rising tells us of the prayers of the people that ought to be sweet smelling to God (that is, without selfishness or marred by sin of any kind), which rise to His throne on behalf of the departed.

Once these prayers are finished, the *In Paradisum* is sung. "May the angels guide thee into Paradise; may the martyrs receive thee on thy journey, and lead thee into the holy city Jerusalem. May the choir of Angels take thee, and with Lazarus, once poor, may you have everlasting rest." Thus, the last prayer said for the departed, before the last time he goes through the doors of his parish, is a perfect expression of hope. It is the nature of hope to be convinced that the sacrifice of Christ at Calvary—at which we were present during the funeral Mass—would make salvation possible for the departed.

One of the fruits of the Sacrifice may be seen at the cemetery. In a cemetery of consecrated ground, you will see the sign of salvation, the cross. The cemeteries and burial places of all other religions are like those of the pagans—no cross, no signs of salvation mark the resting place of their dead; their monuments and tombstones are today like those on the banks of the Nile, or along the roads leading out of Rome, around the site of ancient Athens, in the desert of Arabia, monuments of human folly and pride, while the Church alone surrounds her funeral rites with signs, and figures and symbols, teaching truth to the living, and guarding the remains of her dead.

The word *cemetery* is from the Greek, meaning a sweet station, a place of rest or sleep, for those who die in peace with God go to a sweet station or place on their way to the Last Judgment, awaiting their rising.

The origin of the practice of the cemetery may be found in the burial of Abraham, who bought the double cave (Gen. 23:9), where his bones were laid; there was buried Sarah; there slept the bones of Issac, of Jacob, of Adam and of Eve.

We do not bury indifferently inside the church or in the cemetery. The condition of a person at his death, his station or wealth or the importance of his family, should not be the cause of his monument in consecrated ground, but only his good life and his holiness. St. Augustine says, "Those, who, being oppressed by grievous sins, procure that their bodies at death be placed in consecrated ground, should be condemned for their audacity, and the holy place will not deliver them, but will accuse them of the guilt of temerity." Those who are buried in a church are martyrs or great defenders of their country. Of ecclesiastics, only bishops or founders of orders should be buried in the church.

BIBLIOGRAPHY

Here are a few of the books and journals I used to compose this book.

A Benedictine Monk, *Discovering the Mass*. This came from the monastery of Le Barroux in France and has the stamp of the excellent poetical approach of the late Dom Calvert, O.S.B.

―――. *Four Benefits of the Liturgy*. Excellent reading from Barroux.

―――. *The Sacred Liturgy*. Another gem from Barroux. It is especially good to understand how the Liturgy uses the things of creation to worship God.

Bruyere, Madame L'Abbess Cecile. *The Spiritual Life and Prayer according to Holy Scripture and Monastic Tradition*. Her explanation of the liturgy within the soul, and how it connects to the liturgy of the Temple of Solomon and the Sacrifice of the Mass is excellent.

The Centre International D'Etudes Liturgiques (CIEL). The proceedings from the colloquiums of this center are very valuable, and are translated by CIEL UK.

Crean, Fr. Thomas, O.P. *The Mass and the Saints*. An excellent compendium of what various saints have written about the meaning of the gestures and symbolism of the Mass. Anything written by this priest is worth reading, and in this book is a very good list of sources for anyone who wants to read more about what the saints and ecclesiastical writers have said about the meaning of the ceremonies of the Mass. I used his translations frequently when quoting these saints.

St. Gertrude the Great. *Life and Revelations*. In this work you'll find an account of St. Gertrude's mystical experience of the liturgy in heaven, which has everything to do with the sacrifice and worship that takes place in the soul of one who loves God.

Gihr, Fr. Nicholas. *The Holy Sacrifice of the Mass.* A very thorough book that goes into great detail about the Mass; not only the nature of its symbolism but also the theology of it.

Guardini, Romano. *Sacred Signs.* This little book is a good introduction to thinking about the things we do and use in the liturgy, from kneeling and standing to linens and candles.

———. *The Spirit of the Liturgy.* This is what inspired Cardinal Ratzinger to write his book by the same title. It is a masterpiece to help understand what makes a liturgy good.

Gueranger, Dom Prosper, O.S.B. *The Liturgical Year.* This great work helps you to pray the Mass and familiarizes you with the Eastern Rites. It is organized so that you can follow the entire liturgical year with it.

———. *The Prayers and Ceremonies of the Holy Mass.* A very pious little work, ideal as a good introduction to the basics of the ceremonies, written with great love for the Mass.

Jungmann, Fr. Joseph A., S.J. *The Mass of the Roman Rite.* A massive writing of about 1,000 pages, a treasure trove of the history of the development of the Roman Rite and a comparison with the Eastern liturgies.

Lang, Fr. Jovian P., O.F.M. *Dictionary of the Liturgy.* This work is unabashedly in favor of the Ordinary Form but fair in its description of things "which used to be done."

Meagher, Fr. James L. *Teaching Truth by Signs and Ceremonies: The Church, Its Rites and Services, Explained for the People.* A wealth of symbolic explanation.

Mosebach, Martin. *The Heresy of Formlessness: The Roman Liturgy and Its Enemy.* This is a superbly written look at the Liturgy by an artist.

Ratizger, Joseph Cardinal. *The Spirit of the Liturgy*. Good, solid theology on the nature and purpose of the liturgy.

Vigourel, Fr. Adrian, S.S. *A Synthetical Manual of the Liturgy*. A concise manual that combines basic theology, the old Code of Canon Law, and the rubrics and ceremonies.

Zundel, Maurice. *The Splendor of the Liturgy*. This is a good poetic explanation of the liturgy and deals with symbolism in a poetic mode.

Here are two websites that have been very beneficial to me:

Vultus Christi: http://vultus.stblogs.org/ (the website of Dom Mark Kirby, O.S.B.)

New Liturgical Movement: http://www.newliturgicalmovement. org/ (This site will connect you to the work of Peter Kwasniewski, Gregory DiPippo, Dom Alcuin Reed, O.S.B., and many others.)

Sophia Institute

Sophia Institute is a nonprofit institution that seeks to nurture the spiritual, moral, and cultural life of souls and to spread the Gospel of Christ in conformity with the authentic teachings of the Roman Catholic Church.

Sophia Institute Press fulfills this mission by offering translations, reprints, and new publications that afford readers a rich source of the enduring wisdom of mankind.

Sophia Institute also operates the popular online resource CatholicExchange.com. *Catholic Exchange* provides world news from a Catholic perspective as well as daily devotionals and articles that will help readers to grow in holiness and live a life consistent with the teachings of the Church.

In 2013, Sophia Institute launched Sophia Institute for Teachers to renew and rebuild Catholic culture through service to Catholic education. With the goal of nurturing the spiritual, moral, and cultural life of souls, and an abiding respect for the role and work of teachers, we strive to provide materials and programs that are at once enlightening to the mind and ennobling to the heart; faithful and complete, as well as useful and practical.

Sophia Institute gratefully recognizes the Solidarity Association for preserving and encouraging the growth of our apostolate over the course of many years. Without their generous and timely support, this book would not be in your hands.

www.SophiaInstitute.com
www.CatholicExchange.com
www.SophiaInstituteforTeachers.org

Sophia Institute Press® is a registered trademark of Sophia Institute. Sophia Institute is a tax-exempt institution as defined by the Internal Revenue Code, Section 501(c)(3). Tax I.D. 22-2548708.